"You've heard it before: 'Every pastor needs this book!' Well, it's the truth about *Setting Your Church Free*. Every church that desires to be truly healthy to do effective ministry in the '90s would be wise to work through this biblically profound book."

Dennis N. Baker, General Director
Conservative Baptist Churches of America

"After reading *Setting Your Church Free*, I said, 'If I were a pastor, I would be chomping at the bit to implement it in my church.' The same would be true any place in the world. Churches in mission areas will greatly profit from this approach. For too long, we have tried to ignore the corporate responsibility for sin. At last we have clear, practical guidance for dealing with it."

Timothy M. Warner,
Former Director of Professional Doctoral Programs
Trinity Evangelical Divinity School,
Deerfield, Illinois

"*Setting Your Church Free* deals with one of the basic elements in church growth: the spiritual releasing of a church for the power of God. While many are writing about the principles and programs to make a church grow, and others are featuring the user-friendly aspects of marketing the message to the general public, Anderson and Mylander have dealt with the spiritual factors that prohibit the church from revival and the power of God."

Dr. Elmer L. Towns, Dean
School of Religion
Liberty University
Lynchburg, Virginia

NEIL T. ANDERSON

SETTING

YOUR

CHURCH

FREE

A BIBLICAL PLAN TO
HELP YOUR CHURCH

Regal Books
A Division of Gospel Light
Ventura, California, U.S.A.

CHARLES MYLANDER

Published by Regal Books
A Division of Gospel Light
Ventura, California, U.S.A.
Printed in U.S.A.

Library of Congress Cataloging-in-Publication Data
Anderson, Neil T., 1942-
    Setting your church free / Neil T. Anderson, Charles Mylander.
        p. cm.
    Includes bibliographical references.
    ISBN 0-8307-1682-3 (trade paper)
    1. Church renewal. 2. Pastoral theology. I. Mylander, Charles.
    II. Title.
    BV600.2.A56 1994   93-47886
    250—dc20   CIP

4 5 6 7 8 9 10 11 12 13 14 / 03 02 01 00 99 98 97

Rights for publishing this book in other languages are contracted by Gospel Literature International (GLINT). GLINT also provides technical help for the adaptation, translation and publishing of Bible study resources and books in scores of languages worldwide. For further information, contact GLINT, P.O. Box 4060, Ontario, CA 91761-1003, U.S.A., or the publisher.

CONTENTS

PART ONE

This section presents a biblical analysis of the Church, taking into account the reality of the spiritual world and the need for Christ-centered leaders and ministries.

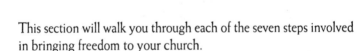

This section will walk you through each of the seven steps involved in bringing freedom to your church.

APPENDICES

FOREWORD

The idea that sin hinders personal spiritual growth is a principle that all Christians would recognize as biblical. Scripture teaches, however, that just as sin can have detrimental effects in the life of an individual, it can also have disastrous effects to a corporate group. Unfortunately, this same principle applicable to the church in a corporate or group sense is rarely considered.

Although the sin of individuals may bring harmful consequences to the group (as in the cases of Achan's greed and the numbering of the people by David), we must realize that a group can also sin directly. Corporate actions may be based upon sinful worldly principles rather than on the truth of Scripture and the leading of the Spirit. The group can also sin collectively by failing to confront the sins of individuals and thereby engage in disobedience to the Lord of the Church.

One reason that such corporate sins are so little mentioned is that the possibility of there being corporate sin is not a part of most discussion on the doctrine of sin. The manner in which the group interacts with its members or leaders, whether according to God's principle of love or not, is seldom properly and fully considered. The rationale is often "action simply has to be taken." In any sinful action, the "I" is easily lost within the "they." Because no one feels directly responsible, corporate sin is difficult to deal with and thus is often buried under time and inactivity. Tragically, responsibility for collective sins is easily shirked.

But the truth of Scripture remains, and sin always robs spiritual vitality. Spiritual power to do God's work with fruitfulness is available only when sin is properly dealt with and a right relationship to God reestablished. This principle, which most believers know personally, must be applied equally to the church as a corporate body! Dr. Neil Anderson and Dr. Charles Mylander are to be commended for bringing this truth before the church and also for providing such thoughtful practical instruction for dealing biblically with sin on the corporate church level. At a time when the effectiveness of the church is being questioned, the insights in this book will help Christian leaders find God's answers for free victorious living and successful ministry in Christ!

Dr. Robert L. Saucy
Distinguished Professor of Systematic Theology
Talbot School of Theology
Biola University

INTRODUCTION

Community Bible Church was only 12 years old. Mark, the founding pastor, had originally been called to the community to pastor another church. He was a gifted evangelist who led many in this nominally Christian fellowship to salvation. Opposition to Mark's leadership style soon began to surface, and the inevitable struggle for power resulted in a church split. Along with the conservative core, Mark started Community Bible Church. Tragically, he eventually had to leave Community Church. It was a bitter departure, resulting from a moral failure.

Mark's successor was a young man named Jerry, who was attempting his first ministry. Jerry did not last long. In guarded language, the calling committee at Community Church admitted that the church had run him off. It was clearly made known, however, that the principal players who orchestrated his departure were no longer in the church. Besides, Jerry probably made a lot of mistakes that inevitably accompany every pastor's first ministry experience. So when Community Church extended a call for yet another pastor, John accepted.

It was a joyful experience for several months, but by the end of the first year the honeymoon was over. Resistance to John's leadership was increasing at every board meeting. Gossip was rampant and rumors were floating around the church. He was spending most of his time putting out fires instead of leading in a responsible way. A spiritual pall hung over the church like a brooding vulture. Worship was an arduous task instead of a joyful celebration. The responses to his messages were neutral at best. Visible signs of anybody bearing any fruit were not evident.

In the past, John would have doubled his efforts, but somehow he knew that was not the answer for this church. Personal needs in his life had caused him to look beyond his previous seminary training, as well as the latest pop psychology, to find some resolution. Through a series of conferences and books, he was made aware of the spiritual battle in which we are all engaged. More important, he discovered who he was in Christ. John found freedom from his past, and began daily to win the battle for his mind. Just trying harder had not helped him personally before, and he now knew it would not help his church corporately resolve its problems.

John began to teach his people who they are in Christ, and that their "struggle is not against flesh and blood, but against the rulers, against the authorities, against the powers of this dark world and against the spiritual forces of evil in the heavenly realms" (Eph. 6:12). At the same time, he began to pour through the minutes of previous board and church meetings. He discovered that many in the church had not dealt fairly with their previous pastors.

John waited for the right time to confront the present board with the corporate sins of their past. Although the primary players were no longer in the church, the same pathology seemed to be continuing. John pointed out to them how Nehemiah and Daniel had prayed, confessing their sins and the sins of their fathers. Being a small church, the board decided to bring the matter before the whole body. It brought up a lot of painful memories, and it was obvious that the issues had only been covered up, not resolved. The church members all sensed a release after acknowledging their sin, and sought God's forgiveness.

The church, however, was not done. They called Jerry, the previous pastor, and asked if he would be willing to come back to the church for a special service of reconciliation. It turned out that he was still hurting from the devastating experience, and had not returned to ministry. He declined at first, but finally agreed to come back for the good of both his family and the church he had to leave.

As Jerry stood before their church body, they read a list of offenses the church had committed against him. Handing him the list, they asked for his forgiveness. They held their breath as he painfully considered the choice confronting him. Finally Jerry said, "Jesus requires that we forgive as He has forgiven us. So I choose to forgive you for what you have done to me and my family." Not a dry eye could be seen in the house.

Mark, the founding pastor, refused their invitation, but they had done all they could to resolve their issues and bring their church into a right relationship with God. Jerry has since returned to ministry as the Lord had called him. The spiritual pall left the church, and the congregation began joyfully to bear fruit. They are still experiencing the normal pains of growth, as well as occasional problems, but they are learning how to resolve those problems by facing the truth and taking into account all of reality.

Community Bible Church, Mark, Jerry and John, are fictional names, but the story is true. As I (Neil) have traveled across America and around the world, I have had the privilege of talking to many denominational leaders and missionary executives. Based on their observations, the most optimistic assessment is that 20 percent of our churches are functioning as a living organism and bearing substantial fruit. They estimate that between 35 and 50 percent are dysfunctional, bearing no fruit at all. Denominational leaders are overwhelmed with problems. They find themselves, like the pastor above, spending most of their time trying to put out fires instead of offering leadership and vision. The average churches are operating as though their transmission were in reverse, and they have jammed on the brakes to halt any further slide in attendance.

When new members join your church, what are they bringing with them? Undoubtedly they will occupy some empty seats and be spiritually endowed with some combination of sorely needed skills, talents and gifts. In many cases, however, they also bring a tremendous amount of baggage left over from unresolved conflicts. Accumulate enough of this in your church and you will have corporate bondage.

By "corporate bondage," we are talking about unresolved personal and spiritual issues that inhibit churches from being the most God wants them to be—free in Christ. These issues may result from painful memories, corporate sins, satanic attacks or simply the weaknesses of the church.

Paul says of the Church, "If one part suffers, every part suffers" (1 Cor. 12:26). The sins of some individual leaders in the Church will cause the whole Body to ache. In addition, many pastors leave bad church experiences hoping for a better congregation somewhere else. Unless the pastors make a conscientious effort to overcome their hurts and disappointments, what will they bring to their next church? If the leadership lacks an adequate theology of resolution, they either lower their standards and expectations, or live in denial while the board meetings continue on with "business as usual." (This is the reason you will find us addressing the subject of leadership so extensively throughout this book. If leaders have not established their identity and freedom in Christ, how can they lead their churches to freedom?)

I recently conducted a conference in Europe, primarily for missionaries. I have never been in a group of called and committed Christians that were hurting as badly as they were. They represented almost every country in Europe, as well as many mission boards. Most were being chewed up personally and interpersonally, and several were chafing under oppressive administrative restraints. Ask any honest missionary executive and they will admit that the casualty rate is high. Ask any honest and experienced pastor and he will tell you that he and his family have experienced malicious personal and spiritual attacks.

Chuck and I want to offer our analysis, but more importantly, we will conclude with steps that have to be taken to free our churches from their bondages and come again under the Lordship of Christ. I have written the first five chapters of this book; Chuck wrote chapters 6 to 13. Together we have collaborated over all the material. Chuck has guided more than 20 churches through the process of "Setting Your Church Free." Each was a learning experience, and we have been instructed and blessed by the honest feedback from the churches' leadership.

Chuck's chapters 8 through 13 will discuss the specific steps of "Setting Your Church Free," which are given in appendix B. We will refer to these steps throughout the book. The procedure we are suggesting is a comprehensive process of personal and corporate assessment and cleansing. The time frame we are recommending is Friday evening and all day Saturday.

I will be addressing the spiritual and leadership issues as they relate to organizational structure. We must take into account the reality of the spiritual world, but only resolving spiritual problems without correcting leadership problems and organizational pathology will prove counterproductive. The need is for balance. Every organized church has personal, spiritual and administrative problems. We need a biblical answer that addresses all three.

A few years ago Talbot School of Theology, where I taught for 10 years, extensively researched its graduates for the purpose of revising its curriculum. As suspected, the results showed that the problems were first interpersonal, second administrative. At the time, we were offering no required courses on leadership and administration for Master of Divinity students, a deficiency now corrected. Many other seminaries saw the need to better equip their students to be spiritual leaders.

Poor leadership and administrative goofs can and do lead to interpersonal problems and spiritual chaos. Trying to resolve personal and spiritual conflicts in a church or mission group without correcting leadership problems is an exercise in futility. It would be like trying to help a rebellious 14-year-old boy and then sending him back into the same dysfunctional family. One would have to ask why he rebelled in the first place.

Chuck will discuss the role of the pastor as a saint (chapter 6), and the role of the church in living communion with Christ. He will share the theological basis and practical procedure for setting your church or missionary organization free. As previously mentioned, the actual steps are given in appendix B ("Seven Steps Toward Setting Your Church Free").

Two overwhelming issues underscore this book.

First, we strongly believe that individual freedom must come to the leadership before organizational freedom can be accomplished. It has taken me years of study and research to discover how God intends His people to live free in Christ. The result is a comprehensive procedure called "Steps to Freedom in Christ," now being used all over the world in many languages. This is a fierce moral inventory that helps believers resolve their personal and spiritual issues between themselves and God.

The basis for this tool and my present conference, "Resolving Personal and Spiritual Conflicts" (a seven-day Bible conference about living free in Christ that includes a comprehensive discussion of the Christian life), is spelled out in my first two books, *Victory over the Darkness* (Regal Books) and *The Bondage Breaker* (Harvest House Publishers). Chuck has used this material, and has had great results in his own ministry. *Released from Bondage* (Thomas Nelson Publishers) gives case studies written from the victims' perspective, and additional insight on how we help people find their freedom from every form of bondage. (For your convenience, we have included the "Personal Steps to Freedom in Christ" in appendix C of this book.)

Organizations are like marriages. Trying to get couples to behave right, before establishing them free in Christ, is like trying to win a race without an engine in your car. It reverses the order of Scripture. It is even more unrealistic to expect a church to function well when many are struggling in one form of bondage or another and most do not know who they are in Christ. Our ultimate purpose is to reach our communities and this world for Christ. But we first have to get our people free in Christ and then our marriages, churches and missionary organizations can come back together. Then, and only then, will we be able to accomplish our purpose.

Second, we believe that the unity of the true Church is essential to accomplish our mission on planet earth. The Lord prayed that we would all be one (see John 17:21). The only basis for that unity is our common heritage: We are all children of God. Frankly, the Church is being patronized in America. As long as we fight one another and find our identity only in our theological positions and denominational heritages, we will not be taken seriously.

Part of our problem in the English-speaking world is that we do not have provision in our language for a plural "you." (Some parts of the country say "y'all" or "youse," but the rest of the country frowns at this use of the King's English.) Therefore, many passages in Scripture where the Lord addresses the corporate Church Body translate as "you." But the "you" is plural. He is addressing the Body of Christ. From God's perspective, there is one Church, one Spirit, one Lord. We have often stressed our personal relationship with Christ at the expense of our corporate relationship to Him. This has been increasingly more evident since the rebellious '60s. The consequence is a cultural commitment to radical individualism. Individual rights have been emphasized over personal and corporate responsibilities.

This book in itself is a statement. Chuck was theologically educated at a Friends college having Wesleyan influence, and at a reformed seminary. I was educated at a more Calvinistic and dispensational school of thought. We both hold to the authority of Scripture and believe that the original manuscripts are infallible. The issues we are addressing do not pit the covenant theologian against the dispensational theologian, nor the Arminian against the Calvinist, nor the evangelical against the charismatic. Not to say that these are not important issues, they are; they will remain issues of discussion until the Lord comes back. But they are not issues we are going to allow Satan to use as points of division. The primary battle is not between differing theological schools, it is between Christ and Antichrist.

All biblically conservative schools of theology have a common core of belief that they find essential for us to live and grow by. You may not agree with all I have to say, or with all Chuck has to say. But would you agree that we all need to find our identity and freedom in Christ, and be "diligent to preserve the unity of the Spirit in the bond of peace" (Eph. 4:3, *NASB*)? It is our prayer that this book will help the Church come closer to fulfilling the prayer of Jesus in John 17, which is where I begin my section of this book.

PART ONE

This section presents a biblical analysis of the Church, taking into account the reality of the spiritual world and the need for Christ-centered leaders and ministries.

PROTECTED FROM THE EVIL ONE

I am coming to you now, but I say these things while I am still in the world, so that they may have the full measure of my joy within them. I have given them your word and the world has hated them, for they are not of the world any more than I am of the world. My prayer is not that you take them out of the world but that you protect them from the evil one. They are not of the world, even as I am not of it. Sanctify them by the truth; your word is truth. As you sent me into the world, I have sent them into the world. For them I sanctify myself, that they too may be truly sanctified. My prayer is not for them alone. I pray also for those who will believe in me through their message.

John 17:13-20

The high priestly prayer in John 17 reveals the concern of Jesus for His disciples and all those who believe in Him. He is returning to the Father, but the disciples and the soon to be established Church will remain on planet earth where "the ruler of the world" (John 14:30, *NASB*), "the prince of the power of the air" (Eph. 2:2, *NASB*), "your enemy the devil prowls around like a roaring lion looking for someone to devour" (1 Pet. 5:8). Unlike concerned parents who may be tempted to isolate their children from the harsh realities of this world, Jesus did not ask that we be removed. That strategy would result in no growth for the children or the Church, and thus no future ministry. His prayer is that we be protected from the evil one.

Scary thought, but Jesus has not left us defenseless. First, "You have been given fullness in Christ, who is the head over every power and authority" (Col. 2:10). The Church is established in Christ and seated with Him in the heavenly realms (see Eph. 2:6). Because of our position in Christ, we have all the authority we need over the evil one to carry out the delegated responsibility of fulfilling the Great Commission (see Matt. 28:18,19).

Second, "Having disarmed the powers and authorities, he made a public spectacle of them, triumphing over them by the cross" (Col. 2:15). "His intent was that now, through the church, the manifold wisdom of God should be made known to the rulers and authorities in the heavenly realms, according to his eternal purpose which he accomplished in Christ Jesus our Lord" (Eph. 3:10,11).

The Eternal Purpose of God

I am a strong believer in the necessity of taking the time to work through a purpose statement for every aspect of Christian ministry. It is what defines our mission and directs our efforts in a meaningful way. And here we have it, the "eternal purpose of God," for the Church! He has committed and apparently somewhat limited Himself to make His wisdom known through the Church. To whom? To the rulers and authorities in the heavenly (i.e., the spiritual) realms. The very existence of the Church reveals God's wisdom to the powers. He "made foolish the wisdom of the world" (1 Cor. 1:20). Satan thought he could stop the plan of God by inciting the rulers of the day to put Jesus to death, but he was wrong. The rulers and authorities in the heavenly realms are seeing salvation come to all those who call upon the name of the Lord. God was able to unite both Jews and Gentiles into one corporate Body.

"The Son of God appeared for this *purpose*, that He might destroy the works of the devil" (1 John 3:8, *NASB*, italics added). Should you be tempted as some are to think that these rulers and the authorities in the heavenly realms are human governments and structures of earthly existence, let me encourage you to read *Powers of Darkness: Principalities and Powers in Paul's Letters* by Dr. Clinton E. Arnold.[1]

If, therefore, the battle is between the kingdom of darkness and the Kingdom of Light, between Christ and Antichrist, and God's eternal purpose is to make His wisdom known through the Church to the rulers and authorities, how are we doing? Half of those who claim membership in the Church do not believe in a personal devil, a standard doctrine of the true historical Church. Most operate as though the devil does not exist, having little understanding of how the spiritual world impinges on the natural world. A few would insist no interaction is taking place. Some, out of fear, make a conscious choice not to deal with the reality of the devil. In some circles, belief in the devil is not academically credible. Many are like blindfolded prisoners who do not know who their enemy is, so they strike out at themselves and each other.

The Church is filled with so many wounded people, it is seen by much of the world as a hospital for sick people. But that is not what Christ established His Church to be. The Church, rather, is a military outpost that has been called to storm the fortresses that are raised up against the knowledge of God (see 2 Cor. 10:3-5). Thankfully, within that military outpost is an infirmary. I have spent a lot of my time in the infirmary, because this war has a lot of casualties. But the Church does not exist for the infirmary, the infirmary exists for the Church. The Church is "the pillar and foundation of the truth" (1 Tim. 3:15). The Bible assures us, "We are more than conquerors through him who loved us" (Rom. 8:37). Why then, if we have all this assurance of victory, are we limping along, and in what ways are we vulnerable?

A Very Real Enemy

As we confront this hostile world, the Lord has not left us defenseless. We have a sanctuary in Christ and He has equipped us with the armor of God. We have all the resources we need in Christ to stand firm and resist the devil, but if we do not assume our responsibility those resources will go unused. He has instructed us to put on the armor of God (see Eph. 6:10-18). What if we haven't? We have been told, "Put on the Lord Jesus Christ, and make no provision for the flesh in regard to its lusts" (Rom. 13:14, *NASB*). What if we have made provision for the flesh? Clearly it is our responsibility to "resist the devil" (Jas. 4:7). What if we don't? God's provision for our freedom in Christ is limited only to the degree that we fail to assume our responsibility.

The most common and naive response in the Western world is to ignore the battle or to make the fatal assumption that Christians are somehow immune. Just the opposite is true. Ignorance is not bliss; it is defeat. If you are a Christian, you are the target. If you are a pastor, you and your family are the bull's-eye! It is the strategy of Satan to render the Church inoperative and to obliterate the truth that we are "dead to sin but alive to God in Christ Jesus" (Rom. 6:11).

How is the devil doing? The divorce rate and disintegration of the Christian family roughly parallels the secular world. Sexual activity among Christian singles is only slightly less. The distinction between a Christian and a pagan is no longer obvious. The tragic fall of many visible Christian leaders indicates that something is dreadfully wrong. Having an intellectual knowledge of Scripture obviously is not enough, because I am sure these leaders had that. "Christianity does not work" is the message many are receiving.

One reason Christianity does not appear to work is found in 1 John 2:12-14. John identifies little children of the faith as those who know the Father and have had their sins forgiven. In other words, they have overcome the penalty of sin. Satan loses the primary battle when we trust in Christ, but he does not curl up his tail, pull in his fangs and slink away. His strategy is to keep the believer under the power of sin. Twice, the young men of the faith are identified in this passage as having overcome the evil one. How are we going to help our people reach their full maturity in Christ if they have no idea how to overcome the evil one? The unfortunate truth is that many of our Christian leaders still have seemingly uncontrollable appetites and behaviors. The sin, confess, sin, confess, sin, confess and sin again cycle does not deal with all of reality. It should be sin, confess and resist.

Do you still think you are immune? Then let me ask three pertinent questions:

1. Have you experienced any temptation this week? Biblically, who is the tempter? It can't be God (see Jas. 1:13). He will test our faith in order to strengthen it, but Satan's temptations are intended to destroy our faith.

2. Have you ever struggled with the voice of the accuser of the brethren (see Rev. 12:10)? Before you answer, let me ask the question in another way. Have you ever struggled with thoughts such as, *I'm stupid,* or *I'm ugly,* or *I can't,* or *God doesn't love me,* or *I'm different from others* or *I'm going down?* I know you have, because the Bible says that Satan accuses the brethren day and night.

3. Have you ever been deceived? The person who is tempted to answer no may be the most deceived of all.

If I tempt you, you know it. If I accuse you, you will know it. But if I deceive you, you do not know it. If you knew it, you would no longer be deceived. Now listen to the logic of Scripture: "If you hold to my teaching, you are really my disciples. Then you will know the truth, and the truth will set you free" (John 8:31,32). Jesus said, "I am the way and the truth and the life" (John 14:6). In the high priestly prayer, Jesus prayed, "Sanctify them by the truth; your word is truth" (John 17:17). When we put on the armor of God, the first thing we do is put on the "belt of truth" (Eph. 6:14).

The Battle for Our Minds

What was the conflict that required God to intervene dramatically in the Early Church when He struck down Ananias and Sapphira? Peter asked, "How is it that Satan has so filled your heart that you have lied to the Holy Spirit and have kept for yourself some of the money you received for the land?" (Acts 5:3). The message could not have been made more clear. If Satan can operate undetected in your church, your home, your marriage or yourself, convincing you to believe a lie, couldn't he control your life? The Lord had to expose the battle for the mind as soon as Satan raised his ugly head in the Early Church. The strategy is not new. Satan deceived Eve, and she believed a lie (see Gen. 3:1-7). The sobering reality is that Eve was spiritually alive and virtually without sin at the time. To assume that a Christian who is spiritually alive and struggling with sin can't be deceived is hopelessly naive!

Is a battle going on for our minds? Absolutely! Steve Russo, an evangelist, and I surveyed 1,725 teenagers who were attending evangelical schools or churches. Here are the results of the high schoolers who participated:

- 47 percent have experienced a presence in their room that scared them;
- 54 percent struggle with bad thoughts about God;
- 37 percent said it is mentally hard to pray and read their Bible;
- 70 percent have heard "voices" in their head as if there were a subconscious self talking to them, or they struggled with really bad thoughts;
- 20 percent frequently entertain thoughts of suicide;
- 24 percent have had impulsive thoughts to kill someone, such as, "Grab that knife and kill that person";
- 71 percent think they are different from others (i.e., Christianity works for others but it does not work for them).

Those percentages get worse if young people have dabbled with the occult, as you can read in my book, *The Seduction of Our Children*. I do not believe that the 70 percent who are hearing or have heard voices are paranoid schizophrenic or psychotic. I believe 1 Timothy 4:1: "The Spirit clearly says that in later times some will abandon the faith and follow deceiving spirits and things taught by demons." Is that happening? It is happening all over the world. It matters not where I go, the problems are basically the same and the answer is always the same.

In the last 10 years, I have counseled more than 500 adults who are hearing voices or are severely struggling with their thought life. With very few exceptions, the problem has been spiritual. It takes us an average of about three hours to help a person find freedom in Christ. Most will experience for the first time "the peace of God, which transcends all understanding" (Phil. 4:7). One pastor wrote to me after reading *The Bondage Breaker*: "I have been in the pastorate for 15 years struggling with three compulsive addictions: workaholism, overeating and my private thought life. Praise God for the freedom in Jesus Christ. I have just experienced this freedom and I am looking forward to enjoying it until death or Christ's return."

Why don't more believers know about and experience this freedom? For one reason, I can't read your mind, and you can't read mine. We really do not have any idea what is going on in the minds of other people unless they have the courage to share with us. In many cases they won't share because in our culture they might wrongly be judged as mentally ill. People will tell us about their abuse or what has happened to them, but rarely do they dare to share what is going on inside. Are they mentally ill, or is a battle going on for their mind? The lack of any balanced biblical contribution to mental health professions has left them with only one conclusion: any problem in the mind must be either psychological or neurological.

Your education and worldview form a grid by which you interpret data and evaluate events. Let me illustrate by using the following testimony that was sent to me by a struggling young lady who found her freedom in Christ:

"Silence"

When I sit and think, I think of many things. My life, what I want to do, what I think about issues and people. I have conversations with myself inside of my mind. I talk to myself and answer myself—I am my own best friend. We get along great! Sometimes I talk to myself so much during the day that I am really tired at the end of the day. But, I keep myself occupied and it helps me to think things through.

Sometimes I think of myself as two people: the one who is me every day of the week...the one I want to change. The one who has a low self-esteem, and is afraid to really be herself in front of everyone. And then there's the one inside of me...the confident me who I wish would come out, but for some reason won't. I call that part of me "her." She is a "she," and I refer to her as such. She is very bold, and everybody loves her; at least that's what I think would happen if I would just let her out. If I could just be myself...life would be so much easier and happier.

But until then, I talk to her inside of me. We talk about what we will do today, where we will go to eat, what we will wear, who we will talk to. Sometimes she comes up with very good ideas and I am impressed with myself that I am so smart and clever. "If only people knew the real me," I think. "They would really love me." And sometimes I hear her say things to me that don't make sense. "I shouldn't really do that," I think. "That isn't very nice. That would hurt someone. That is a stupid thing to do...." And I don't listen to her that time. But, I don't mind. I like talking to her, so I continue talking.

Before you hear the rest of her story, ask yourself some questions. Is what this lady describes "normal"? Is this self-talk? Does she have a split personality? Is she psychotic? Maybe she is struggling with multiple personalities. Is this an inner child of her past? Your education and worldview will certainly affect your diagnosis. Let's finish her story:

One day, things changed between her and me. My life was going okay, but I wanted a closer relationship with God. I wanted to be free from the past and to be healed in my heart from the pain that I had been carrying. Someone told me that I should go through something called "The Steps to Freedom in Christ," and I made an appointment with a counselor. I wasn't thinking about my friend inside of me; I was thinking about me.

In the counseling session I was asked to read some prayers and Scripture out loud. While doing this, my mind became fuzzy and I couldn't concentrate. Most of all, when I tried to speak to her in my mind, I became confused. I couldn't hear her clearly. I became scared, my heart raced and I became very enraged inside. I shook. Where was my friend inside of me? Why all of a sudden was she mad? What was going on? What was wrong with me?

Then I found out. She wasn't my friend. She wasn't really me. She didn't want me to be friends with Jesus, and she didn't want me to get my life right with God. It didn't make sense because these were things that I wanted to do. I thought she was on my side. But I was wrong. I had to tell her to leave—out loud. Out loud? That seemed weird when I was told that she couldn't read my thoughts. But it made sense; she wasn't God, and she wasn't omnipresent. So I told her to leave out loud, and she was gone.

And there was silence. There were no more conversations going on in my mind anymore. And I missed her. I knew I shouldn't, but I did. I knew that she wasn't good for me and that God wanted me to talk to Him and not her. I struggled with the thought of talking to her and not talking to her. I couldn't stand the silence—I felt alone. She tried to come back, and when she did it scared me. She was angry and hostile. I felt betrayed. But after time, I got used to the silence. I used it to remind me to talk to God, and I did. He didn't answer like she did. I could not hear His voice like I could hers. But I began to love talking to Him, singing to Him. I really felt close to Him—like He cared. And after awhile I forgot about the silence.

After some time I found myself lonely again. I forgot about the silence and found myself in conversation without even realizing it. My life was in confusion and I couldn't figure out why...until one day I had to really pray. My friend who had been discipling me wanted to help me and I wanted help. She was talking to me about my rebellion, and I needed to stop living independent of Him. It was then that I heard a very loud voice inside of me say, "I am independent of God." It scared me. Was that me? Did I really feel this way? No, I didn't. She was back. Then I got angry because I had let her back. I wanted her gone, but I couldn't move and I couldn't say anything. My friend prayed with me and I bowed my head. She told me to picture heaven with a light, the lampstands and the throne of God. I started to really see it and to feel calm again. But then the voice started yelling, "No! No! No!" So I opened my eyes and gave up. My heart became hard and I didn't really want to give everything to God. I wanted control still. There were some things that I did not want to give up.

But inside I longed for the silence again. *How ironic,* I thought. Something that I didn't like at first had become my freedom. How I fought inside, trying to struggle with praying to God or running away from Him. It was so easy to run, so easy to put off what I could do right now. But I didn't feel repentant. I didn't feel like letting go, even though I knew I needed to. I wondered if I would ever feel like it again.

And that is when I saw the words from "The Steps to Freedom in Christ" jump at me from the page. It read, "Faith is something you decide to do, not something you feel like doing." So I did it.

And now I live in wonderful silence.

Who Has the Answer?

Could someone have this young lady's symptoms and the problem be neurological or chemical? Probably, but in too many cases, neurological and chemical problems are the only possibilities considered. In our Western world, a natural explanation for everything is assumed. Every medical possibility has to be explored first, and when doctors cannot find any cause, people say, "There is nothing left to do now but pray." I think the order is reversed. My Bible reads, "But seek first his kingdom and his righteousness" (Matt. 6:33). Why not go to God first?

I have a great respect for the medical profession, and I think the Church should work hand in glove with committed doctors. But we should not be intimidated as though the Church has no valid contribution. When it is assumed that someone who is hearing voices has a chemical imbalance, ask for an explanation of how that could be. How can an impersonal chemistry create a personal thought? How can the neurotransmitters in my brain randomly fire in such a way as to create a thought that is totally foreign to what I would choose to think? I am open; explain it to me. It can't be explained, however, any more than I can explain to someone how Satan puts thoughts into our minds. It is much easier for me to believe the latter because of 1 Timothy 4:1 and other passages, especially because I have seen it to be true in thousands of people around the world.

The problem is much like the debate between creationists and evolutionists. Creation is a hard thing to accept if you do not believe in God. But if you do believe in God, creation is easier to accept because you do not have to deal with all the unsubstantiated assumptions that have to be made in the case of evolution. For instance, 1 Corinthians 15:39 says that all creatures are not the same. Human beings have one kind of body; animals have another, birds another and fish another. If you believe in God it is much easier to accept God's explanation of His created order than it is to justify spending the rest of your life looking for a missing link that does not exist.

A committed Christian lady brought her husband and son in to see me because she thought for sure that I would side with her argument that they needed psychiatric help. After hearing their story, it was obvious to me that their problem was far more spiritual than psychiatric. When I shared with her that I believed their story, she was disappointed in my diagnosis. I then asked her if she believed in evolution.

"Of course not," she said.

"You mean to tell me that you don't believe in the scientific explanation of the origin of the species?" I asked. Again the answer was no, so I asked her if she believed in the social scientists' explanation of mental illness. "Yes," she said.

Although I was unable to convince her of her faulty logic or the incongruity of her statements, I did have the privilege of seeing her husband and son come to freedom in Christ.

Sadly, many Christians would probably answer the same way this lady did, but why? If we do not accept the natural scientists' explanation of reality, why do we accept the social scientists' explanation of mental illness? The natural sciences are far more precise than the social sciences. In fact, the social sciences make no claim for precision at all. It is a study of probabilities and statistics. Sociologists and psychologists are often poles apart and can vary all over the charts, even in their own schools of thought. Yet many Christians labor under the assumption that they are precise sciences.

In addition to my seminary degrees, I have a research doctorate in the social sciences, as well as a scientific degree in engineering. I have some understanding of the scientific method of investigation. By definition, it leaves out the reality of the spiritual world. God Himself does not submit to our methods of investigation. Rest assured, the god of this world is not going to cooperate either, because his major strategy is deception.

Research is not wrong; it is just incomplete. I have done my own research and will be sharing more of it with you in this book. If the research is done right, it can give us a fairly good picture of reality. When the research is descriptive, it is very helpful. When it becomes prescriptive, then it is not helpful. The only way we are going to overcome the father of lies (see John 8:44) is by revelation, not research nor reasoning. This is why the Lord prayed that we be sanctified "by the truth; your [His] word is truth" (John 17:17) as the only means by which we can be protected from the evil one.

One leading Christian educator indicated that he was mildly interested in what I was saying about the reality of the spiritual world, but he wanted to do some of his own research to validate my statements. I said I was open, but when I went on to explain what I perceived to be the limitations of research, he said he was no longer interested. So I asked him, "Do you need research to validate revelation?"

On the contrary, I believe we need revelation to validate research. We must look at research through the grid of Scripture, not Scripture through the grid of research. But if we close our eyes and ears to valid research, we will not be as effective in the application of God's eternal truth when we seek with wisdom to apply it to the changing needs of this world. I believe the credibility of the Church is at stake. Is Christ the answer? Does truth set us free?

A False Dichotomy

I am often asked how I know whether a person's problem is spiritual or psychological. I believe this is the wrong question and forces us into a false dichotomy. Our problems are never not psychological. At no time are our minds, wills and emotions not involved or pertinent to the situation. Our humanity is never in doubt this side of eternity. On the other hand, our problems are never not spiritual. At no time is God absent or irrelevant. He is right now "sustaining all things by his powerful word" (Heb. 1:3).

To my knowledge, at no time is it safe to take off the armor of God. The possibility of being tempted, accused or deceived is a continual reality. The Bible teaches that the unseen world is more real than the seen world: "For what is seen is temporary, but what is unseen is eternal" (2 Cor. 4:18). If we could just accept this truth, we would stop polarizing into psychotherapeutic ministries that ignore spiritual reality, or jump into some kind of deliverance ministry that ignores developmental issues and human responsibility. We must take into account all of reality and strive for a balanced message.

As we strive for biblical balance, consider Diagram 1.A. Keep in mind that I am assuming a correct biblical understanding of God (theology), man (psychology), the natural world and the spiritual world. I am not pitting one against the other. I want to show what can potentially happen if one is emphasized at the expense of the other.

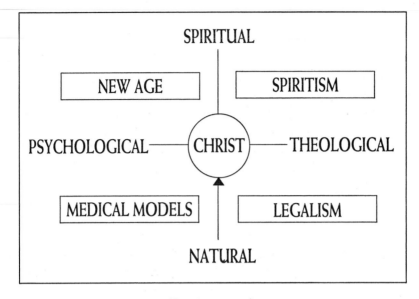

Diagram 1.A

Psychological and Medical

First of all, we need to realize that the Western world has been skewed substantially toward the natural, although that has been changing rather dramatically in the last quarter of the twentieth century. In the lower left quadrant of Diagram 1.A, medical models have dominated the helping professions. Man and nature are the only players, humanism being the dominant philosophy. Secular psychology entered into the Christian arena out of this quadrant. Many are trying to integrate these models into Christianity. In some cases, the result is nothing more than nice Christian people doing secular counseling. Others are sincerely trying to incorporate these approaches from a Christian perspective. I do not believe the latter will be successful or balanced until two issues are thoroughly embraced.

First, do you have a gospel? Does it make any difference whether the person is a Christian or not? Are we just a product of our past, or are we a product of the work of Christ on the cross? Does 2 Corinthians 5:17 have any practical relevance to us today? "Therefore, if anyone is in Christ, he is a new creation; the old has gone, the new has come!" Are we trying to fix our past, or be free from it? Does our hope lie in God, or does it lie in some technique or group? I will have more to say about that in the next chapter.

Second, does our Christian counseling take into account the reality of the spiritual world? In other words, do we have a biblical worldview? Is our struggle just against flesh and blood? Are we trying to accomplish God's will without depending upon the Holy Spirit? Does your method or concept of helping people change if the person is a Christian or not? If we are trying to help people establish their identity, find purpose and meaning in life, and seek to meet their needs without Christ, then we need to know that it is precisely the agenda of Satan on planet earth. Sobering!

New Age
A dramatic shifting of these secular models moves upward on Diagram 1.A. Unfortunately, the spiritual reality is not Christian; it is demonic. In the absence of an adequate theology, demons have been renamed spirit guides, and mediums are called channelers. Humanism as a viable philosophy is waning. Man as only man is unable to save himself, but man as god has a better chance, reasons the New Ager. The New Age philosophy can be appealing. You are not a sinner in need of salvation; you are a god and just need to be enlightened. You can have spiritual power *and* materialism. Wow!

The rise of paganism as a religious philosophy among the elite and the influential in England is an interesting offshoot of the New Age in the United States. These people look at the Church in disdain because it lacks spiritual substance. The New Age, the occult and the ancient religions appear to offer much more spiritual reality. Power is what they want, and satanism offers it. The lure of esoteric knowledge and power has trapped many a traveler in the web of the occult.

Spiritism
The movement upward on the right side of Diagram 1.A has also been rapid. The Holy Spirit seemed to come out of hiding in the '60s and '70s for conservative Christians, but the devil is coming out in the '80s and '90s. Much of this new spiritual and personal awareness has been sorely needed, but distortions are evident when it becomes unbalanced. Personal needs and responsibilities are often overlooked. People are judged by others as having a spirit of this or a spirit of that. They reason that if the person can just get rid of that

spirit, they will be okay. Some pray and pray for God to do something, when He has already done all He needs to do for us to be free in Christ. He will not do for us what He has required us to do.

Legalism

The lower right quadrant of Diagram 1.A is diminishing, but the legalistic remnant has a tendency to drift even further to the right as they encounter people who are not interpreting Scripture as they believe it should be interpreted. The further legalists remove themselves from hurting humanity, the more controlling and judgmental they get. Legalists are the "defenders of the faith," similar to the Pharisees. They are right and if you do not agree with them, you are wrong. Their major characteristic will become evident when you try to get personally close to them; they won't let you.

Legalists motivate through fear and guilt. If you tried to help them understand how they got so hard and bitter, they would castigate you for psychoanalyzing them. In their churches, people are perceived as sinners in the hands of an angry God. That is not the case. We are saints in the hands of a loving God. I have never been able to understand how that simple truth is often distorted by those who claim most vehemently to uphold the authority of Scripture. I think the Lord would say to them, "Go and learn what this means: 'I desire mercy [compassion], not sacrifice'" (Matt. 9:13), for "the goal of this command is love" (1 Tim. 1:5).

Please do not draw the wrong conclusion from Diagram 1.A that I am giving man an equal billing with God. Nothing could be further from the truth. Christ, the God-Man, is the center. We will see in the next chapter how everything radiates from Him. What I am saying is that theology can never be an end in itself. There is a time to pray, and a time to serve, a time to worship and a time to share. Prayer and worship come first. But if we say we love the Lord, then we need to care for and feed His lambs (see John 21:15-19). If we say we love the Lord, Scripture requires that we love our brother (see 1 John 4:19-21).

The Only Perfect Balance

The above is a simple analysis of those who stray too far from the center. So who is perfectly in the center of the diagram? Only Christ! There are no

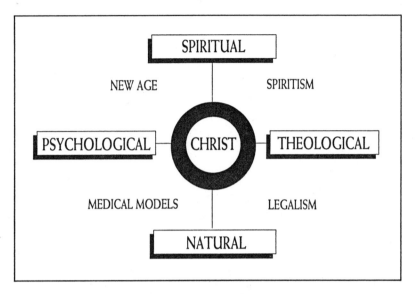

Diagram 1.B

perfectly balanced people, so I will add two circles to Diagram 1.A (see Diagram 1.B).

The inner circle of Diagram 1.B would constitute orthodox teaching by those who hold to the absolute authority of Scripture. If only God were interpreting His Word, the circle would be a dot. For us it is a circle, because there will always be minor disagreements, even among the most intellectually gifted theologians. No one man will ever be able to achieve omniscience. Where one would fall on the inner circle is also affected by giftedness. For example, those who have the gift of prophecy would probably be more oriented to the right because they are calling for holiness, the administrators to the bottom because they work in the world of facts and figures, those who have the gift of helps to the left because they are motivated to serve people.

The outer circle indicates that we need to exercise tolerance to a certain point. People are in various stages of transition and growth. People outside this circle need to renounce what they are doing and the lies they have believed. They are in bondage to the lies they have believed and the acts they have committed. So how do we help them find their freedom in Christ?

Basically the answer is, "Submit yourselves, then, to God. Resist the devil, and he will flee from you" (Jas. 4:7). Trying to resist the devil without first submitting to God is a dogfight. This is often the error of confrontational kinds of deliverance ministries. By this, I mean deliverance where demons are directly confronted without the person in bondage first submitting to God. On the other hand, you can submit to God without resisting the devil and stay in bondage. The tragedy of our time is that many recovery ministries are not doing either one. Submitting to God requires us to deal with the sin in our lives. Sin is like garbage; it attracts flies. So get rid of the flies! No, get rid of the garbage. If you get rid of the garbage, the flies will have no reason or right to be there.

I did not ask for my first encounter with the powers of darkness; it was thrust upon me. My feeble attempt was based on the most commonly perceived process of calling up the demon, getting its name and rank, and then casting it out. I found the process ugly, exhausting and potentially harmful to the victim. Often the process had to be repeated and the results did not seem to last. In this procedure, the deliverer seems to be the pastor, counselor or missionary. The information is obtained from the demons. Why would we believe them?

We are clearly told, "There is no truth in him [Satan]. When he lies, he speaks his native language, for he is a liar and the father of lies" (John 8:44). I have found it unnecessary to know the name of the demons or their rank. I do not dialogue or deal with the demonic nor advise others to interact with them. I do not want demons to manifest themselves; I desire that the Lord be manifested and thereby glorified. I don't think we should ever let the devil set the agenda.

I also found the process nontransferable. The procedure is often based on giftedness, or an office of the church, as in the case of the Roman Catholics. I think there is a better and much more transferable procedure. I believe Jesus is the Deliverer, and He has already come. Second, we should get our information from the Holy Spirit because He is "the Spirit of truth" and "he will guide you into all truth" (John 16:13).

The shifting of my thinking began when I realized it is truth that sets us free, and Jesus is the Truth. His prayer in John 17 is that we be kept from the evil one by being sanctified in the Word of God, which is the truth. That is why I prefer to think of our battle as more of a truth encounter as opposed to a power encounter. I know of no place in the Bible that instructs us to seek power, except to seek that which we already have available to us in Christ (see Eph. 6:10). We already have all the power we need because of our incredible position in Christ.

> I pray also that the eyes of your heart may be enlightened in order that you may know the hope to which he has called you, the riches of his glorious inheritance in the saints, and his incomparably great power for us who believe. That power is like the working of his mighty strength, which he exerted in Christ when he raised him from the dead (Eph. 1:18-20).

The power for Christians lies in their ability to believe the truth, and the power of the evil one is in his ability to deceive. When you expose the lie, the enemy's power is broken. Often when Christians struggle, they wrongly conclude that they lack power. The temptation is to pursue some experience that will give them more power—it will be a false trip. Satanists pursue power because it has been stripped from them. Christians are to pursue the truth and carry out their ministry in the power of the Holy Spirit.

We have the authority to carry out our ministry because of our position in Christ, and we have the power because of the indwelling presence of the Holy Spirit. These are operative only as we live a life dependent upon God. We are "strong in the Lord and in his mighty power" (Eph. 6:10). If we operate in the flesh, independent of God, we will be defeated. A Jewish chief priest sadly found this out.

> One day the evil spirit answered them, "Jesus I know, and I know about Paul, but who are you?" Then the man who had the evil spirit jumped on them and overpowered them all. He gave them such a beating that they ran out of the house naked and bleeding (Acts 19:15,16).

Occasionally, we will be called to confront the powers of darkness directly. I was working with a young lady who was extremely abused in her youth. She briefly lost mental control and a vile voice said through her, "Who the (blank) do you think you are?" If that happened to you, how would you respond? "I'm a child of God," I said and commanded the spirit to be silent in the name and authority of the Lord Jesus Christ. The lady returned to her right mind and that night found her freedom in Christ in a quiet and controlled way.

Another time, a large lady slowly got out of her chair and started to walk toward me in a menacing way. What would you do? Based on 1 John 5:18 I said, "I'm a child of God and the evil one cannot touch me." She immediately stopped and returned to her seat. By the way, authority does not increase with volume. We do not shout out the devil, we calmly take our place in Christ. You have lost control if you end up screaming and shouting. In such cases, fear is the controlling issue, not faith. Fear of anything other than a healthy fear of God is mutually exclusive of faith in God.

The classic approach of confronting and dealing with demons was primarily developed from the Gospels because they are the only New Testament historical books that show how the Lord confronted the demonized. Prior to the Cross, Satan had not yet been defeated, and the Holy Spirit had not yet come in His fullness. Therefore, it required a specially endowed authority agent to accomplish the deliverance. This is why we read in Luke 9:1, "When Jesus had called the Twelve together, he gave them power and authority to drive out all demons." If we are to continue driving out demons in the Church Age, where are the instructions in the Epistles? The Epistles contain no instructions for a person to cast a demon out of someone else. Why not?

A Great Hope for Deliverance

After the Cross, deliverance is no longer the outside agent's responsibility; it is the individual's responsibility. I can't put on the armor of God for you, or confess for you, or repent for you, or believe for you, or take every thought captive to the obedience of Christ for you. I can't even resist the devil for you. Those are your responsibilities, but I can help you. Now we have a very definitive passage for helping Christians find their freedom in Christ in the Pastoral Epistles.

And the Lord's servant must not quarrel; instead, he must be kind to everyone, able to teach, not resentful. Those who oppose him he must gently instruct, in the hope that God will grant them repentance leading them to a knowledge of the truth, and that they will come to their senses and escape from the trap of the devil, who has taken them captive to do his will (2 Tim. 2:24-26).

This is not a confrontational model; it is a kind, compassionate and able-to-teach model. It requires a dependency upon the Lord, for only He can grant the repentance that gets rid of the garbage. This model identifies truth as the liberating agent and implies that the battle is for the mind. It is totally transferable because all it requires is a lovingly mature servant of the Lord who knows the truth. I know the latter is true because we have had the privilege of training thousands of pastors, missionaries and laypeople all over the world who are at this time setting captives free in Christ. To illustrate how transferable this model is, let me share with you a letter I received from Dr. David Finnell, director of the International Network of Church Planters and a teacher at Columbia Bible College and Seminary.

I came across your materials a couple months ago and really sensed that they expressed the truths that I have been struggling with concerning power encounter. I have been involved with power encounter on the mission field and as a teacher here at Columbia Bible College and Seminary. I have really been concerned with the lack of personal involvement of the counselee in power encounter. I have utilized your materials in counseling situations over the last few weeks with dramatic and powerful results.

All of my students in my Prayer and Evangelism class are reading *The Bondage Breaker* and going through the "Steps to Freedom." I am spending personal sessions with those whose bondage is too great for them to deal with on their own, with very positive results.

I had to use the same procedures when I taught at Talbot School of Theology. It would be a tragic mistake to think that all Christians or all our Christian leaders are free in Christ. Does Christ want us free? Of course! "It is for freedom that Christ has set us free. Stand firm, then, and do not let your-selves be burdened again by a yoke of slavery" (Gal. 5:1). The context is free-dom from the law; so if you are on the far right side (theological) of Diagram 1.A, chances are you lost your freedom. Should you be tempted to throw off constraints and go too far to the left (psychological), then consider Galatians 5:13: "You, my brothers, were called to be free. But do not use your freedom to indulge the sinful nature."

Does this process work for nonbelievers? No, we have to lead them to Christ first. But I personally do not believe we will be very effective in our evangelistic effort until we better understand how Satan holds unbelievers in bondage. "Even if our gospel is veiled, it is veiled to those who are perishing. The god of this age has blinded the minds of unbelievers, so that they can-not see the light of the gospel of the glory of Christ, who is the image of God" (2 Cor. 4:3,4). When the children of God take their rightful place in Christ and pray against the blinding of Satan, we will see a greater harvest of souls.

I believe we are locked in a paralysis of analysis. We consider those brilliant who can show with great precision what the problems of society are. We love to share the results of polls, indicating how sick we are. But what is the answer? If you were lost in a maze, would you want a "maze-olo-gist" to come and explain all the intricacies of how a maze works? Would you want a sick, legalistic pastor to tell you what a jerk you are for getting into the maze in the first place? I think you would want to know the way, the truth and the life (see John 14:6). We can go wrong in innumerable ways; but only one path leads back to God. You could have been abused in countless ways; but you will still have to forgive if you want to be free from your past. You can sin myriad different ways, but the answer is the same. People in bondage need a clear road map to show the way out. If they already knew the way out, they would have taken it long ago. Nobody likes to live in bondage.

I believe God has made some people smart, and some not so smart. I do not believe His plan for salvation or living the Spirit-filled life is available only for the smart. Those who think they are smart should make God's answer simple enough so that the simplest of His creation can understand it; howev-er, in keeping our message simple, we dare not be simplistic or naive.

The "Steps to Freedom" are just a tool to help people resolve the issues that are critical between themselves and God, and then to go on to resist the devil. No "tool" will set you free. *What* sets you free is complete repentance. *Who* sets you free is Christ. But we have the privilege of being the Lord's bondservants. You can't hurt anybody with the process unless you create some false hope. The worst thing that can happen is that they are truly going to be ready for communion the following Sunday.

When we go to see our doctor, he may prescribe some tests to see if he can determine the cause of our illness. When they do not reveal a problem, you do not get mad at him, do you? Shouldn't people be able to attend our churches and ascertain whether or not their problem is spiritual? Do not get mad at the secular world for not taking into account the reality of the spiritual world. It is not their responsibility, it is the Church's responsibility to resolve spiritual conflicts. In a similar fashion, we need a safe way to resolve the spiritual problems that dog our churches.

Pastor John is a friend of mine. I got a call from him after he and his staff attended my conference. John shared with me that he had often discerned a heavy spirit that seemed to grip his church. Efforts to move the ministry forward were often challenged. A lot of prayer and much soul-searching had little, if any, effect. From most people's perspective, the church was doing fine and good things were happening, but John believed something was not quite right.

The founding fathers of John's church were a faction that had split off from another church. The whole affair of splitting had been a bad witness in the community. John wondered if this could be Satan's opening to keep this church in bondage. He talked it over with his board, and they decided the church should confess their corporate sins and the rebellious nature of their beginning. It was a moving experience for the church body. According to John, the general spirit of heaviness does not seem to be present anymore, and the willful resistance to authority also seems to be gone.

Chuck and I believe that many churches are in bondage; like people, churches need to resolve the issues that are critical between the church body and the Head of the Church. The Lord is praying that we be kept from the evil one. If your church is ready to walk in the light, speak the truth in love and face the issues for the purpose of resolving them, then great hope is in store for you.

Note

1. Clinton E. Arnold, *Powers of Darkness, Principalities and Powers in Paul's Letters* (Downers Grove, IL, InterVarsity Press, 1992).

PRAYER FOR UNITY

My prayer is not for them alone. I pray also for those who will believe in me through their message, that all of them may be one, Father, just as you are in me and I am in you. May they also be in us so that the world may believe that you have sent me. I have given them the glory that you gave me, that they may be one as we are one: I in them and you in me. May they be brought to complete unity to let the world know that you sent me and have loved them even as you have loved me.

John 17:20-23

Having requested our protection from the evil one by being sanctified in truth, the Lord now asks that we all be one. Jesus is praying that the Church be unified. John 17:20-23 seems to indicate the world would know that the Father has sent the Son if we dwell together in unity. If that is the case, how are we doing? Terrible! The Western Church has been incredibly split by denominational distinctives, church practices (especially the ordinances), theological differences and traditions. Churches may agree on these issues, but they still split because of personal differences and animosities. The Lord must be grieved.

So pervasive is the problem of unity that several leading and highly influential Christian periodicals and organizations that minister and speak to the masses have consciously steered away from theological issues. Theology is perceived as being divisive by some. This absence has prompted the theologian, David F. Wells, to write *No Place for Truth, or, Whatever Happened to Evangelical Theology?* (Wm. B. Eerdmans, 1993). Wells argues that "modernity" has abandoned absolute truth for a psychologized, pragmatic and subjective view of truth. "What is true" has been replaced by "what works." Is theology divisive? It can be if the truth is not proclaimed in love (see Eph. 4:15), or if we allow doctrine to be an end in itself.

What is the purpose of good theology or right doctrine? I think it is summed up in the great commandment, "'Love the Lord your God with all your heart and with all your soul and with all your mind.' This is the first and greatest commandment. And the second is like it: 'Love your neighbor as yourself.' All the Law and the Prophets hang on these two commandments" (Matt. 22:37-40). A proper understanding of the Word of God should govern our relationship with God and man. If we make doctrine an end in itself, we will distort the very purpose for which it was intended. Good teaching should result in the Body of Christ falling in love with God and each other.

The Goal of Our Instruction

I have 25 years of formal education, and I have taught in a graduate level seminary for 10 years. I honestly believe that the major problem in Christian education is that it has the wrong goal. Paul says, "The goal of our instruction is love from a pure heart and a good conscience and a sincere faith" (1 Tim. 1:5, *NASB*). What can be more frightening to the Church at large than to graduate a seminary student purely on the basis that he answered most (not even all) of the questions right!

It is too easy in our culture to extol the virtues of theologians and apologists at the expense of the soul winner and the lover. "He who wins souls is wise" (Prov. 11:30), and, "By this all men will know that you are my disciples, if you love one another" (John 13:35). A godly theologian and humble apologist have their rightful place and should not intimidate you with their brilliance. They will utilize their God-given capabilities to bolster your confidence in God, set you free in Christ and put you on the right path of knowing Him. Without godliness and humility, even the brightest and best can get into trouble. Paul was a religious zealot and leading candidate for theologian of the year when Christ struck him down. Only then was Paul able to say, "I consider everything a loss compared to the surpassing greatness of knowing Christ Jesus my Lord" (Phil. 3:8).

Do not get me wrong; I am totally committed to the truth of God's Word, but it is intended by God to unite and liberate us, not to be intellectually discussed without personal appropriation. Godly character is the primary requirement for spiritual leaders. Theology does not divide; intellectual arrogance does. "Knowledge puffs up, but love builds up" (1 Cor. 8:1).

When academia is substituted for godliness, Christianity gets reduced to an intellectual pursuit instead of a personal relationship with a living God. We can know all about God theologically, but not know Him at all. We can develop our skills, exercise our gifts and learn better ways to become a professional Christian, yet totally miss the mark.

> If I speak in the tongues of men and of angels, but have not love, I am only a resounding gong or a clanging cymbal. If I have the gift of prophecy and can fathom all mysteries and all knowledge, and if I have a faith that can move mountains, but have not love, I am nothing (1 Cor. 13:1-3).

If we think we are theologically right, then others ought to know it because of our love, not by our ability to win arguments.

So what is the basis for unity? It is certainly not common traditions or common practices: It is common heritage. We are all children of God. That is why Paul writes, "Make every effort to *keep* the unity of the Spirit through the bond of peace" (Eph. 4:3, italics added). The unity is already present; it is our responsibility to preserve it. Look again at the Lord's prayer quoted at the beginning of this chapter: "That they may be one as we are one: I in them and you in me" (John 17:22,23). Unity is the result of Christ within us. The world will know that the Father has sent the Son because of His presence within us.

Unity is the effect, not the cause. The model is the Godhead. Sound doctrine should enable us to be firmly rooted in Christ.

A parallel concept can be seen by examining John 15. Verse eight says, "This is to my Father's glory, that you bear much fruit, showing yourselves to be my disciples." Does this verse and the preceding context require us to bear fruit? No it does not; it requires us to abide in Christ! If we abide in Christ, we will bear fruit. Trying to bear fruit without abiding in Christ is fruitless, because Jesus says, "Apart from me you can do nothing" (John 15:5).

Trying to establish unity by insisting that all adhere to denominational distinctives and common practices will prove counterproductive. That is not to say we should not be submissive and remain loyal to our spiritual leaders. We must, but I learned years ago that whenever two hard-nosed fundamentalists get together, they will have at least three opinions! I see no hope for unity ever coming from those who insist they are right and everyone else is wrong. Only God is right, and the rest of us are just starting to have one eye slightly open. "Now we see but a poor reflection as in a mirror; then we shall see face to face. Now I know in part; then I shall know fully, even as I am fully known" (1 Cor. 13:12).

When I pastored, I used to tell the new members' class that somewhere my theology was wrong. I paused for a moment to let that sink in. Then before any mass exodus could occur, I said, "If you think about it, how presumptuous to believe otherwise!" Then I committed myself to them to preach the Word of God as honestly and accurately as I could. Too many times we end up defending our previously learned doctrine that may or may not be right, rather than teaching the Word of God. I have no commitment to any systematic theology written by any one man or school. I am thankful for all their contributions, but I doubt if any one man or school is going to get it perfectly right. We will never learn so much that we will no longer need to be dependent upon the Lord. A greater sense of dependency upon the Lord should be the result of continuing Christian education.

Laboring Under Half a Gospel

The corporate unity the Lord is praying for cannot be accomplished without individual awareness of who we are as children of God. The one common denominator of all the people whom I have had the privilege of helping to find their freedom in Christ was the complete lack of assurance for salvation and ignorance of their spiritual heritage. When we are established free in Christ, "The Spirit himself testifies with our spirit that we are God's children" (Rom. 8:16). The practical significance of having "Christ in you, the hope of glory" (Col. 1:27) can't be overstated.

I believe the greatest determinant of our success in ministry is conditioned by our own sense of identity and security in Christ. One pastor wrote a thank-you note to me saying:

> I am in the first steps of recovering from a church split. I have never known pain like this, Neil, but I am finding it to be a tremendous time of learning and growth in the Lord. Your *Victory over the Darkness* book has been especially helpful in that I have tried to find too much of my identity in what I do as a pastor and not enough in who I am in Christ.

Let me further illustrate by quoting a shortened version of a missionary's personal testimony he sent to his own mission:

> I grew up in a family of high achievers. I felt that I did not receive as much affirmation or affection as I needed to balance their expectations. I believed I had to be perfect the first time and every time in order to win their approval. I saw myself as a failure, a quitter and a loser.
>
> I got involved with a great Christian organization my first week in college. Their high standards made me feel comfortable with them. A lot of love, acceptance and affirmation came from the guys who discipled me. They taught me by personal example how to meet the organizational standards (i.e., quiet times, Bible study, Scripture memorization, prayer, witnessing, etc.). They became, in a very real way, my family and my God.
>
> Although I was learning good things about God and His Word, my security and identity were primarily being developed in the relationships I had within the organization and not in God Himself. It was more important to be an integral part of this ministry than it was to be a Christian.

Being associated with this group was the peak of my spiritual experience. Spiritual pride was setting me up for a fall. Had it been a cult that had met my needs for affirmation and acceptance, I would have swallowed it hook, line and sinker. In spite of the mistakes I made, the training I received was excellent, and there were many positive results in my life.

As I "matured" in my walk with God, and as my ministry responsibilities increased, I found myself getting fewer strokes from my relationship with people, especially the leadership. It was even more true when I served on my first tour of duty overseas. Although I struggled with this, I fully expected my lifetime career to be with them. During my first furlough I was told that I would not be invited back. I thought God had rejected me. I felt I had been kicked out of my family where I had found my love, acceptance and identity for the past 10 years. Since I had not built my identity on my position in Christ, the only identity that I had to fall back on was that of a failure who was never good enough.

My wife and I joined another missionary organization, and the only reason we stayed with them for eight years was because of the love and acceptance we found with them. However, I have always been afraid that they would find out what I was really like, and they would kick me out, too. My wife said they did see what I was really like, and that is why they kept me. I never could accept other people's positive belief in me until I came across Dr. Anderson's materials.

I realized that I was living in bondage to perfectionism, fear and bitterness. I also learned that the first and most foundational step to freedom from living in bondage to the lies of the devil is to firmly establish my scriptural position and identity in Christ, which was something I had never done.

I was believing the lies of Satan. Events in the past were blown out of proportion, and they had become my judge and jury without being balanced by the truth of Scripture. It was almost impossible to meet with God, and there was no motivation for ministry (especially to the nationals whom I did not know or trust). My life on the mission field was characterized by guilt, depression, confusion and lack of desire to learn the language.

I have found immediate freedom and release from my bondage to perfectionism, fear and bitterness by these truth encounters as I verbally challenged the enemy's lies with the truth of God's Word.

I believe much of the Church in America is laboring under half a gospel. We have presented Jesus as the Messiah who came to die for our sins, and if we believe in Him our sins will be forgiven. Then we will get to go to heaven when we die. What is wrong with this? Two things. First, it would give us the impression that eternal life is something we get when we die. That is never taught in Scripture. "He who has the Son has life; he who does not have the Son of God does not have life" (1 John 5:12). Second, it is only half the gospel.

For instance, if you wanted to save a dead man, what would you do? If you just gave him life, he would only die again. You would have to first cure the disease that caused him to die, and "the wages of sin is death" (Rom. 6:23). So Jesus went to the cross and died for our sins. Is that the whole gospel? No, finish the verse! "The gift of God is eternal life in Christ Jesus our Lord." Further, John 10:10 proclaims, "I have come that they may have life, and have it to the full." The most repeated phrases in the New Testament are "in Christ," or "in Him," or "in the beloved." You will find 40 such references in the book of Ephesians alone. One pastor called up his Bible software program and directed his computer to print out every text that included those and similar phrases. As he showed his congregation, the computer printout extended from the pulpit to the front row of the church. We were dead in our trespasses and sins, but now we are alive in Christ.

Finding Our Identity

It is this life in Christ that gives us our identity.

"Yet to all who received him, to those who believed in his name, he gave the right to become *children of God*" (John 1:12, italics added).

"You are all *sons of God* through faith in Christ Jesus" (Gal. 3:26, italics added).

"How great is the love the Father has lavished on us, that we should be called *children of God*" (1 John 3:1, italics added).

Why is this so essential? Because no person can consistently behave in a way that is inconsistent with how they perceive themselves. It is not what you do that determines who you are; it is who you are that determines what you do. This is so critical in our discussion, because any fool can divide a fellowship. A heretic is someone who causes divisions in the Body. The Spirit of God brings unity, and godly people work with Him to bring people together. "Blessed are the peacemakers, for they will be called *sons of God"* (Matt. 5:9, italics added).

From the earliest beginning of the Church to this day, people are prone to follow men and seek their identity from that association. "For when one says, 'I follow Paul,' and another, 'I follow Apollos,' are you not mere men? What, after all, is Apollos? And what is Paul? Only servants, through whom you came to believe" (1 Cor. 3:4,5). So what is a Baptist? What is a Presbyterian or an Assembly of God? And who is Billy Graham? Only servants and organizations through whom we came to believe, for which we should all be thankful. "For we are God's fellow workers; you are God's field, God's building" (1 Cor. 3:9).

Paul wrote, "My God will meet all your needs according to his glorious riches in Christ Jesus" (Phil. 4:19). The most critical needs in our lives are the being needs, and they are the ones most wonderfully met in Christ. He met our greatest need of eternal life, but He also meets our need for identity, acceptance, security and significance. Let me encourage you to read aloud the following truths, and personally appropriate them for yourself. We have also provided this list on the last page of the book for easy removal and use.

In Christ:

I am accepted

John 1:12	I am God's child
John 15:15	I am Christ's friend
Romans 5:1	I have been justified
1 Corinthians 6:17	I am united with the Lord and one with Him in spirit
1 Corinthians 6:20	I have been bought with a price; I belong to God
1 Corinthians 12:27	I am a member of Christ's Body
Ephesians 1:1	I am a saint
Ephesians 1:5	I have been adopted as God's child
Ephesians 2:18	I have direct access to God through the Holy Spirit
Colossians 1:14	I have been redeemed and forgiven of all my sins

Colossians 2:10	I am complete in Christ
	I am secure
Romans 8:1,2	I am free from condemnation
Romans 8:28	I am assured that all things work together for good
Romans 8:31	I am free from any condemning charges against me
Romans 8:35	I cannot be separated from the love of God
2 Corinthians 1:21	I have been established, anointed and sealed by God
Colossians 3:3	I am hidden with Christ in God
Philippians 1:6	I am confident that the good work God has begun in me will be perfected
Philippians 3:20	I am a citizen of heaven
2 Timothy 1:7	I have not been given a spirit of fear, but of power, love and a sound mind
Hebrews 4:16	I can find grace and mercy in time of need
1 John 5:18	I am born of God and the evil one cannot touch me
	I am significant
Matthew 5:13,14	I am the salt and light of the earth
John 15:1,5	I am a branch of the true vine, a channel of His life
John 15:16	I have been chosen and appointed to bear fruit
Acts 1:8	I am a personal witness of Christ's
1 Corinthians 3:16	I am God's temple
2 Corinthians 5:18	I am a minister of reconciliation
2 Corinthians 6:1	I am God's coworker
Ephesians 2:6	I am seated with Christ in the heavenly realm
Ephesians 2:10	I am God's workmanship
Ephesians 3:12	I may approach God with freedom and confidence
Philippians 4:13	I can do all things through Christ who strengthens me [1]

My understanding of discipleship and counseling is all based in our relationship with God. Colossians 2:6,7 *(NASB)* says, "As you therefore have received Christ Jesus the Lord, so walk in Him, having been firmly rooted and now being built up in Him." I believe we have to be firmly rooted *in Him* before we can be built up *in Him*. And we can't expect people to live (walk) *in Him* as mature Christians if they have not first been built up *in Him*. We would be like cars without gas. We may look good, but we won't be able to run. If the root issues are not faced and resolved, growth will be stymied. In *Victory over the Darkness,* I tried to identify levels of conflict and levels of growth spiritually, mentally, emotionally, volitionally and relationally. I have included these two tables in appendix A for your consideration.

To illustrate what I am trying to say, consider Diagram 2.A on individual disciplines. Luke 2:52 says, "Jesus grew in wisdom and stature, and in favor with God and men." Some have seen from this passage the necessity to grow in a balanced way: spiritually, mentally, physically and socially. To accomplish this, many of us have gone to our concordances and found everything God has to say about marriage, parenting, rest, prayer, meditation and other relevant topics. Tremendous books have been written about each discipline, most of them accurately portraying what God has to say on the subject. Over the years I have either taught, preached or given seminars on almost every one of these topics. So have most pastors if they have been in ministry long enough. So what is wrong? Considering all the available resources, why isn't our Christianity bearing more fruit?

Individual Disciplines

Each discipline is like the spoke in a large Christian wheel. The problem is, the spokes may not be connected to the Hub, which is Christ. The result is a subtle form of Christian behavioralism that results in a try-harder methodology. "You're not trying hard enough. If only you will try harder maybe your Christianity will work!" Guilt! Condemnation! Defeat! We have shifted from negative legalism (you *shouldn't* be doing that), to positive legalism (you *should* be doing that). Instead of being called, we are driven. The further we are from the Hub, the harder we try until something snaps. Some run around like fanatics who have lost their way, so they double their efforts.

Those who are the closest to the Hub are sweet-spirited and gentle people. They seem to bear fruit with little effort. They are living testimonies of the beatitudes (see Matt. 5:3-12). Those furthest from the Hub become judgmental and legalistic. They are the big wheels who run over and intimidate others. They insist they are right and, ironically, they may be right in a legalistic and moralistic sense. They can tell you, using Scripture to prove their

Diagram 2.A

point, how to behave. They know what is right and what is wrong. They have captured the letter of the law, which kills, but not the Spirit, which gives life (see 2 Cor. 3:6). They have no deep and meaningful relationships. Everything remains on the surface. They are driven to do everything right, but the one discipline they can't stand is solitude. They often use their theology as a smokescreen to keep everybody else on the defensive. Any effort to break through the barriers to get at their inner man will be repulsed. Their insecurity results in complete withdrawal and passivity, or they become sick controllers.

Most of these people have never had any bonding relationships. None of them are free in Christ. I hurt for these people, but I hurt even more for their families and congregations. They are the victims, but unless they are set free in Christ, they will continue the cycle of abuse. Hundreds of books have been written about these dysfunctional families, and many books have been published recently describing churches that abuse. Many of these books are excellent and, if applied in the proper order, will bear a lot more fruit. Let me illustrate.

I recall statements made prior to the '60s that claimed if families had devotions and prayed together, only one in 1,000 would separate. We do not hear such statements being made today. The rebellious '60s wreaked havoc within the family. Consequently, the Church went into high gear to save this God-ordained institution. Seminaries developed programs and offered degrees in marriage, child and family counseling. The old ministerial faculty in pastoral care was slowly replaced by clinical psychologists. Most were educated in secular schools because in those days Christian schools did not offer doctoral degrees in psychology. Evangelism and discipleship took a backseat because the other needs were so overwhelming.

Some of the largest parachurch ministries and radio programs are now geared to the family. More Christian books are sold to this market than any other by far because it is the number-one felt need in the United States. Never in the history of the Christian faith has such a concerted effort been made to save the family. How are we doing? Have our families become any stronger? Are our children doing any better? What is wrong?

I think what we have done is to jump to the second half of Paul's Epistles without understanding and appropriating the first half. Characteristically, the first half has been categorized as being "theological," the second half as being the "practical" or application portion of his teaching. If you were only concerned about the family, then you would probably address only those practical passages. The problem with this approach is that it is the first half of Paul's Epistles that establish us in Christ.

It is my strong contention that if we can help people understand and appropriate the first half of Paul's Epistles, they instinctively will do the second half. It would be the "natural" thing for children of God to do if they were filled with the Holy Spirit. Trying to get people to act as though they are children of God when they have little or no clue as to who they really are in Christ is going to prove fruitless. We must get them out of bondage and connected to the Hub first.

I have candidly told many couples, "Forget your marriage. You are both so torn up on the inside that you couldn't get along with your dog much less each other!"

When are we going to learn that it is not what goes into a man that defiles him, it is what comes out (see Matt. 15:11)? The problem is not primarily external and resolved by learning to behave better; it is internal and resolved by learning to believe and speak the truth in love. I have seen marital conflicts resolved and stay resolved through internal change, but never through external or behavioral changes. We are spending too much time trying to change behavior, and not enough time trying to change what people believe about God and themselves.

Proverbs 23:7 *(NKJV)* says, "For <u>as he thinks in his heart</u>, so is he." What do we see? The "so is he." What do we try to change? The "so is he"! Back up a notch and find out what is going on inside. If someone's belief is wrong, so will the behavior be wrong. Now do you see why the battle for the mind is so critical? If we do not "take captive every thought to make it obedient to Christ" (2 Cor. 10:5), we will not behave in a way that is Christian. If we first establish people free in Christ (connect them to the Hub) so they know who they are as children of God, then all those good books will be effective. All those studies on family systems and role relationships will work. The individual disciplines diagram should look like this:

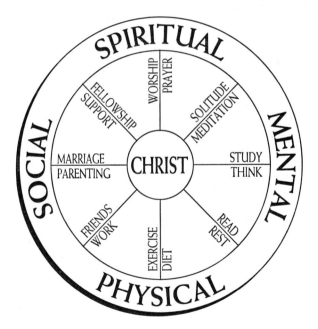

Diagram 2.B

Church Disciplines

We have done the same thing corporately in our churches as we have done individually. Look at the following diagram (2.C) for church disciplines. We have developed some incredibly good material as it relates to evangelism, discipleship, leadership and worship. Having taught practical theology for 10 years, I can't think of one spoke that I have not taught or used as a seminar, as have most seminary professors who teach pastoral ministry. At least we are abreast of and have a working knowledge of what is being said in these areas.

Diagram 2.C

The most obvious example of increased interest in the areas of church discipline is the tremendous effort that was made toward church growth in the late '70s and '80s. Pastors flocked to seminars that shared programs and strategies that would enable their churches to grow. Many pastors committed great time and expenditure to obtain their Doctor of Ministry degrees. The most popular programs were in church growth. (Incidentally, counseling and family ministries were the two other major emphases.) Church consultants seemed to come out of the woodwork. Ironically, many had not been successful as pastors, and some had never even been pastors! Many of the leading contributors were sociologists or businessmen. Some were missiologists. Very few theologians contributed significantly to the church growth movement. Never in the history of the Church has there been such a concerted effort to understand church growth. How are we doing?

Reports will vary, but overall I would say the Church as a whole declined in America during the '80s, both in numbers and influence. Much of the numerical loss can be attributed to the tremendous decline of attendance in liberal churches. The contribution and focus of the church growth movement probably kept the decline from being far worse. I am deeply thankful for the focus on the Great Commission and for the biblical principles that benefited many. But, as with individual disciplines, church disciplines must be centered in Christ as well.

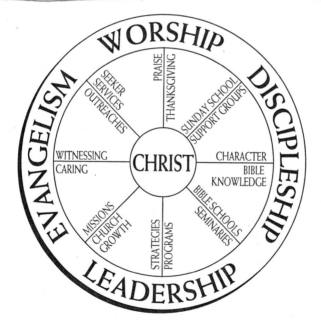

Diagram 2.D

Nothing is wrong with the programs and strategies developed by the church growth movement if Christ is at the center. The problem comes when our confidence and dependence upon God shifts to confidence and dependence upon programs and strategies. Instead of searching for God, we search for a better program. Some pastors have allowed such a guilt trip to be put on them for not being able to see measurable growth that they burn themselves out trying to produce fruit. God, however, has not called us to *produce* fruit, only to *bear* it as we cling to Christ, the true vine and source of all life.

The churches that did profit greatly from the church growth movement had Christ at their center, and they were motivated to share Christ because they cared for the lost. It is interesting that, although their situations are hardly perfect, churches in third world countries have grown significantly during this time. Several factors make their situation different than in our country. First, the Church in Africa, South America, Indonesia and China is not as sectarian as it is in America. They have a greater sense of unity because Christ is more preeminent. Second, they have a greater appreciation for the reality of the spiritual world. Third, they are far less self-centered and narcissistic than the Western world.

When I taught evangelism at Talbot School of Theology, I heard a pastor share in chapel his strategy for reaching his city for Christ. Being the chairman of the chapel committee, I invited him to come back to give a series of lectures on church growth. On the first day of the lectures, he made it abundantly clear that the key to effective church growth was "brokenness" (i.e., a growing recognition of the need for total dependence on God). Then he went on to share his strategy, which I thought was excellent. My evangelism class was meeting every day after his lecture. On the last day, I asked the class what they thought the key was to his success. They all brought out various aspects of the visiting pastor's strategy. Not one person, however, said brokenness, even when I pushed them to think again. It is so easy to lean on our own understanding, and not trust in the Lord with all our heart (see Prov. 3:5).

For instance, David had a whole heart for God. He knew it was not he who slew the giant. What marked his early years was his complete confidence and reliance upon God. Then one day, "Satan rose up against Israel and incited David to take a census of Israel" (1 Chron. 21:1). So what is wrong with taking a census? After all, David was the commanding officer; he should know what his military strength is, right? Joab, however, knew it was wrong, and asked David why he was bringing guilt upon Israel (see 1 Chron. 21:3). David had been successful before because he knew that, "The king is not saved by a mighty army; a warrior is not delivered by great strength. A horse is a false hope for victory; nor does it deliver anyone by its great strength" (Ps. 33:16,17, *NASB*).

Satan knew he could not sit down face-to-face with David and get him to serve anything other than the Lord his God. So the devil subtly worked at shifting David's confidence off the resources of God and onto his own resources. Is that happening today? I doubt if any satanists will be reading this book, but I am sure many readers who have had their faith very slowly and subtly eroded will read it. Only when our hope and confidence is in God can we say with Paul, "For it is we who are the circumcision, we who worship by the Spirit of God, who glory in Christ Jesus, and who put no confidence in the flesh" (Phil. 3:3).

Christ-Centered or Program-Centered?

I know of no church that contributed any more to the dynamics of church growth in a positive sense than First Baptist Church of Modesto, California. Thousands flocked to their "Institute of Church Imperatives." I attended twice when I was a pastor. I also got the chairman of our church board to go and see how a church should function according to the New Testament principles of evangelism and discipleship. It became a model church for some consulting groups who in turn taught First Baptist's principles to other churches. As a seminary professor, I offered credit to any student who attended the conference. Tremendous church growth took place, much of it by conversion. Few churches had as many good spokes in their church disciplines wheel as this church did. Most of their present staff is homegrown.

After several years of growth, the ministry reached a plateau. Their dynamic pastor, Bill Yaeger, retired and Wade Estes was handed the mantle. I had the privilege of conducting a conference in this fine church. Here is Wade's story as he shared it with me.

Pastor Bill Yaeger is a man for whom I have great affection. In a very real sense he has been a father in ministry to me, much as Paul was to Timothy. I cannot imagine having a finer or greater ministry legacy than that which I have received from him.

During the 1970s when Bill and the pastoral staff were putting their ministry plan together, the Church in America was struggling to understand its mission and its methods to get the gospel out. In 1972, First Baptist Church in Modesto undertook a survey of churches around the country and found that small group discipleship was almost unheard of. Laymen did not know how to express their faith. Campus Crusade for Christ and Evangelism Explosion took the lead and came through with some great tools. As Bill told me, "There was much to be done just in the basics of 'how do we fly this thing?'" That was the challenge of the day.

The Lord led in a powerful way, as revival broke out. Hundreds of people came to Christ and became a part of small group Bible studies. In the 24 years that Bill was senior pastor, the church grew tenfold. In the early 1970s a vision for training men and women for professional ministry was born. Today, the pastoral staff is almost entirely a second-generation team, trained in our church. More than 200 men and women from our internship training ministry have been sent out over the past 24 years.

The ministry skill training that was imparted to our young pastoral staff (while they were involved in our internship program) was superb in content, modeling and supervision. However, for many of the younger staff, our confidence slowly came to rest in our ability to duplicate and fine-tune the ministry programs that were entrusted to our leadership.

As with many second-generation ministries, a "program mind-set" (institutionalization) can subtly take over and replace a conscious and intentional dependence upon Christ, without whom we can do nothing (see John 15:5).

Teaching other pastors and leaders through "The Institute of Church Imperatives" only added to our youthful deception, heightening our sense of self-sufficiency. We would teach the need to seek God's wisdom through prayer, but unconsciously, that was really secondary to hard work and the execution of biblical principles. We slowly became aware that our hard work was no longer bearing the fruit it once had.

A growing sense of discontent began to characterize our staff. We were fine-tuning, tweaking and renovating every program we had, but the fruit neither increased nor remained (see John 15:16). We were stymied. We began to realize that program motivation was not the answer. But what was? We found ourselves in the same position that Bill was in 24 years earlier. We had to seek the Lord's will and leading for the work to which He had called us.

When we finally saw our helplessness, the Lord began revealing the need to fully rely upon Him and not our ability to work for Him. The Lord powerfully led us to spend increasing amounts of time in prayer. We devoted two pastoral staff retreats to prayer and fasting, seeking the Lord's direction and blessing. It became clear that the Lord was calling us to lead the church into a life of dependence upon Him, expressed through prayer.

I preached on prayer for four months in morning worship services. We worked with the leaders of the church to equip them to lead their groups in prayer. I must emphasize that this call to prayer was not a program. It was seeking forgiveness and looking for the blessing and leading of God in our church. It was a resignation to His perfect will, whatever it might be. It was a recognition that without His strength empowering us, without His leading and guiding us, and without the manifestation of His presence in our midst, we were doomed to mediocre ministry.

During this time, a church in our town hosted a "Freedom in Christ" conference. We sent a few pastoral staff members and some lay people. They returned with such a glowing report that a few of us began to read *Victory over the Darkness* and *The Bondage Breaker*. Later, at a pastoral staff retreat, the Lord totally disrupted our schedule following a time of prayer. We shifted gears and viewed a video of a counseling session conducted by Dr. Anderson. I told our staff, "We're not going to just watch this; we need to go through it." As he led the counselee through the "Steps to Freedom in Christ," we would listen, turn off the VCR and go through the steps ourselves. Later in the week, the Lord led us to contact Freedom in Christ Ministries regarding a conference for our church. We agreed to hold a communitywide conference.

To prepare for the conference the entire pastoral staff, board of deacons and other leaders, along with our spouses, blocked out a week and went through the entire conference on video. By the time the conference arrived, about 200 leaders had worked through the process and the "Steps to Freedom." Two hundred key leaders walking in spiritual freedom is quite an army with which to begin a conference!

On Saturday evening before the event began, Dr. Anderson and I talked about the conference and what the Lord had been doing in our congregation. As we talked, I was overpowered with a renewed assurance that the Lord had been guiding us through the changes we were experiencing. Dr. Anderson explained the trap we had fallen into and the need to be Christ-centered in our ministry as opposed to being program-centered. He made the same presentation to our entire staff later in the week. It crystallized in our hearts and minds the deception we had fallen into and the new path we were on.

When the conference began, the attendance and level of participation were incredible! More than 2,200 people from our church and community were involved. God was working so powerfully in people's lives that we changed our plans for the Sunday morning worship services. We invited people to share with the congregation what God had done in their lives that week. The degree of transparency and love that was openly shared was amazing. It was apparent that people were truly free in Christ!

We are continuing to strive to be a ministry that depends upon Christ and not ourselves or the programs we are able to create and maintain. The patterns of the flesh don't change easily, but we are seeing remarkable progress in our thinking and actions. We still work hard, but we realize that if we only receive the fruit that comes from our hard work, we are missing God's blessing upon our lives and ministry.

Is Your Bag Empty?

Learning to rely entirely upon the Lord is a process. Patterns of the flesh can be deeply entrenched. I suppose every pastor has at one time possessed a little bag of tricks. When we start out as youth pastors, we reach into that bag and pull out a skit that delights the kids. We share the 10 best messages we have. Then one day the bag is empty, and the crowd begins to dissipate. Time to move on to the next ministry, but this time we are going with more tricks in our bag. So the crowd stays longer, but eventually the bag is empty again. The bag gets bigger as the years go by, but there will always be a day when it will be empty again.

Is your bag empty? Are you willing to let the Lord fill it up this time? Do you see the necessity? Nothing is wrong with the skits, the gags and the worked-over sermons as long as they are under the Lord's control and your confidence is in Him. But if we can account for everything that happens in our church by our own hard work and human ingenuity, then where is God? Remember, self-reliant service for God may be the biggest enemy of devotion to Him.

The Body of Christ is like a big ocean. When the spiritual tide is in, all the fish swim together. Effortlessly they glide through the water and each movement is synchronized as though something is guiding them. The storms are only on the surface where the big waves create all the turbulence. But when the spiritual tide is out, every little fish wants his own little tidepool in which to swim. There is unity in the Body of Christ because the Holy Spirit has made us one, and we can learn to swim together only if we are united to the One who synchronizes us. Then we can swim in truth, in unity and in love. And the high priestly prayer will be personally answered in our lives.

Note
1. Neil Anderson, *Living Free in Christ* (Ventura, CA: Regal Books, 1993).

BALANCE OF POWER

Then they said, "Come, let us build ourselves a city, with a tower that reaches to the heavens, so that we may make a name for ourselves and not be scattered over the face of the whole earth." The Lord said, "If as one people speaking the same language they have begun to do this, then nothing they plan to do will be impossible for them."

Genesis 11:4,6

What an incredible statement made by God, "Nothing they plan [*NASB* says "purpose"] to do will be impossible." They must have had something special going for them to prompt the Lord to make such an optimistic assessment. I first saw this idea pointed out in a book by Myron Rush.[1] He identifies four key ingredients that are essential for the success of any Christian ministry. They are, in my words, *purpose, unity, effective communication* and a *desire to do the will of God.* Because the men did not possess the desire to do the will of God, the tower was not built. Looking at these ingredients from a practical perspective, let's see if we can integrate these four prerequisites for effective ministry into a balanced organizational structure in our churches.

"There is no more powerful engine driving an organization toward excellence and long-range success than an attractive, worthwhile, and achievable vision of the future, *widely shared,*"[2] says author Burt Nanus (italics added). I emphasized "widely shared" because I think that is a major key to unity. Although the book by Nanus, *Visionary Leadership,* is secular, it is helpful for those who want to understand how a clear purpose (mission) statement is essential to keep a ministry moving cohesively in a meaningful direction. *Vision-Driven Leadership*[3] by Merrill Oster, and *The Power of Vision*[4] by George Barna are also helpful.

Defining Your Purpose

A purpose statement is the basis for all future planning. It asks the question, "Why are we here?" Having Scripture in mind, how do you specifically determine God's unique purpose for your church? Some pastors may be tempted to climb into the clouds like Moses, descend with the final answer and announce it to the people. That is how cults operate, and in rare occasions that may work when the followers are immature and the situation calls for immediate action, as we shall see in the next chapter. If the purpose is to make a name for yourself, the Lord will thwart your plans. He will build His kingdom, but not a Tower of Babel. If the purpose is to do God's will, even the gates of hell will not be able to overcome it (see Matt. 16:18). The Lord may initially impress His vision for the church upon the pastor, but others will also sense God's leading.

A responsible pastor will honestly and openly share with the rest of the leadership team what the Lord is doing in his life. If God is leading the church in a new direction, all the leadership and eventually the entire church family must be incorporated into the process. Let me suggest a workable plan to bring this about. Divide the church body into relatively small groups, and invite each cluster to an evening of sharing hosted by one of the board members or staff. Invite them to talk openly about their perceptions of the church. Ask questions such as:

• What are the strengths of our church?
• What are the weaknesses?
• What are we doing right?
• What are we doing wrong?
• What kind of church would you like to see us become?
• What needs are being overlooked?

Although needs don't constitute a call, they certainly do contribute to establishing a purpose statement. You may want to consider this evening of sharing before you have your leadership go through the process of "Setting Your Church Free" described in part two of this book.

Once the congregation has been heard, the leadership needs to evaluate their contribution and collectively establish a purpose or mission statement. Messages from the pastor to the church body may be necessary, because you cannot move any faster than you can educate. When there is unanimity on the board and the staff, share the results with the congregation in a service of celebration. If the process is done right, the congregation will be united around a common purpose. They will be committed because they have been heard, and because they actually contributed to the process. In chapter 7, Chuck will share a model for drafting the purpose statement itself.

In working toward consensus, understand that not everyone will agree with everything that is said or done, nor is it realistic to expect that the final decision will be everybody's first choice. The fact that everyone had an equal opportunity to express their views while working toward a group decision is what is important. I believe that a lot of the lethargy evident in churches today is because the people have no sense of ownership. Consequently, we identify churches by the pastor, not the congregation.

Consensus implies conflict—it thrives on conflict in a constructive sense. Not everybody will perceive the present condition of the church the same way, nor perfectly agree with what it should be. The best picture will emerge when all perspectives are heard and appreciated. By entertaining diverse ideas and perspectives, the group has the potential to unearth more alternatives from which to choose. If not handled right, the process can lead to stalemates rather than decisions, and cause major interpersonal hostilities. Whether it is constructive or destructive will be determined as follows.

Destructive When:	Constructive When:
Members do not understand the value of conflict that naturally comes when other opinions and perspectives are shared;	Members understand the need to allow all to share so that group consensus can be achieved;
There is a competitive climate that implies a win-lose situation; "Getting my own way" is all important;	There is high team spirit and commitment to the group and mutually agreed upon goals; when doing it God's way is all important;
Members employ all kinds of defense mechanisms including: projection, suppression, blame, withdrawal and aggression;	Members are not defensive and assume that disagreements evolve from another person's sincere concern for their church;
Members are locked into their own viewpoints, unwilling to consider the value of other ideas and perspectives;	They believe that they will eventually come to an agreement that is better than any one individual's initial suggestion;
Members resort to personal attacks instead of focusing on the issues;	Disagreements are confined to issues rather than personalities;
Personal ideas and opinions are valued over relationships.	Relationships are valued higher than the need to win or be right.

In destructive situations, cliques form, subgrouping emerges, deadlocks occur, stalemates are common and tension is high. In these settings a lot of unresolved personal conflicts occur that need to be resolved first before anything constructive can take place. In constructive situations, unity and a high level of trust occur. Sharing between members is open and honest.

The Power of Words

The key to all this is communication. All the Lord had to do to totally stop the Tower of Babel building program was to destroy the builders' ability to communicate with one another. "Come, let us go down and confuse their language so they will not understand each other" (Gen. 11:7). That is about all the devil has to do to stop the progress in your church. Find some disgruntled member, whisper a lie in his ear, and he will wreak havoc in your church. I do not believe the average church leader has any idea how effective the father of lies is in creating havoc and confusion in the church.

A pastor friend of mine shared how a board member in his church started to rant and rave uncontrollably at a business meeting, making incredible accusations. He had no knowledge of spiritual warfare, but somehow he knew he had to pray out loud. The man stopped as abruptly as he started. Everyone knew what the problem was, but nobody knew what to do about it.

An exceptionally sharp seminary student stopped by my office to make sure that what he had done to resolve a disciplinary problem with his son was enough. He had three wonderful children. His most loving and pious child suddenly started to lie and steal things around the house. Being strong and responsible parents, they lovingly disciplined him. The problems continued until one day the eight-year-old boy suddenly blurted out, "Daddy, I had to, the devil said he would kill you if I didn't." The father told me that if he had not heard me talk about the battle for our mind, he would not have responded properly and the real problem would have gone unresolved.

Instead of saying, "How dare you blame it on the devil," he asked his son if he was hearing voices that were threatening him. The boy said he was, and then the father explained that the devil was only trying to destroy their family and future ministry. Once the boy understood that he was paying attention to a deceiving spirit, he stopped lying and stealing. I wish I could say that was an isolated experience, but we are running into similar situations all over the world, especially with the children of spiritual leaders. If that is happening in our Christian families, is it happening in our churches?

I recall an experience several years ago when I was on an early morning walk with my wife. By the time we finished the walk, I knew I had to preach a certain message. Ten minutes into the sermon the next Sunday, a young man who was something less than a spiritual giant suddenly fell out of his chair and had a seizure. Two of our doctors in the church immediately attended to him. When the nature of the problem was made known to me, I stopped and prayed. Somehow I knew it was a spiritual problem designed to distract the people from the message. Publicly I asked for God's protection and commanded Satan to release the young man. He did. After the service, the chairman of the board said he did not like the way I prayed because it implied that the young man had a spiritual problem. I told him that I didn't imply it; I clearly said it. Then I asked him to inquire what happened to the young man after I prayed. He never brought up the subject again.

Consider the words of James:

The tongue also is a fire, a world of evil among the parts of the body. It corrupts the whole person, sets the whole course of his life on fire, and is itself set on fire by *hell*....Out of the same mouth come praise and cursing. My brothers, this should not be (Jas. 3:6,10, italics added).

Could you say it any stronger than that? What is the origin of this?

If you harbor bitter envy and selfish ambition in your hearts, do not boast about it or deny the truth. Such "wisdom" does not come down from heaven but is earthly, unspiritual, of the *devil*. For where you have envy and selfish ambition, there you find disorder and every *evil practice* (Jas. 3:14-16, italics added).

I cannot overstate how essential it is to personally "take captive every thought to make it obedient to Christ" (2 Cor. 10:5).

Therefore each of you must put off falsehood and speak truthfully to his neighbor, for we are all members of one body....Do not let any unwholesome talk come out of your mouths, but only what is helpful for building others up according to their needs, that it may benefit those who listen (Eph. 4:25,29).

But if we walk in the light, as he is in the light, we have fellowship with one another, and the blood of Jesus, his Son, purifies us from all sin (1 John 1:7).

God does everything in the light; the devil does everything in the dark. The Lord can speak only the truth; the devil is the father of lies. Do you have secret meetings going on in your church? You are in trouble!

I tried to tell every seminary student I taught that their loyalty to their senior pastor would be tested. Should anyone come to them for the purpose of talking about the pastor, they should immediately stop the conversation because they are talking to the wrong person. They should go first to the pastor in private. If you are around church members who are talking negatively about the pastor (or anybody for that matter), do all you can to stop the ungodly chatter. Instead of gossiping, these people should be praying. If someone points out to you some minor little character defect in another, you cannot help but notice it the next time you see that person. With a pastor it gets amplified. The next time you sit under his teaching, that little defect that went unnoticed before will now stand out like a sore thumb. No pastor will survive disloyalty.

Our churches are being destroyed by gossip. What is it about us that wants to hear all the garbage? If you think you are innocent because you only listen, then consider Proverbs 17:4: "A wicked man listens to evil lips; a liar pays attention to a malicious tongue." You cannot hear without it contaminating you.

I played golf one day with the music director of the church I was attending. I had just left engineering to attend seminary. I was impressed with the pastor of the church until I asked this man what he thought of the pastor and what it was like to work with him.

"Frankly, I can't stand the man," was his response.

For the next 18 holes I heard about every little defect the pastor had. I never noticed them before, but he was right. This man was definitely not qualified to be a member of the Trinity! (And, of course, we all know that is a prerequisite for the pastorate.) Within a matter of months I actually hated that pastor. I finally made an appointment to see him and ask his forgiveness for not loving him. The pastor continued to have a great ministry, but the music director ran off with another woman.

Before you hear the dirt, ask the person five questions:

1. What is your reason for telling me this?
2. Where did you get your information?
3. Have you gone directly to the source?
4. Have you personally checked out all the facts?
5. Can I quote you if I check this out?

Much of Satan's strategy is to discredit spiritual leaders or destroy them through relentless accusation and temptation. I am sure Paul had this in mind when he wrote, "Do not entertain an accusation against an elder unless it is brought by two or three witnesses" (1 Tim. 5:19). Hearsay does not count; it must be witnessed by two or three people. The accusations must be based on observed behavior, not on the judgment of character. You can't bring an accusation against a pastor simply because you do not like him. If in fact you do not like the pastor, find another church or keep your judgments to yourself, and start praying for God to bless the pastor's life.

> Obey your leaders and submit to their authority. They keep watch over you as men who must give an account. Obey them so that their work will be joy, not a burden, for that would be of no advantage to you (Heb. 13:17).

As we entered a city to conduct a conference, my wife and I were over-whelmed by the spiritual opposition. This was not passive resistance; it was active opposition. Without saying a word, we knelt by our hotel bed to pray before we did anything else. The pastor of the church where we were conducting the conference had resigned to keep the church from splitting. He had a tremendous ministry for more than 20 years before an associate pastor undermined his authority. Both were now gone and out of ministry. The staff, board and church were split down the middle.

At the same conference, a denominational leader asked for my help. One of his pastors was accused of being a satanist. The accusation came from a Christian counselor. Her client, who had since committed suicide, made the charges. We were able to clear the pastor and his wife of all charges, but why was that necessary? We had no witnesses, only a "testimony" from the grave of a deceived girl.

Development of Leadership Roles and Responsibility

Obeying your leaders is only half the equation. Spiritual leaders will give an account for watching over the souls of others. How does the leadership in a church do this in a balanced way? To answer that question, let me shift gears for a few pages and explore the development of leadership roles and responsibilities.

In Deuteronomy 17:14—18:21, the Lord set forth the roles and responsibilities of the prophet, priest and king. The concept of checks and balances, as well as the idea to have executive, judicial and legislative branches in government, originated from these passages. The king would be roughly parallel to our president or the executive branch of government. The Lord never told the Israelites to have a king, but He anticipated that they would ask for one in order to be like other nations (see Deut. 17:14,15). Notice the restrictions the Lord put upon the king in Deuteronomy 17:16,17:

> The king, moreover, must not acquire great numbers of horses for himself or make the people return to Egypt to get more of them, for the Lord has told you, "You are not to go back that way again." He must not take many wives, or his heart will be led astray. He must not accumulate large amounts of silver and gold.

As a united nation Israel only had three kings. Saul sinned and lost his crown. The prophet Samuel brought the word of the Lord to him, "To obey is better than sacrifice, and to heed is better than the fat of rams. For rebellion is like the sin of divination, and arrogance like the evil of idolatry" (1 Sam. 15:22,23). Why did Saul sin? Because he feared the people and listened to their voice (see 1 Sam. 15:24). David slew Goliath, drove the evil spirit away from Saul by playing his harp, but he also sinned and lost his son. Solomon violated every restriction God had placed on the king, and he lost it all. Listen to the sad summary of Solomon in 1 Kings 10:21,26,28; 11:3:

All King Solomon's goblets were gold, and all the household articles in the Palace of the Forest of Lebanon were pure gold. Nothing was made of silver, because silver was considered of little value in Solomon's days....Solomon accumulated chariots and horses; he had fourteen hundred chariots and twelve thousand horses....Solomon's horses were imported from Egypt....He had seven hundred wives of royal birth and three hundred concubines, and his wives led him astray.

One other restriction was placed on the king: "When he takes the throne of his kingdom, he is to write for himself on a scroll a copy of this law, taken from that of the priests, who are Levites" (Deut. 17:18). The king was not to interpret the law; he was to execute it as it was interpreted by the priests. This takes us to the judicial branch of government. The priests were not lawmakers; they were to ensure that the law was correctly carried out. They had one major restriction: "They shall have no inheritance among their brothers; the Lord is their inheritance, as he promised them" (Deut. 18:2). In other words, no conflict of interest.

One of the biggest breakdowns of the check and balance system in the United States is in the judiciary branch of government. Judges are not to create law, only interpret it. It is presently estimated that 60 percent of the laws of our country are being generated by our courts. Once a court precedent is established, it becomes law unless it is overturned by a higher court. Most of our judges are not elected, so they neither speak for nor represent the people. For instance, *Roe vs. Wade* was not a legislative decision. The people did not vote on this issue. If the people had voted at that time, they would have defeated abortion on demand. To overturn the Supreme Court by the legislative branch requires a two-thirds majority.

A prophet is a lawgiver, and represents the legislative branch of government. He had one major restriction: "But a prophet who presumes to speak in my name anything I have not commanded him to say, or a prophet who speaks in the name of other gods, must be put to death" (Deut. 18:20). Sounds a little bit like, "Not many of you should presume to be teachers, my brothers, because you know that we who teach will be judged more strictly" (Jas. 3:1). The prophet was not to speak presumptuously. Prophets were to announce only God's words. Our legislative lawmakers are supposed to represent those who elected them, not just themselves.

God gives the law through the prophets; the priests interpret it and the king rules the people by it. Sounds good, but false prophets started to spring up; the priests lost their commitment, and the kings were mostly corrupt. Not one godly king ruled Israel after the nation divided. Jeroboam led the rebellion against Solomon (see 1 Kings 11:26). In monotonous repetition, Scripture records for every king that followed, "He did evil in the eyes of the Lord, walking in the ways of Jeroboam and in his sin, which he had caused Israel to commit" (1 Kings 15:34). Instead of worshiping God in Jerusalem, the Israelites built high places and worshiped Baal. Israel's official calf idol was set up by Jeroboam. Prophets were sent to Israel, but repentance never came. Eventually God raised up Assyria as a rod of His anger to bring down Israel (see Isa. 10:5,6).

Obviously the sins of previous generations can affect following generations unless they are dealt with specifically. The Ten Commandments clearly reveal this:

> You shall not make for yourself an idol in the form of anything in heaven above or on the earth beneath or in the waters below. You shall not bow down to them or worship them; for I, the Lord your God, am a jealous God, punishing the children for the sin of the fathers to the third and fourth generation of those who hate me, but showing love to a thousand generations of those who love me and keep my commandments (Exod. 20:4-6).

One possible reason for the demise of the theocratic government in the Old Testament was the Israelites' failure to carry out the command given in Deuteronomy 18:9-13:

> When you enter the land the Lord your God is giving you, do not learn to imitate the detestable ways of the nations there. Let no one be found among you who sacrifices his son or daughter in the fire, who practices

divination or sorcery, interprets omens, engages in witchcraft, or casts spells, or who is a medium or spiritist or who consults the dead. Anyone who does these things is detestable to the Lord, and because of these detestable practices the Lord your God will drive out those nations before you. You must be blameless before the Lord your God.

Requirements of Leadership

"But when they [Israel] said, 'Give us a king to lead us,' this displeased Samuel; so he prayed to the Lord. And the Lord told him: 'Listen to all that the people are saying to you; it is not you they have rejected, but they have rejected me as their king'" (1 Sam. 8:6,7). The Israelites were no longer connected to the Lord, their Hub. Judah faired only slightly better, having 7 godly kings out of 20. They did experience periods of revival, and the one under Hezekiah (see 2 Chron. 29) reveals what must happen if ever we are to see true freedom and renewal in the Church.

It started with Hezekiah: "He did what was right in the eyes of the Lord, just as his father David had done" (2 Chron. 29:2). Similarly, renewal in the Church has to begin with ourselves. God has done all He has to do for us to have a right relationship with Him. Choose now to do what is right in the eyes of the Lord. Pastor, do not wait for others; it begins with you. The Church cannot be renewed without your leading the way. Nor can it be done without the church staff and board. As Hezekiah said: "Listen to me, Levites! Consecrate yourselves now and consecrate the temple of the Lord, the God of your fathers. Remove all defilement from the sanctuary" (2 Chron. 29:5).

Just getting the spiritual leaders consecrated was not enough. They had to right what was wrong in their worship setting. The priests had to be cleaned up, however, before the Temple could be cleaned up. Once that was done, Hezekiah "ordered the burnt offering and the sin offering for all Israel" (2 Chron. 29:24). True worship followed and the revival spread. I leave the details and thrilling results of this revival up to you for further study.

One aspect of this revival, however, has especially caught my attention. The sin offering came first. In the Old Testament, only the blood was sacrificed in the sin offering. The carcass was taken outside the city gate and disposed of. Jesus was our sin offering. After the crucifixion, Jesus' body was taken outside the gate and buried. The burnt offering came next. Unlike the sin offering, the entire animal was sacrificed. Question: Who is the burnt offering in the New Testament? We are!: "Therefore, I urge you, brothers, in view of God's mercy, to offer your bodies as *living sacrifices*, holy and pleasing to God—this is your spiritual act of worship" (Rom. 12:1, italics added).

Revival will not come simply because your sins are forgiven. All Christians have their sins forgiven, but in most cases we are not experiencing revival. Notice what happened when the burnt offering was given: "Hezekiah gave the order to sacrifice the burnt offering on the altar. As the offering began, singing to the Lord began also" (2 Chron. 29:27).

Burnt literally means "that which ascends." We must consciously yield ourselves to God as living sacrifices. Notice what happens when we offer ourselves to the Lord and He fills us with His Holy Spirit: ✳

Do not get drunk on wine, which leads to debauchery. Instead, be filled with the Spirit. Speak to one another with psalms, hymns and spiritual songs. Sing and make music in your heart to the Lord, always giving thanks to God the Father for everything, in the name of our Lord Jesus Christ (Eph. 5:18-20).

What happens? The music begins! People start speaking and singing to one another (communicating). Hearts are made right. People are connected to Christ, the Hub. Unity returns because the Lord is King of their lives. How can we bring about this kind of New Testament revival? Like the revival under Hezekiah, it must start with those who are responsible. This prerequisite for the spiritual renewal of our churches is the intended purpose for the "Steps to Setting Your Church Free," in appendix B. True, our churches are not governed by kings, prophets and priests as was the Old Testament kingdom. But we do have pastors *(poimen)*, elders *(presbuteros)* and overseers *(episkopos)*. Let's examine these roles.

Let's look at the elder first. The root word *presbus* is often used to represent age (see John 8:9). An elder could not be a new convert (see 1 Tim.

3:6). In reference to church leadership, the term "elder" emphasizes the maturity and dignity of the office. Titus 1:5-9 requires an elder to be spiritually mature and above reproach. Elders are always referred to in Scripture in the plural sense.

The word "overseer" is derived from two root words: *epi* means "over," and *skopeo* means "to look or watch." Hence an overseer (or bishop) provides oversight or administration. In reference to church leadership, the overseer emphasizes the duty or function of the office. The spiritual requirements are the same for the overseer as they are for the elder. Also, like elder, bishop is always plural in Scripture except where the passage is describing what a bishop should be (see 1 Tim. 3:2; Titus 1:7).

Poimen, or pastor, is one who tends herds or flocks and is used metaphorically of Christian pastors. The pastor guides as well as feeds the flock. In the Bible, all three titles—elder, overseer, and pastor—represent the same office. Elder and overseer are interchanged in Titus 1:5-9, pastor and overseer in Acts 20:28 and 1 Peter 2:25, pastor and elder in 1 Peter 5:1-2. No special gifts or talents are required. The first requirement is to have a desire (see 1 Tim. 3:1), combined with the right motive (see 1 Tim. 6:6-9) and then to meet the character requirements as set forth in 1 Timothy 3:1-7 and Titus 1:5-9.

Movement to Ministry

Why then does the Church make a distinction between a pastor and elders or deacons? First Timothy 5:17,18 indicates that double honor was due those who did well in teaching and preaching. It also allows for a possible distinction between a ruling elder and a teaching elder, although all elders should be able to teach (i.e., know and apply the Word of God). Financial support was needed in order that some could be free to give their full attention to spiritual things (see Acts 6:2). The elders appear to be responsible for and to the church. Within this plurality of elders, some are pastor-teachers who are to equip the body so that they may do the work of the ministry (see Eph. 4:12). It would seem that during the Church Age, God has uniquely called evangelists and pastor-teachers to equip the Body of Christ. As we seek to move people to maturity and ministry, consider Diagram 3.A.

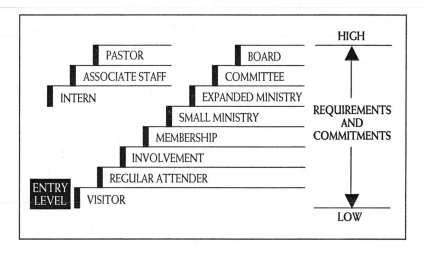

PASTOR	BOARD
ASSOCIATE STAFF	COMMITTEE
INTERN	EXPANDED MINISTRY
	SMALL MINISTRY
	MEMBERSHIP
	INVOLVEMENT
	REGULAR ATTENDER
ENTRY LEVEL	VISITOR

HIGH

REQUIREMENTS
AND
COMMITMENTS

LOW

Diagram 3.A

Movement to ministry requires the called professional staff to see them-selves as equippers. The pastor is on the same level of leadership organiza-tionally as the board of the church. The associate staff are on the same level as the standing committees. Together they comprise the major leadership of the church. They are to exercise oversight and watch over the souls of the saints. Let me point out some differences that exist between small fruitless ministries and growing ministries.

A small church—and one destined to stay small—thinks the decisions should be made by all the membership and the work done by a few, usually the pastor. A growing church sees that the work of the ministry should be done by all, as equipped by the pastoral staff, and the decisions made by the few who are spiritually qualified and recognized by the church. This can only be possible if the congregation holds the leadership in high regard, and they in turn seek to represent and meet the needs of the people.

It is critical to make a distinction between form and function. I am describ-ing the function of leadership, not the form. Scripture gives little instruction about the form church government should take, and denominations vary considerably. Church growth research indicates that small churches usually function with a congregational style of government, no matter what the official polity of the church or denomination. As the church grows, the government becomes more and more representative. In a larger organization, decisions cannot be made on a monthly basis. They have to be made on a daily basis by people who represent the body. Churches that fail to make the transition stop growing.

Another important concept is to see the necessity to increase the commitment and the requirements for leadership as the movement to ministry continues upward. A growing church makes the initial entry as easy as possible, no commitments or qualifications required. Visitors should feel loved and accepted just as they are. On the other hand, the requirements and commitment level should increase for each level of ministry, holding the staff and board to the character requirements of 1 Timothy 3:1-13 and Titus 1:5-9. The unfruitful church will slide to the middle from both ends, increasing membership requirements and backing off from board and staff requirements. In some weak churches, any volunteer can teach or serve on a committee. It can get so bad that some of these churches start looking for bodies to fill slots rather than spiritually alive saints to assume responsibility.

As members show themselves faithful in small things, be prepared to entrust them with greater things (see Luke 16:10; 19:17). Some will experience the call of God as they continue their movement to ministry. An expanded ministry should go beyond the boundaries of the local church. Ministry should be taking place in neighborhoods and places of employment. Ideally, nobody should consider themselves eligible to be on an established committee until their Christianity has made itself known in the community. The church then becomes an equipping center for worldwide ministry.

Although the terms "pastor," "elder" and "overseer" refer to the same office, they do not describe the same function. Other than the pastoral staff, in any church you can usually divide the board into two groups: those who are more gifted to do administrative work, and those who are more gifted to shepherd the flock. They roughly parallel the roles of prophet (pastor), priest (elder) and king (overseer). In chapter 8, Chuck will show how the functions of cause, community and corporation relate to having a balanced ministry. Diagram 3.B is a simplistic model enabling all the people and ministries of the church to be represented by the elder board.

ELDER BOARD		
PASTOR *Poimen* (Pastor-Teacher)	SHEPHERD *Presbuteros* (Elder)	ADMINISTRATOR *Episkopos* (Overseer)
Pastoral Staff (Professional/Called)	Shepherding Ministries	Standing Committees
Equippers	Counseling	Missions
Associate	Visitation	Evangelism
Intern	Teaching	Finance
Enablers	S.S. Leader	Worship/Music
Secretary	Small Group	Christian Education
Custodian	Outreach	Building & Grounds

Diagram 3.B

Balanced Leadership Breeds Unity

Regardless of a church's specific polity, unity on the highest leadership level will be present if all the leaders are free in Christ and are qualified spiritually according to 1 Timothy 3:1-13 and Titus 1:5-9. If a balanced leadership team is functioning properly, an opportunity for effective communication should be possible, because every person and ministry is represented on the board. Purposeful planning will be possible if the people are being cared for and listened to as described earlier, and if the leaders are committed to do the will of God. I believe this balance of power and ministry is essential to working together in harmony.

One church I visited was deeply divided between the staff and the board. The pastor was a godly man, but he came to the church thinking that God had called him to give vision to the church. He saw himself as being in authority of the board, or at least that is how the board perceived their working relationship. Because the board was made up of highly successful people, they agreed that the pastor was not going to control them; so they informed him that he was indeed subordinate to them.

This arrangement will not work any better than the pastor being in control of the board. The pastor and board members should occupy the same level of leadership and have the same degree of authority. No person is mature enough to function as prophet, priest and king. Only Jesus can fulfill all functions. This delicate balance works when leaders know their place and faithfully serve in the capacity to which they have been called. If you are tempted to grab for more power by stepping beyond your borders, remember that absolute power corrupts absolutely. King Uzziah was rewarded with leprosy when he tried to enter the temple and perform the functions of a priest (see 2 Chron. 26:16-23).

How can a church work with a plurality of leaders? No other organization does. Society appoints only one president, one governor, one mayor and one chairman of the board. The answer of course is Christ. He is the Head of the Church. People are no different today than they were in the days of Moses. Rejecting God as King, the Israelites wanted their own king, as did the pagan nations. And a few will always want to be king.

Servant leaders (which I will discuss in chapter 5) are dependent upon the Lord. They are accountable to one another, and see the need for one another. Only these kinds of leaders will be able to set their churches free in Christ. The remaining chapters in part one are devoted to understanding that kind of leadership.

I have mentioned 1 Timothy 3:1-13 and Titus 1:5-9 as the passages that present the requirements of elders. Nobody perfectly measures up to these requirements because perfection belongs only to Christ. Disqualification can and should come, however, to any elder for two reasons:

First, if an elder willfully chooses not to accept these standards as God's credentials for leadership. This becomes evident when an elder chooses some other standard for leadership, such as talent or position, or if the elder willfully commits some act of immorality.

Second, if the elder fails to deal with an inadequate characteristic, either through self-justification or an unrealistic evaluation, hence refusing to accept the truth.

I recall telling my young seminary students that the best asset they will have in ministry is spiritually mature saints. They won't have a generation gap or a communication problem with them. They are sweet people, seasoned by time and the ministry of the Holy Spirit, having wisdom only time can teach.

On the other hand, I told my students that the greatest liability they will have is old saints who never matured. They are no more loving now than they were 20 years ago. The fruit of the Spirit is no more evident in their lives. All they do is censor and critique. Brothers and sisters in Christ, this ought not to be. The life of Christ should become more and more evident in our lives every year. Are the basic qualifications for leadership evident in your life? Use the following 20 questions extrapolated from Timothy and Titus to evaluate yourself.

1. Do you have a good reputation in your church as a mature Christian who speaks the truth in love?
2. Do you have an intimate and loving relationship with your spouse? How well are you handling sexual temptations?
3. Do you have a biblical philosophy of life? Does it reflect temperance? Are you living what you profess?
4. Are you prudent and humble, realizing that all gifts are from God and apart from Christ you can do nothing?
5. Are you respected because of your Christian character?
6. Are you hospitable (i.e., exhibiting a love for strangers)?
7. Are you able to teach (i.e., understand and apply the Word of God)?
8. Are you free from addictions to tobacco, alcohol, gossip, etc.?
9. Are you self-willed? Do you always have to be right and have your own way?
10. Do you lose your temper easily or harbor feelings of resentment?
11. Are you pugnacious (i.e., do you use physical means to get even or control others)?
12. Are you contentious? Do you purposely take the opposite point of view, stir up arguments, destroy unity, or are you a peacemaker?

13. Are you a gentle person, reflecting forbearance and kindness?
14. Are you free from the love of money?
15. Are you able to manage your household? Do your spouse and children love and respect you?
16. Do you have a good reputation with non-Christians?
17. Do you pursue after that which is good and right? Do you desire to associate yourself with truth, honor and integrity?
18. Are you just and able to make objective decisions and be openly honest in your relationships with other people?
19. Are you pursuing personal and practical holiness?
20. Are you in the process of continual growth in your Christian life, becoming more and more like Christ?

Notes

1. Myron Rush, *Management: A Biblical Approach* (Wheaton, IL: Victor Books, 1983).
2 Burt Nanus, *Visionary Leadership* (San Francisco, CA: Jossey-Bass Publishers, 1992).
3. Merrill J. Oster, *Vision-Driven Leadership* (Nashville, TN: Thomas Nelson Publishers, 1991).
4. George Barna, *The Power of Vision* (Ventura, CA: Regal Books, 1992).

SITUATIONAL LEADERSHIP

Jim was an exceptional seminary student. He graduated with honors in Christian education and had several offers from churches because of a fine track record. He was happily married and excited about his first full-time position as Minister of Christian Education. He was challenged by his senior pastor to give leadership to their church's Sunday School ministry, which was bulging at the seams. Recent church growth had made the position both necessary and possible.

Mary, the Sunday School superintendent for the past 25 years, was looking forward to working with Jim. She had been a public school teacher for many years. Her love for the church and education was evidenced by her many years of loyal and sacrificial service. The ministry had grown too big, however, for a working layperson, no matter how dedicated. She was part of the search team that recommended Jim, so Mary felt relieved that help was on the way.

Jim was anxious to implement some of the wonderful ideas he had learned at seminary. What the church had been doing was okay, but he knew it could be done better. So he took charge and began to exercise his leadership to improve the Sunday School. He felt personally called to take the ministry of Christian education into the twenty-first century. Although the people initially received his energy and ideas well, opposition to his leadership soon began to arise and his relationship with Mary began to deteriorate. Then a letter arrived, which read:

Dear Pastor Jim,

I have been praying about my involvement in the Christian Ed ministry at our church. I have been at it for a long time, too long, my husband says. So, effective immediately, I am resigning my position as Sunday School Superintendent. I have been asked to do a number of things at my school, which I have not been able to do in the past because of my involvement in church work. I wish you God's best.

Sincerely,
Mary

Six months later, Mary was teaching Sunday School at another church. What went wrong? Was Mary being overly sensitive and resentful? Had she wrongly assumed ownership of the Sunday School? Was Jim "messing with her baby," or did he unwittingly drive her off? Wasn't he called to take over the Christian education ministry and give it new leadership and direction? Which brings up two questions: What is leadership? and, How does one give direction? Should direction be given? Does the church need leadership? (Does it ever!) But what kind of leadership? Will the wrong leadership create conflicts in the church, no matter how good the intentions are?

Commonly Accepted Definitions of Leadership

To answer these two questions let's examine several definitions of leadership. The most popular notion is that of the pied piper. This type of leader is a charismatic person who has the ability to inspire people to follow him or her. In this narrow definition, the leader gathers a following because of personality and/or power. Power is the ability to rule or influence through charm, persuasion or threat. The con artist wins followers by using charm and clever persuasion. The cult and occult leaders have a spiritual hold over their subjects that is nothing less than diabolical. Church leaders who operate only from this perspective usually develop a ministry around themselves that will fall when they leave, or else they become authoritarian and rule through intimidation. Question their rule, and you will be charged with not being submissive. I will address abusive leadership in chapter 5.

Let's try another definition of leadership: A leader is the one who comes closest to realizing the norms that the group values highest. This conformity gives the leader the highest rank, which attracts people and implies the right to assume control. This definition best describes the unofficial leader or leaders that every church has. The church sees them as their champions, and usually that view is legitimate. These leaders are quality people who have the ability to represent and unite the church. They have tremendous influence, whether or not they hold any leadership position. Pastors must never be threatened by the popularity of these people. If a strong personal bond exists between the pastoral staff and these leaders, tremendous things can be accomplished in the church. If an adversarial relationship exists, a split or staff dismissal is imminent.

Pulpit committees look for a pastor who will "fit" based on this definition of strong leadership. If the pastor does not represent the norm of the church in any dimension, they will not follow him in that respective area. For instance, the pastor can be a great fit theologically but not socially. In that case, the pastor's leadership may be appreciated in the church but not in the community.

I knew of a pastor who was having an exceptional ministry. His church had grown from 200 to 800 in a relatively short time, although geographically it was situated in what would be considered a difficult place to grow a church. One evening during devotions, the pastor had an unusual encounter with the Lord. He wondered if he should share it with the congregation. He chose to, and that was the end of his ministry at that church. Because of his experience with the Lord, he no longer represented the norm of that church theologically, and he had to go. Tragic, but true.

A founding pastor who stays with a church for a number of years is the norm of that church because every person who joins the church has done so because they relate to his teaching, personality and style of leadership. He is the center of a bell-shaped curve and people on either side identify with him. The numbers drop off rapidly as you move further from the center. Every church has a norm that is often more cultural than theological. If you are far from the center of that norm, you will feel a little out of place if you attend that church. It is unlikely that anyone could be chosen from the body to a leadership position if they did not represent the norm.

Unless he is a clone, the new pastor will not represent the norm to the degree the first pastor did. If he is far from the center, he will probably never feel like "one of them," nor will he be accepted as such. If he is fairly close to the center, people on the extreme other side of the bell-shaped curve will probably drift away, and the center of the curve will shift in the direction of the pastor as he attracts new people who identify with him. One of the greatest rejection or acceptance factors for any pastor will be his leadership style.

A Functional Definition of Leadership

Let's look at another definition of leadership. Leadership is the ability to gain consensus and commitment to common objectives, beyond organizational requirements, which are attained with the experience of contribution and satisfaction on the part of the whole church. Although awkward, this is the best *functional* definition of leadership I know, because it includes five critical elements.

First is the "ability to gain." This is the one aspect of leadership that has caused some to believe that leaders are born not made. I do not know how to teach this ability. Some just seem to have it. Whenever a group is in a stalemate, natural-born leaders have the ability to pull the group together and get them moving in the right direction.

The second element found in this functional definition of leadership is the result of the leader's ability to gain: consensus and commitment. Without this, there will be no substantial movement forward. Tragic is the pastor who thinks he has won a great battle because the board finally gave in and voted with a narrow majority to do what he wants. He will do it, yes, but all by himself. He has neither consensus nor commitment.

The consensus and commitment is to "common objectives," which is the third element. If I had to determine the spiritual health of a church on only one issue, I would find out if the governing board of the church consisted of people coming together to persuade each other of their own independent will, or if they were spiritually mature children of God who were coming together to collectively discern the will of God. What a group holds in common is the strongest link in the organizational chain by which objectives are determined. If we are bonded to Christ and He alone is who we have in common, we can collectively and easily come up with meaningful objectives.

In this setting, the center of the bell-shaped curve is Christ. In spiritually dead churches, the common bond can be similar occupations (we are all blue collar or white collar), social interests (we are all hunters or golfers) or politics (we are all conservative or liberal). The common norm of a church becomes more and more influenced by culture as it drifts further and further from Christ, the Hub. Healthy churches do not primarily establish programs around social norms because, in most churches, very few people hold everything in common socially.

Now, do not get me wrong. Some churches may have wonderful social events. Friendships are usually established because of common social interest, but fellowship can only be established around the one person we all have in common. "Here there is no Greek or Jew, circumcised or uncircumcised, barbarian, Scythian, slave or free, but Christ is all, and is in all" (Col. 3:11).

The fact that what was mutually agreed upon was also attained is the fourth element in this functional definition of leadership. I have seen visionary leaders possess the first three elements, but seem to lack the crucial follow-through. The people were all excited and agreeable to do something, but they never achieved their goal. Nothing will torpedo leadership faster than good ideas that never get off the ground. You can create only so much hype before the people become disillusioned.

I once heard Bob Biehl, president of Master Planning Group International, give the following definition: "Leadership is knowing what to do next, why it is important, and what resources are needed to make it happen." The leader who lacks this fourth element of obtaining his objective needs to know why his direction is important and what resources the people need to make it happen. If the leader is successful, the church will experience a sense of accomplishment.

For which one of you, when he wants to build a tower, does not first sit down and calculate the cost, to see if he has enough to complete it?

Otherwise, when he has laid a foundation, and is not able to finish, all who observe it begin to ridicule him, saying, "This man began to build and was not able to finish" (Luke 14:28-30, *NASB*).

A manager will see that the work conforms to plan, but a leader will accomplish something beyond organizational requirements. And when it is accomplished, the whole church will enter into the experience of contribution and satisfaction of a ministry well done, which is the fifth element of the definition. They will be satisfied because they had a part in it, and because it was carried through. The body is functioning as a whole, and Christ is at the center.

Historical Development of Leadership Theory

So far we have looked at what leadership is, but this is not the whole story. Let me trace the historical development of leadership theory. Prior to the industrial revolution, the "great man" theory was the most prominent. The idea was to study the great leaders and find out what made them tick. Until the '60s, this approach was by far the most common among Christians. It is still quite prominent and has value, but has limitations we will mention later. The Church has studied the leadership characteristics of Moses, Nehemiah, David, Paul, and most of all, Jesus. We observe their character and study their ways. For instance, I will draw some critical spiritual principles from Moses in the next chapter.

The industrial revolution brought forth the "traitist" theory. The question then was: What traits do successful leaders possess? They studied mannerisms, compared physical statures, observed personalities, as well as personal grooming, to see what traits produced the greatest results. The concept of "dressing for success" was a product of this kind of thinking. All other things being equal, the taller man got the nod over the shorter man, the quicker thinker over the contemplative thinker and so on. Every conceivable feature, characteristic, personality and intellect was studied, compared and evaluated. But the theory left many questions unanswered. Why was Napoleon such a great leader? He, along with many others, seemed to defy the odds.

In the early '50s, the focus changed from leadership traits to leadership behavior. Studies were conducted to find out what successful leaders do and should do. The studies were narrowed down to two primary activities: consideration of people and initiating structure. In other words, relationships and tasks. The tool most used by researchers was the "Leader Behavior Description Questionnaire"[1] (LBDQ). In 1964, Blake and Mouton wrote *The Managerial Grid*.[2] The grid is shown in Diagram 4.A.

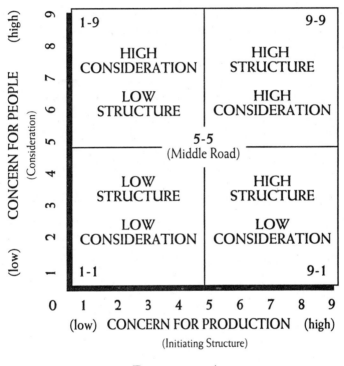

Diagram 4.A

Blake and Mouton concluded that the best leaders were both proficient at initiating structure and showing consideration toward people. According to the diagram, they were 9-9 leaders. A 9-1 leader was task oriented (i.e., high in structure but low in consideration). A 1-9 leader was high in consideration, but low in initiating structure. Does this have any application to Christianity?

When I was finishing my doctorate in institutional management at Pepperdine University, I wanted to find out, so I conducted my research on church leaders and wrote my dissertation on the results. My theory was that the administrative duties of pastors and their desire to bear fruit roughly paralleled task behaviors, or initiating structure. Showing consideration should be a high need for pastors known for their love. In *Strategy for Leadership*, authors Edward Dayton and Ted Engstrom write, "Christian leaders are continually faced with the unresolvable tension between moving the work forward and caring for those doing the work."[3]

In researching my dissertation, 94 associate ministerial staff were contacted and asked to complete two Leader Behavior Description Questionnaires (LBDQ), a morale test and a demographic sheet. They were asked to take the LBDQ as they perceived the leadership behavior of their senior pastor, and then take it a second time as they would perceive an "ideal" pastor. The demographic sheet was used to determine their age, sex, length of paid ministerial service and whether or not they were seminary graduates.

The results[4] showed a positive correlation of .62 (range is from 0 to 1, 0 showing no correlation) between staff morale and the perceived leadership behavior of the pastor. Correlation does not establish causation, but by squaring the derived correlation (.38), one can arrive at a coefficient of determination. Thus, 38 percent of the variance in staff morale can be accounted for by its correlation with perceived pastor's leadership behavior. More revealing were the comparative results with other studies. The mean score of the pastor's leadership behavior was lower in both initiating structure (task), and consideration (relationships) than of air force commanders and public education administrators. One would hope that pastors would have tested higher in consideration, but such was not the case. Let me point out that the LBDQ was an objective questionnaire. The participants answered questions purely on the basis of observed behavior.

When the participants were asked to take the LBDQ as they would perceive an ideal pastor behaving as a leader, every participant in the study perceived the ideal pastor as being high in both initiating structure and consideration. In addition, there was no correlation between the perception of an ideal pastor and the age, sex, length of ministerial service or whether the participant in the study had graduated from seminary. In other words, there was a uniform perception of the ideal pastor being 9-9 on the managerial grid. It would seem that the pastor who really loves people, but has no ability to initiate structure, will struggle in bearing fruit. On the other hand, the task-oriented leader who does not know how to love may also fall short of the ideal. Before you are quick to agree, let's see what developed next.

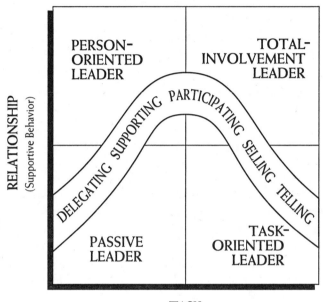

Diagram 4.B

In 1969, Kenneth Blanchard and Paul Hersey, authors of *Management of Organizational Behavior*,[5] added another important dimension. They suggested a curvilinear relationship between leadership style and the maturity of the follower. (See Diagram 4.B.) If the group is immature, the leadership style should be predominantly task oriented. Leaders should provide specific instructions and closely supervise performance. As the group matures, the leader should become less directive. This style is much like being a player coach. He works toward team unity by fostering good relationships. He welcomes the feedback of the members and encourages them to share their opinions in the decision-making process.

As the group continues to mature, the leader becomes more person oriented and less task oriented. The group is assuming a greater responsibility and sense of ownership. They are becoming less dependent upon the leader and more dependent upon the Lord. The leader is shifting from directive behavior to supportive behavior. When the group is mature enough, the leader shifts to a passive style of leadership. He has helped the group to mature to the point that he can delegate with confidence. He then turns over to the group the responsibility for decisions and implementation.

Choosing and Training Leadership

Choosing the right style of leadership is very much determined by who the followers are. Every leader must determine the followers' readiness and adapt a leadership style that best relates to the followers' ability and maturity. Those who are unable to do a task must be shown how. Only a task-oriented leader will be effective when the maturity and ability level of the follower is low.

As a pastor, suppose you have been doing it all when it comes to weddings in your church. You sense the need to recruit a wedding hostess to relieve you of this task. After prayerful consideration, you ask Nancy if she would consider such a responsibility.

"It is just what I have been praying for," she responds. So you say, "That's wonderful, Nancy. Let me show you where all the stuff is, and you can begin by leading the rehearsal for the Smith and Olsen wedding this Friday night. By the way, I won't be able to make it!"

Is that a good leadership move? It is disastrous! This is a passive style of leadership when it requires a task orientation.

The pastor who understands leadership will have Nancy observe at the first wedding rehearsal as he walks her and the wedding party through the whole process. At each successive wedding rehearsal, Nancy assumes more and more responsibility. The pastor is moving away from the role of a task-oriented leader to the style of total involvement. Nancy has progressed from being unable to being capable. At first, she felt insecure at the prospect of being the wedding hostess because she did not fully know how to do it. Many are unwilling to commit themselves to accept an assignment or volunteer to a ministry because of the insecurity they feel at being inadequate. The only way to get them over that hurdle is to let them learn first by example, then follow up with a lot of instruction and close supervision.

Nancy was feeling pretty secure in working with the pastor until he informed her that she would be in charge at the next rehearsal; he would be there to provide moral support only. He was in the process of shifting his leadership style to one of personal orientation. Taking on a greater responsibility caused Nancy to feel a little insecure. However, the pastor's presence at the rehearsal helped her become more secure as her confidence and ability increased. Nancy was eventually ready, willing and able to be the wedding hostess of the church, so the pastor fully delegated the responsibility to her.

It is important to note that a good leader never stops being a loving, relational person, regardless of the maturity of the followers. The point is that immature people need instruction and supervision. As they mature, they want and need more involvement in the decision-making process. As they start to assume more responsibility, they need the emotional support of their leader. When they have been fully delegated the responsibility, they may resent the constant interference and intrusion of the one who entrusted the ministry to them. Ask yourself a question: If your immediate supervisor delegated a responsibility to you because you were competent enough to do it, would you appreciate his looking over your shoulder and evaluating your every move? On the other hand, if you are new in your ministry, do you appreciate it if your senior pastor is unavailable to you, leaving you alone to sink or swim?

Let's apply this to evangelism. Have you ever tried to teach evangelism from the pulpit? It does not work. Why not? The majority of the congregation will go home intimidated or even terrified. They feel totally insecure and, in some cases, unable to witness. This is the wisdom behind Evangelism Explosion developed by Dr. James Kennedy. Rather than tell people to witness, Evangelism Explosion shows them how.

I conducted a school of evangelism in my early years of ministry. I had the privilege in a large multistaff church to see a nonproductive visitation program grow from 20 coerced volunteers to 100 selected and trained people who were winning an average of 10 people a week to Christ. How did we get there? I started with myself. I followed up on enough visitors until I felt competent to train others. I carefully selected a few whom I personally taught in a classroom until they felt they were ready to give it a shot. I teamed up the more experienced with the less experienced until they all felt comfortable going on visitations on their own.

Then we selected another visitation group, which doubled our numbers. The first few times, these new recruits went on visits with their trainer only to observe. As they felt comfortable, they were invited to participate with their trainer. The feeling of security grew as they continued making visits with their trainer, and eventually the night came when they were asked to take the lead. The trainer would be with them only for support. The trainer had just shifted from a total-involvement style of leadership to a person-oriented style. The process is complete when the trainee is ready to train others.

This is what the Lord modeled for us. He began His public ministry by Himself. Many started to follow Him. After a year of public ministry, He prayerfully selected the 12 apostles. They walked together for the next two years before the Lord sent them out (see Luke 9:1,2). Then Jesus appointed 70 others (see Luke 10:1). He gave them authority and power over demons, and charged them to proclaim the kingdom of God. Finally, they were delegated the responsibility to go into all the world. You could summarize the leadership strategy of Jesus as follows:

1. I'll do it, you watch;
2. We'll do it together;
3. You do it, I'll watch;
4. You do it!

Can Leadership Style Be Changed?

Keeping this in mind, let's return to the story of Pastor Jim and Mary at the beginning of this chapter. Mary was a mature and responsible person, but Jim came in with a task- or, possibly, a total-involvement leadership style. Mary was not used to being told what to do at the church, and she should not have to suffer under it now. What should Jim have done? I would suggest that he sit down with her and say something like this:

"Mary, I am so impressed with what you have been able to do in this church for so many years while being a mother and a teacher. You probably know more about education and teaching than I will be able to absorb in the next 10 years. I'm going to spend the first few months getting to know our teachers and Christian Ed staff. I need to know where we have been, what we are presently doing and who we are as a ministry team. This is my first full-time ministry position, so I'm likely to make a few mistakes. Naturally, I have a lot of ideas that I would like to see implemented, as well as a sense of direction for this ministry. I need someone of your experience with whom to discuss my ideas and to give me some feedback on how they might fit this church. I can't abdicate the position and responsibility that God has called me to, but I can't do it alone either. Would you help me?"

In my early years of ministry, I was asked to oversee a thriving high school group while having other responsibilities in a large multistaff church. I recruited five mature people to serve with me on the youth committee. Between them, they had more than 75 years of combined experience working with young people. I eventually searched and found a gifted and talented youth pastor to take my place as I shifted to adult ministries. He was one of the most effective youth pastors I have ever known when it came to working with kids. However, working with the committee he inherited was another story.

After every committee meeting, this youth pastor was in my office and had bullet holes all over him. "They're all loyal to you," he complained, which may have been true, but that was not the problem. Coming from a small church, he had run a solo ministry. He never learned how to work with mature people. He would go into the youth committee meetings with a lot of wonderful plans, looking for a rubber stamp. When he was not trying to tell them what to do, he was trying to sell them on what he wanted to do. Their response was, "No you're not!" Eventually, two of the committee members resigned and one left the church.

After teaching a Doctor of Ministry class on church administration, I asked the pastors what they were going to do when they got back to their churches. One young pastor said, "I'm going home and begging the forgiveness of my elders!" His church was an affluent body and had a strong board of extremely capable people. You guessed it; he had been laboring under a wrong leadership style.

Can a leader easily change from one orientation to another? Within limits, yes. Some pastors who are called into ministry are more gifted at initiating structure. These task-oriented leaders should search for ministries that can best utilize their skills. Church planting would be one. They have the drive to organize, motivate and accomplish a lot when the church is immature and struggling to get on its feet. They often will take a church to about 200 people in a hurry, but it will plateau if they continue to exercise a task style of leadership. If they can't adjust their leadership style to allow others to participate with, assume ownership of and finally delegate to, they should move on to another task that is more in keeping with their calling.

Some task-oriented leaders adopt an authoritarian style of leadership, yet continue to add numbers to their membership. I hesitate to say they continue to grow, because, although the numbers are growing, the people are not growing. These leaders attract people who are willing to let others think for them. It seems to absolve them of their responsibility if others tell them what to do. I am always amazed at how many people are like that. Such is the birth of cults.

I also know of several pastors at the other extreme who do well in certain settings. They are the passive, laissez-faire kind of leaders. They function well because they are surrounded by mature people. They are fully capable of loving people and giving direction, but prefer to work with and relate to those who do not need that love and direction. Do not work for these people if you are looking for strokes or direction. They will assume that you need neither one, although they may be capable of giving it to you. If you are the kind of person who likes a lot of freedom to work within broad parameters, then this kind of pastor may be just what you are looking for.

Everybody has a predominant leadership style. If you are about as equally adept at initiating structure as you are at relating to people, you will be more capable of adjusting your leadership style. If you would like to know what your leadership style is, I recommend that you read *How to Be a More Effective Church Leader*[6] by Norman Shawchuck, which includes a test followed by examples and explanations.

Leadership That Releases from Bondage

The development of leadership theories introduced another vital component in the '70s. Leadership is not just a function of the leader and the follower; it is also a function of the situation. In other words, situations greatly determine what kind of leadership will be most effective. Let's say a missionary group decided to have a major leadership conference in Indonesia. They gathered all their top executives and experts onto a plane and flew them there. A newly converted tribesman was also on the plane as it crash-landed in the middle of a vast jungle. Assuming they all survived, who would arise as the leader who would most likely be able to get them out of that situation?

Ken Peters was a faithful member of a church I pastored. Other than finances, I knew of no other contribution he made to our church. His name was never mentioned for any leadership position. He was a relatively successful civil engineer. When our church decided to relocate and build new facilities, guess who came to the forefront? The leadership he provided as chairman of the building committee was incredible. He was the right man in that situation for us.

Sometimes this is referred to as *expert power*. People rise to the top, or to the occasion, because they have a certain expertise. That is not the only dimension of situational leadership, however. Various situations call for certain leadership styles. If there are definite limits of time, then someone needs to take charge. The relational leader does not function as well under time pressure as does the task-oriented leader. What's more, the group will be more cohesive when somebody takes charge and gives much needed direction. This is not the time to seek group consensus. Under times of pressure, rest assured that the group consensus is, "Somebody do something!" If the designated leader does not, probably someone else will, saving the day. When the time pressure is off, however, the group is more cohesive with a relational leader. Moses never called for a committee when the Egyptians were breathing down his neck. He held up his staff and said to the Red Sea, "Part!"

If the pastor's support base is strong, he can initiate a lot more structure than if it is not. When the support base is moderate, a relational style of leadership will be more effective. Interestingly enough, research seems to reveal that if the support base is weak, a task orientation seems to be more effective.

102 SITUATIONAL LEADERSHIP

I suspect that is so because critics will be more likely to respond positively if something constructive is getting done, or at least being attempted. Leadership is not just determined by the leader; it is a function of the leader, the follower and the situation. Just because a pastor does well in one situation does not guarantee he will do well in another. Because a pastor shepherds one flock well does not mean that he can pastor any flock. The history of World War II clearly shows that Winston Churchill was a task-oriented leader who was the right man for that situation. General Patton was also the right man during the war. When the war ended, however, neither one was in demand for further leadership positions.

Why are we spending so much time on leadership in a book written to set our churches free? Because many of our church problems are caused by dysfunctional leadership and organizational pathology. In his years as a denominational leader, Chuck has observed that the first and foremost factor in church growth is the Christ-centered leadership ability of the pastor. The second most important factor is the Christ-centered leadership of the influential lay leaders. When both pastor and church leaders have exceptional competence and commitment, the church moves forward in both spiritual health and numerical growth.

When I was sharing with a group of missionaries who were struggling to overcome their experiences on the mission field, one young lady insisted she would never return. As we met privately, she related that their relationship with the nationals was great. She loved that part; it was her own missionary organization and fellow team members that caused all the pain. The conflict between the missionaries was traceable to an administrative nightmare, a problem since corrected.

It is much like helping a child in spiritual bondage. You may be able, with the cooperation of the child, to help him or her find freedom. But what have you really solved if the child goes back into the same dysfunctional family? The root of the problem has not been dealt with. That is why my book with Steve Russo, *The Seduction of Our Children*, contains so much material on parenting. We can't deal effectively with the child without dealing with the parent. It is interesting to note that the effective parenting styles presented in *The Seduction of Our Children* closely parallel the leadership styles in this book.

The last step in setting your church free is to work toward correcting whatever it is that caused the church to be in bondage. The cause can be poor leadership and/or organizational pathology. But dealing with the symptoms will only bring temporary relief. We have to get rid of the garbage, not just chase off the flies.

Conflicts in leadership can happen to the best of us. A sharp division arose between Paul and Barnabas about who should go on the second missionary trip. "Barnabas wanted to take John, also called Mark, with them, but Paul did not think it wise to take him, because he had deserted them in Pamphylia and had not continued with them in the work. They had such a sharp disagreement that they parted company" (Acts 15:37-39). Who was right is a matter of conjecture. Barnabas was certainly more relational in his leadership style. Possibly under the pressure of the moment he did not act wisely in wanting Mark to go. Mark apparently had not yet proven that he was mature enough, at least not to Paul. The fact that Paul knew how to reconcile and move people to maturity and ministry is demonstrated in his last letter: "Get Mark and bring him with you, because he is helpful to me in my ministry" (2 Tim. 4:11).

The important thing to keep in mind is that you can correctly choose the right style of leadership and behave admirably, yet still not be connected to Christ, the Hub. If God is not in it, no leadership style or organizational structure will work. If He is in it, any style will work, but it will be far more effective if it is done right. Dedicated incompetency is still, unfortunately, incompetency.

"Brothers, choose seven men from among you who are known to be full of the Spirit and wisdom. We will turn this responsibility over to them" (Acts 6:3).

Notes
1. Andrew W. Halpin, *Manual for the Leader Behavior Description Questionnaire* (Columbus, OH: Bureau of Business Research, College of Commerce and Administration, Ohio State University, 1957).
2. Robert R. Blake and Jane S. Mouton, *The Managerial Grid* (Houston, TX: Gulf Publishing House, 1964).

3. Edward Dayton and Ted Engstrom, *Strategy for Leadership* (Grand Rapids, MI: Fleming H. Revell, 1979).
4. Neil Anderson, "The Perception of Pastoral Leader Behavior and Its Correlation with the Morale of the Associate Staff in the Southwest Baptist General Conference," unpublished Ed.D. dissertation, Pepperdine University, 1982.
5. Kenneth Blanchard and Paul Hersey, *Management of Organizational Behavior* (Englewood Cliffs, NJ: Prentice-Hall, 1969).
6. Norman Shawchuck, *How to Be a More Effective Church Leader* (Glendale Heights, IL: Spiritual Growth Resources, 1990).

5

SERVANT LEADERSHIP

Moses said to the Lord, "You have been telling me, 'Lead these people,' but you have not let me know whom you will send with me. You have said, 'I know you by name and you have found favor with me.' If you are pleased with me, teach me your ways so I may know you and continue to find favor with you. Remember that this nation is your people." The Lord replied, "My Presence will go with you, and I will give you rest."

Exodus 33:12-14

Can you imagine the responsibility Moses was saddled with? When Pharaoh would not voluntarily let God's people go, the Lord orchestrated a few object lessons—10 to be exact. Finally Pharaoh capitulated with a little arm-twisting. Even then Pharaoh changed his mind and chased them part way through the Red Sea. Safely on the other side, however, all the Israelites had left to do was survive in the wilderness. Moses was charged by God to lead them to the Promised Land.

I once took 125 high schoolers to a Christian camp. Somebody prepared our meals for us, we had clean bunks to sleep in and the scenery was spectacular. But after one week, my wife was so exhausted that if I even mention the word "camp" 20 years later she breaks out in hives. Moses was about to embark on a 40-year camping experience in a wilderness so bad that modern-day Israel gave it back to Egypt after winning it in a war. They would have no showers, no commodes, and Moses' assignment was to lead multitudes of ex-slaves to only God knew where! No wonder Moses asked the Lord to remember that they were His people!

Overwhelmed by the task before him, Moses petitioned God: "Who are you going to send with me?" and "Teach me your ways." If I had a lifetime to come up with the two most critical issues for effective spiritual leadership, I could not do better than that. The Lord answered, "My Presence will go with you, and I will give you rest" (Exod. 33:14). Rest? Forty years of wandering in a wilderness is not my idea of a rest. Did the Lord give Moses rest? The only way to evaluate whether an event is restful or not is to determine how you feel afterward. Have you ever taken a "restful" vacation and come home more tired than before you went? Forty years later Moses stood on Mount Nebo to view the Promised Land that he could not enter. He had successfully led God's people. Deuteronomy 34:7 records, "Moses was a hundred and twenty years old when he died, yet his eyes were not weak nor his strength gone." God gave him rest.

The Principle of Biblical Rest

Biblical rest is not a cessation of labor, nor an abdication of responsibility. Biblical rest is made possible only by the presence of God and by living responsibly according to God's ways. Moses actually experienced biblical rest. In his youth, Moses had tried to do God's work his way with his own power. He pulled out his sword and spent the next 40 years tending his father-in-law's sheep. Then one day he turned aside to see a marvelous sight. Although the bush was burning, it was not being consumed. If that bush was burning because of the substance it was made of, it would burn up almost immediately. It continued to burn because God was in the bush. Moses could not set the people free; only God could do that, and it was not going to be done the way Moses had tried. It was going to be done God's way or not at all. The same is true today. We can't set any person or group of people free; only God can do that, and He will do it His way.

"Off Center" Leadership

I believe most of the leadership burnout we hear of today is not because the burden is too heavy or the task too difficult. I believe it is because we are trying to serve God in our own strength and in our own way. I sometimes think of the local church as an industrial factory regulated by a sophisticated set of gears. Suppose one of the gears suddenly becomes eccentric. It is slightly off-center or lacks the same center as all the others. What would happen to production? It would certainly create havoc with all the other gears connected to it. Imagine what would happen if many of the gears are eccentric. If Christ is not the center of people's lives, it will affect every person connected to them. If the leadership is eccentric, it will affect the whole church.

The Need for a Wilderness Experience

If we are serious about our walk with God, He will bring us to the end of our resources so that we may discover His. "For we who are alive are always being given over to death for Jesus' sake, so that his life may be revealed in our mortal body" (2 Cor. 4:11). All of us will have to go through a wilderness experience in order to live in the Promised Land. It took 40 years to reeducate Moses after the training he received in Egypt. The Lord would not allow him to rely upon the lofty position he occupied in Pharaoh's court. Only the lofty position we occupy in Christ will be of any use in the kingdom of God. Chuck Colson was of no use to God in the White House, but he was mightily used of God in prison, and now even more.

That is why new converts cannot be elders. They will attempt to serve God in their own strength and in their own way until they are broken and learn His ways. Paul says of an elder, "He must not be a recent convert, or he may become conceited and fall under the same judgment as the devil. He must also have a good reputation with outsiders, so that he will not fall into disgrace and into the devil's trap" (1 Tim. 3:6,7). Woe to any church if one of their elders has fallen into the devil's snare. If left unresolved, the whole church factory may grind to a halt because of that one gear. His personal problem will quickly become their corporate problem.

Falling Prey to Deception

When Satan incited David to take a census, it brought judgment upon the whole nation. "So the Lord sent a plague on Israel, and seventy thousand men of Israel fell dead. And God sent an angel to destroy Jerusalem" (1 Chron. 21:14,15). David was deceived by Satan. Nevertheless, he was responsible for giving the order to number the troops. His elders were also guilty because they went along with it. God will not let anyone off the hook because they were deceived. The devil did not make David do it. David chose to believe a lie and ordered a census that was forbidden by Scripture (see 1 Chron. 21:1-7). It is our responsibility not to sin and it is our responsibility not to be deceived. Because David's personal problem was now a corporate problem, it had to be dealt with as such.

> David looked up and saw the angel of the Lord standing between heaven and earth, with a drawn sword in his hand extended over Jerusalem. Then David *and the elders,* clothed in sackcloth, fell facedown. David said to God, "Was it not I who ordered the fighting men to be counted?" (1 Chron. 21:16,17, italics added).

Properly Fitted Together

Spiritual leaders need to be geared together by responding to the greatest invitation in the New Testament: "Come to me, all you who are weary and burdened, and I will give you rest. Take my yoke upon you and learn from me, for I am gentle and humble in heart, and you will find rest for your souls. For my yoke is easy and my burden is light" (Matt. 11:28-30). Jesus is inviting us to His presence, not to a program or organization. Only then can we truly learn from Him and be able to carry out His program in the organization He calls us to.

"Take my yoke," Jesus says. You may feel as though so many yokes are already hanging around your neck that one more would only be a noose! What kind of yoke is Jesus talking about? Yoke is a metaphorical reference to the heavy wooden beam that fits over the shoulder of two oxen. Look at the picture. Would the yoke work if only one ox had it on? No, it would only serve to bind the beast of burden and work would be incredibly hard. Only when both oxen are properly fitted together can the work be done easily.

At the time of Christ, as in several countries today, a young ox was yoked together with an old seasoned one who had long since been broken. The old ox knew he had a whole day's work ahead of him, so he no longer fell into the temptation of running on ahead and burning out by 10:00 in the morning. If he strayed off to the left or the right, he knew he would get a sore neck. In other words, the old ox "learned obedience from what he suffered" (Heb. 5:8). Young oxen often want to run on ahead because the pace is too slow, but all they get from their efforts is a sore neck. "Even youths grow tired and weary, and young men stumble and fall; but those who hope in the Lord will renew their strength. They will soar on wings like eagles; they will run and not grow weary, they will walk and not be faint" (Isa. 40:30,31). Some are tempted to sit down or drop out, but life goes on, dragging the irresponsible with it.

Walking with Jesus

I have a neurotic dog named Buster, and I have long since given up on training him. When Buster was young, I sent him off to dog obedience training with my son. After two weeks, the dog had thoroughly trained my son! Before I finally gave up, I thought I would give it one more shot by taking the dog for a walk. (Notice I did not say "run.") So I put a choke chain on Buster and off we went. Dumb Buster nearly choked himself to death! He wanted to run, but I did not. After all, I was the master and I knew the way. When he stopped to sniff a flower (or some gross thing), I kept walking. Whenever he strayed to the right or the left, I kept on walking. Did Buster ever learn to walk by his master? No! He never did, and I have met a lot of Christians who have not either. Some want to run on ahead. Others stray off to the left or the right; still others drop out entirely. The Master is still saying, "Come to Me."

What would we learn if we walked with the Lord? We would learn to take one day at a time. We would learn the priority of relationships. We would learn to be compassionate. We would learn to be like Jesus. We would learn to be dependent upon Him because He is our lead ox. How do you put on this yoke that fits? He made it just for you, but you can't put it on unless you are willing to throw off all others.

Do you find yourself huffing and puffing your way through life? "There remains, then, a Sabbath-rest for the people of God; for anyone who enters God's rest also *rests from his own work*, just as God did from his. Let us, therefore, make every effort to enter that rest, so that no one will fall by following their example of disobedience" (Heb. 4:9-11, italics added). In summation, when the task seems overwhelming, learn the principle of biblical rest.

The Principle of Shared Leadership

There is a temptation to see Moses as an authoritarian leader, the lawgiver who struck fear into the hearts of God's people. But I see another Moses, a servant leader who was burdened for the needs of those he was called to lead. Scripture records that the people began to grumble:

> If only we had meat to eat! We remember the fish we ate in Egypt at no cost—also the cucumbers, melons, leeks, onions and garlic. But now we have lost our appetite; we never see anything but this manna! (Num. 11:4-6).

The people of every family began to wail. Listen to how Moses responded:

> The Lord became exceedingly angry, and Moses was troubled. He asked the Lord, "Why have you brought this trouble on your servant? What have I done to displease you that you put the burden of all these people on me? Did I conceive all these people? Did I give them birth? Why do you tell me to carry them in my arms, as a nurse carries an infant, to the land you promised on oath to their forefathers? Where can I get meat for all these people? They keep wailing to me, 'Give us meat to eat!' I cannot carry all these people by myself; the burden is too heavy for me. If this is how you are going to treat me, put me to death right now—if I have found favor in your eyes—and do not let me face my own ruin" (Num. 11:10-15).

Burdened by People's Needs

Have you ever been there, church leader? Have you ever been so burdened by the needs of your people, yet felt so inadequate for the task that you would rather die than to be around for your own demise? It matters not how good you are at preaching and teaching, you will still hear someone say, "I'm not getting fed around here." Where are you going to get meat to feed them? Can a pastor feed everyone in the congregation? Should he even try? It cuts even deeper when older saints say that. I think the Lord would respond to them, "You have been a Christian for over 10 years; are you still expecting someone to spoon-feed you? No pastor in the world can give you enough food on Sunday to live on, much less grow. Why aren't you feeding yourself every morning in your devotions that you are supposed to be having with Me? Aren't you mature enough yet to start feeding others who are not yet able to feed themselves?"

When the burden is overwhelming, does it help you to know that the two most powerful Kingdom figures in the Old Testament, Moses and Elijah, both cried out to God that they wanted to die? Jesus wept over Jerusalem. In addition to the incredible physical hardship that Paul endured, he said, "I face daily the pressure of my concern for all the churches. Who is weak, and I do not feel weak? Who is led into sin, and I do not inwardly burn?" (2 Cor. 11:28,29). If you care, it hurts to see people living in bondage when they can be free in Christ. I have a terrible time saying no to these people; I am sure you do as well.

Distributing the Burden

The Lord told Moses to tell the people that He was going to give them meat to eat every day until it came out of their nostrils, and they loathed it because they had rejected the Lord (see Num. 11:18-20). To Moses the Lord said:

> Bring me seventy of Israel's elders who are known to you as leaders and officials among the people. Have them come to the Tent of Meeting, that they may stand there with you. I will come down and speak with you there, and I will take of the Spirit that is on you and put the Spirit on them. They will help you carry the burden of the people so that you will not have to carry it alone (Num. 11:16,17).

This is similar to the advice given to Moses by his father-in-law, Jethro, in Exodus 18:17-23:

What you are doing is not good. You and these people who come to you will only wear yourselves out. The work is too heavy for you; you cannot handle it alone. Listen now to me and I will give you some advice, and may God be with you. You must be the people's representative before God and bring their disputes to him. Teach them the decrees and laws, and show them the way to live and the duties they are to perform. But select capable men from all the people—men who fear God, trustworthy men who hate dishonest gain—and appoint them as officials over thousands, hundreds, fifties and tens. Have them serve as judges for the people at all times, but have them bring every difficult case to you; the simple cases they can decide themselves. That will make your load lighter, because they will share it with you. If you do this and God so commands, you will be able to stand the strain, and all these people will go home satisfied.

There is a temptation to look at this passage as support for authoritarian or hierarchical rule over others. I believe that misses the point. The purpose for appointing others was to relieve the burden of Moses who was trying to do it all by himself. The hierarchy was just a means to effectively accomplish the task of meeting needs, not so some could rule over others. The needs were far too great for any one person to meet. Although Jethro suggested a hierarchy to Moses, God did not. The Lord simply said to him, "They will help you carry the burden of the people."

Choosing Helpers

Moses was told to select elders who were known to him as leaders. They were already available; why hadn't Moses turned to them himself? Why don't we? Because some of us are codependents who need to be needed. Others are overly conscientious, thinking, *I've been called to do this so I better do it.* For some, it just never crossed their minds to enlist the help of others. Others have a messianic concept of themselves. They reason, "I alone can help this person." That is the danger of professionalism. This type of leader is one of those who created the notion, "Only professionals (pastors, counselors, etc.) can really help these people." There are not enough "professionals" in the United States to meet the spiritual needs of our people. If we do not equip and mobilize the church laity, it won't be done. Paul says to all of us, "Carry each other's burdens, and in this way you will fulfill the law of Christ" (Gal. 6:2). The text we are looking at, however, reveals an even more insidious reason.

Fear of Competition

When the Spirit rested on the 70 elders, they prophesied but did not do it again (see Num. 11:25). "However, two men, whose names were Eldad and Medad, had remained in the camp. They were listed among the elders, but did not go out to the Tent. Yet the Spirit also rested on them, and they prophesied in the camp" (Num. 11:26). Joshua, Moses' aide, said, "'Moses, my lord, stop them!' But Moses replied, 'Are you jealous for my sake? I wish that all the Lord's people were prophets and that the Lord would put his Spirit on them!'" (Num. 11:28,29).

I would pray that every Christian leader could say what Moses said. Do we really want God's Spirit to rest upon others to the same degree that He rests upon us? Do we desire the Lord's anointing to be as obvious on others as we would have it rest on ourselves? Do we get as much delight when others have the spotlight in the Kingdom as we do when it is our turn? Do we earnestly seek to help every person in our church reach their highest potential, even if it is higher than our own? Does it threaten us to share the pulpit with a gifted layperson who is often requested by the congregation to speak? Does it bother the youth pastor when he invites a sharp college student to speak to his kids and they respond better to the guest speaker than they do when he talks?

I know competition bothers some people; probably every pastor has experienced some twinge of envy or jealousy. I personally know of several former students who were run off by the senior pastor in their first ministry, not because they were doing a bad job, but because they were getting too popular. I know of several insecure pastors who keep a thumb on every ministry and protect the pulpit as if it were their own. Some even refer to it as "my pulpit." In too many cases, the number-one hindrance to every member reaching their fullest potential is the pastor. What a tragedy! A pastor's greatest desire should be to see every member reach his or her highest potential. It is for this reason that I believe a Christian leader's personal identity and security in Christ is what will determine success in ministry more than anything else.

Again, if the burden is too heavy, learn the principle of shared leadership.

The Principle of Humble Intercession

Have you ever had a staff member rebel against you? How about the whole congregation? The elder or deacon board? How did you handle it? Moses had all three rise up against him. First it was his staff:

> Miriam and Aaron began to talk against Moses because of his Cushite wife, for he had married a Cushite. "Has the Lord spoken only through Moses?" they asked. "Hasn't he also spoken through us?" And the Lord heard this (Num. 12:1,2).

Moses' staff's attack on his marriage was a pretext. The real issue was the prophetic gift of Moses and his special relationship with the Lord. Their rebellious attitude angered the Lord, and He ordered them out to the Tent of Meeting to speak to them. Numbers 12:6-8 records the message:

> When a prophet of the Lord is among you, I reveal myself to him in visions, I speak to him in dreams. But this is not true of my servant Moses; he is faithful in all my house. With him I speak face to face, clearly and not in riddles; he sees the form of the Lord. Why then were you not afraid to speak against my servant Moses?

Moses Pleads for Miriam

When the Lord departed, Miriam was leprous. God judged her, and she deserved it. How about Aaron, Lord? Nothing for him? I think he deserves at least a cold sore or maybe a boil. Wouldn't the best of us have a little tendency to think that way? After all, they were both attacking Moses' character and it was God who judged Miriam. And if God did it, it must be right. Aaron, however, upon seeing Miriam's leprosy, suddenly realized that they had sinned and was ready to confess it. How did Moses respond? "Moses cried out to the Lord, 'O God, please heal her!'" (Num. 12:13). The Lord relented, but not totally. Miriam had to remain outside the camp for seven days with her leprosy. The whole camp had to wait for seven days until she healed. As I go through these three accounts, keep in mind Numbers 12:3: "Now Moses was a very humble man, more humble than anyone else on the face of the earth."

Moses Considers the Needs of the People

The next thing this humble man Moses had to face was the rebellion of his whole congregation. One member of each tribe had been sent to spy out the Promised Land. Ten came back with a negative report; they said there were giants in the land. The whole community rose up against Moses and Aaron. Moses and Aaron immediately fell on their faces before the assembly. Joshua and Caleb begged them not to rebel against the Lord, but the congregation wanted to stone Moses and Aaron. The glory of the Lord again appeared at the Tent of Meeting. The Lord said to Moses, "How long will these people treat me with contempt? How long will they refuse to believe in me, in spite of all the miraculous signs I have performed among them? I will strike them down with a plague and destroy them, but I will make you into a nation greater and stronger than they" (Num. 14:11,12).

Can't you just hear Moses saying, "Thank You Lord, they were about to stone me to death. I've gotten a little tired of these folks myself. By the way, great choice in starting this new nation!" It would be tempting to think that way, but what did Moses do? He asked the Lord to withhold judgment by appealing to the good reputation of God and His character. Moses did not consider himself; he considered the needs of the people and the reputation of God. The Lord forgave the people, but all those who witnessed His miraculous works could not go into the Promised Land.

Moses Asks God to Withhold Judgment

Finally Moses had to face the rebellion of his board as recorded in Numbers 16. Korah, Dathan and Abiram led the rebellion, but 250 Israelite men who were well-known community leaders and chosen members of the council joined them.

They came as a group to oppose Moses and Aaron and said to them, "You have gone too far! The whole community is holy, every one of them, and the Lord is with them. Why then do you set yourselves above the Lord's assembly?" (Num. 16:3).

Again, Moses fell on his face. Then he told Korah that the Lord would show tomorrow who belongs to Him and who is holy. Numbers 16:16-21 records what happened:

> Moses said to Korah, "You and all your followers are to appear before the Lord tomorrow—you and they and Aaron. Each man is to take his censer and put incense in it—250 censers in all—and present it before the Lord. You and Aaron are to present your censers also." So each man took his censer, put fire and incense in it, and stood with Moses and Aaron at the entrance to the Tent of Meeting. When Korah had gathered all his followers in opposition to them at the entrance to the Tent of Meeting, the glory of the Lord appeared to the entire assembly. The Lord said to Moses and Aaron, "Separate yourselves from this assembly so I can put an end to them at once."

"Thank you Lord for vindicating me, and how far should I separate myself from them?" Was that how Moses responded? Hardly! "But Moses and Aaron fell facedown and cried out, 'O God, God of the spirits of all mankind, will you be angry with the entire assembly when only one man sins?'" (Num. 16:22). God relented and spared the assembly, but the ground swallowed alive the entire families and possessions of Korah, Dathan and Abiram. In addition, fire came down and consumed the 250 leaders who participated in the rebellion. It is important to note that judgment did not come just to those who instigated the rebellion, but also to those who participated in it, although the judgment was less severe. Their families were spared.

How many times have we been tempted to pray that God would bring judgment upon those who oppose us? Moses demonstrated his humility by praying that God would withhold His judgment. This man, Moses, was truly a servant leader. Rest assured that God will bring judgment upon those who reject Him, but what He is looking for is someone who will intercede on behalf of the people:

> I looked for a man among them who would build up the wall and stand before me in the gap on behalf of the land so I would not have to

destroy it, but I found none. So I will pour out my wrath on them and consume them with my fiery anger, bringing down on their own heads all they have done, declares the Sovereign Lord (Ezek. 22:30,31).

There was no Moses to intercede for the people.

For us there is Jesus. "He is able to save completely those who come to God through him, because he always lives to intercede for them" (Heb. 7:25). Would our churches profit more if they had a pastor who prayed for God's judgment upon his church, or would they profit more if they had a pastor who prayed for God's mercy? Has God called us to a ministry of condemnation, or a ministry of reconciliation?

Repenting of Individualism

In my first role as a senior pastor, I found myself embroiled in a power struggle with a board member. It was the worst case scenario for a pastor. He was a charter member and rumored to be the biggest contributor in the church. I went to see him personally in his home to see if we could work out any differences. It was not going to happen then, so I asked if he would have breakfast with me once a week. I thought we could work out any personal differences we had. It was a sparring match for six months. I can honestly say that I was not trying to change him; all I wanted to do was establish some kind of meaningful relationship with him. I thought I could get along with anybody. Realizing I could not develop a relationship if the other person did not want to was a hard lesson for me to learn.

When I asked permission of the board to use my vacation to conduct a tour of the Holy Land, that board member opposed it. "I know how that works," he said. "If he gets enough people to go, he can go for nothing and that is like giving him a bonus!" So I used my vacation and went by myself. It was a tremendous time of spiritual renewal. The Garden of Gethsemane was especially meaningful. I spent an afternoon in the Church of All Nations, which enshrines the rock believed to be where Jesus surrendered His will to the Father. It was there that He decided to take upon Himself the sins of the world. I left that place knowing that I had to take the sin of that elder upon myself if I was going to forgive him as Jesus had forgiven me. At least, I thought I had made that decision.

The storm seemed to pass until that elder decided to go after my youth pastor. That did it. I made a stand against the man and told the board that if they did not do something the entire staff was going to resign. They arranged a time for us to meet and we were to ask each other for forgiveness. I thought, "Great, sweep it under the carpet, and we can trip over it later." I did ask his forgiveness for not loving him, because I did not, and I did not feel good about that. The meeting ended in a stalemate. I realized the board was not going to do anything so I decided to resign.

One morning I wrote my resignation letter at home. By that evening my temperature was 103.5 and I totally lost my voice. It does not take a genius to recognize that God was not pleased with my decision. My original plan was to read my resignation the next Sunday, but I was too sick to do that. Flat on my back with no way to look but up, I came across the story in Mark 8:22-26. Jesus had touched the eyes of a blind man who was brought to Him. The result was that he saw men walking around like trees. The Lord touched him a second time, and now he saw everything clearly. I got the message.

I was seeing this man as though he were a tree; he was blocking my goal. On second thought, he was not—I was! I wanted the man out of the way; I wanted justice. God wanted me to love the man. I cried out to God, "I don't love that man, Lord, and I know You do. There is nothing within me that is able to do that, so if You want me to love him, You are going to have to touch me." God did! The next Sunday I preached from the passage of Mark 8:22-26 with a husky voice. Although it has been years since this happened, I can still remember the message and the results. I confessed my individualism and shared my desire to love people and never again to see them as trees. I then gave an invitation for those who needed God to touch their lives in order to love people.

I could never have anticipated what happened next. People came forward by the droves. Some were going across the aisle to ask forgiveness of others. The front of the church could not handle the numbers, so the doors swung open and the people spilled out onto the lawn. It was a revival! But it came only after I got my heart right. If I had had my way years ago, I would not be writing this book. I am forever thankful that God struck me down.

To this you were called, because Christ suffered for you, leaving you an example, that you should follow in his steps. "He committed no sin, and no deceit was found in his mouth." When they hurled their insults at him, he did not retaliate; when he suffered, he made no threats. Instead, he entrusted himself to him who judges justly (1 Pet. 2:21-23).

So when people question your leadership, learn the principle of humble intercession.

The Principle of Servant Leadership

Leaders who are not secure in Christ often try to establish their worth by seeking prominent positions. Parents even desire it for their children. Such was the case when the mother of Zebedee's sons approached Jesus to ask a favor. She wanted one of her sons to sit on His right and the other to sit on the left of Jesus in His kingdom. The Lord said it was not His to offer, and asked if they were prepared to drink the cup He was about to drink. They said they were. When the other 10 disciples heard about this, they became indignant (see Matt. 20:20-28).

When people are clamoring for position in any organization, it will create major problems in staff relationships. What are the legitimate people supposed to do when one or two are obviously climbing over the backs of others? They neither want those kinds of people in position over them, nor do they want to succumb to the same self-serving, competitive tactics. In Matthew 20:25-28, the Lord used this occasion to teach about spiritual leadership:

> You know that the rulers of the Gentiles lord it over them, and their high officials exercise authority over them. Not so with you. Instead, whoever wants to become great among you must be your servant, and whoever wants to be first must be your slave—just as the Son of Man did not come to be served, but to serve, and to give his life as a ransom for many.

Luke records, "A dispute arose among them as to which of them was considered to be greatest" (Luke 22:24). After the above instruction, Jesus came to Peter and said, "Simon, Simon, Satan has asked to sift you as wheat. But I have prayed for you, Simon, that your faith may not fail. And when you have turned back, strengthen your brothers" (Luke 22:31,32). Peter then said he was ready to die or go to prison with Jesus, but the Lord answered, "I tell you,

Peter, before the rooster crows today, you will deny three times that you know me" (Luke 22:34). This passage clearly shows the opportunity available to Satan to have access to the Church when leaders succumb to pride. You can see the same connection in James 4:6,7 and 1 Peter 5:6-10.

Leaders Must Serve Their Followers

Nothing is lower in position than a servant or a slave. How are we to understand this? What is every leader subject to or the servant of? I believe it is to the needs of those they are called to lead. As a father, I am subject to the needs of my wife and my children. Should something happen to my wife that requires my attention, I am not free before God to ignore that need and do as I please. I must love my wife as Christ loved the Church. My children have no such commandment. When a crisis occurs at an industrial plant over the weekend, they do not call all the employees, do they? No, they call the leader who is responsible. That is why leadership can be lonely and burdensome. Nobody should strive to be a pastor or elder in a church in order to inflate his or her ego, or because they desire the power that comes from position. Look again at 1 Peter 5:1-4:

> To the elders among you, I appeal as a fellow elder, a witness of Christ's sufferings and one who also will share in the glory to be revealed: Be shepherds of God's flock that is under your care, serving as overseers—not because you must, but because you are willing, as God wants you to be; not greedy for money, but eager to serve; not lording it over those entrusted to you, but being examples to the flock. And when the Chief Shepherd appears, you will receive the crown of glory that will never fade away.

Lines of Authority

Does this mean there are no lines of authority? Of course there are, but the instruction to those who are in authority is different than to those who are under authority. Authority is the right to rule based on position. The requirement of God to those who are under authority is to be submissive. Scripture does allow for times when you must obey God rather than man, namely when authority figures are operating outside the scope of their authority or when they are telling you to do something that is a clear violation of Scripture. These positions of authority can be summarized as follows:

- Civil Government (see Rom. 13:1-5; 1 Tim. 2:1-3; 1 Pet. 2:13-16);
- Parents (see Eph. 6:1-3; Col. 3:18-21);
- Husband (see Titus 2:5; 1 Pet. 3:1-3);
- Employer (see 1 Pet. 2:18-21);
- Church Leaders (see Heb. 13:17).

In position-based authority, people are actually obeying God by respecting the person's position, although they may not necessarily respect the person. I may or may not like police officers, but it is best to obey them. Part of our spiritual protection is being under authority. We are never excused from being submissive because we don't like or respect a person in leadership. Civilizations would experience absolute chaos if there were no governing authorities.

Basis of Authority

The instruction differs for those who are in a position of authority. After preaching the Sermon on the Mount, "The crowds were amazed at his teaching, because he taught as one who had authority, and not as their teachers of the law" (Matt. 7:28,29). Jesus, of course, was God but His listeners did not know it at that time, and He had no earthly position of authority. He was not a representative of the Roman government, nor a member of the Sanhedrin. He was not even a Levite. So what was the basis of His authority? It was based in the quality, conduct and character of His life, and His intimate oneness with the Father. So should all spiritual leadership be. Moses never defended his position as a prophet of God when rebelled against. The Bible records no passages of Jesus saying, "Listen, people, shape up and do what I tell you to do because I am God!" He certainly could have, because He is God.

What happens to the quality of your relationship with your wife, husbands, if you say to her, "You have to obey me because I am your husband?" Obeying you is her responsibility; loving her as Christ loved the Church is your responsibility. Submission should be initiated by the ones under authority, not demanded by the ones in authority.

Being in a submissive position is like "riding shotgun" in a car. The rider will feel secure and have no problem letting the other person drive, provided two things are true. First, the driver must know where he is going. If the driver is lost and the rider knows the way, what will the rider be tempted to do? Second, the rider will feel secure if the driver is obeying the rules of the road. If the driver starts speeding and running red lights, the rider is going to become very insecure. In many cases, rebellion is the result of faulty leadership, not just a rebellious spirit. Leaders should make sure they know where they are going and obey all the laws as they go, rather than demanding that the rider be submissive.

Serving by Example

Let me summarize. All the passages in Scripture relating to those who are under authority instruct them to be submissive to those who are in a biblical position of authority over them. Authority is purely based on position. Those who are in authority are not to rule over others based on their position, but rather are to serve by example. That is a character-based authority. Spiritual leaders should strive to be such an example that others will want to follow, not be forced to follow. What qualifies a person to be an elder is his godly character and knowledge of God's Word. Biblical gifts and talents, as well as secular positions of power and influence, do not qualify a person for leadership in the Church. Notice the words of Paul in 1 Thessalonians 2:5-8 (*NASB*, italics added):

> For we never came with flattering speech, as you know, nor with a pretext for greed—God is witness—nor did we seek glory from men, either from you or from others, *even though as apostles of Christ we might have asserted our authority.* But we proved to be gentle among you, as a nursing mother tenderly cares for her own children. Having thus a fond affection for you, we were well-pleased to impart to you not only the gospel of God but also our own lives, because you had become very dear to us.

There is a tremendous need for accountability, and many are calling for it. How can we have legitimate accountability? Look at the following four words and ask yourself an important question: From which end of the list did God come to you?

- Authority;
- Accountability;
- Affirmation;
- Acceptance.

Whose Servants Are We?

How you answer the previous question will say more about how you understand parenting and ministry than any other question I could ask. I have no doubt in my mind that God started with acceptance. "But God demonstrates his own love for us in this: While we were still sinners, Christ died for us" (Rom. 5:8). Then comes the affirmation. "How great is the love the Father has lavished on us, that we should be called children of God! And that is what we are!" (1 John 3:1). People who know they are accepted and affirmed will voluntarily be accountable to the authority figures who grant that acceptance and affirmation to them. But when authority figures demand accountability without love and affirmation they will never get it. Oh sure, under duress, those who have an authoritarian leader will fill out a report form, giving a bunch of superficial answers, but they will never share what is going on inside. They will only be vulnerable to the one they know really loves them. Even pastors have a tremendous need to be affirmed.

Paul makes a strong personal declaration in Galatians 1:10: "Am I now trying to win the approval of men, or of God? Or am I trying to please men? If I were still trying to please men, I would not be a servant of Christ." If Paul were trying to please men, whose servant would he be? This does not just apply to Paul. All spiritual leaders have the responsibility to help people live lives dependent upon God alone. Paul says in 2 Corinthians 5:9 that we are to "make it our goal to please him [God]."

In a general sense, we are all supposed to "submit to one another out of reverence for Christ" (Eph. 5:21), because we are all called to love one another. You are not being a codependent if you are legitimately subject to the needs of others. You are being a codependent if you let the other person control your life and dictate to you how you are supposed to meet their needs. Every believer has all the necessary authority in Christ to overcome the kingdom of darkness because we are seated with Christ in the heavenlies (see Eph. 2:5-7). Let's make it our goal to be the kind of leaders who will enable our people to live free in Christ. Remember, when people question your right to lead, learn the principle of servant leadership that is based in character.

In chapters 6 and 7, Chuck will share some helpful concepts on the pastor as a saint, and the Church as a communion. In the remaining chapters, he will take you through the process of setting your church free. May I encourage you to familiarize yourself with the seven churches in Revelation 2 and 3 before you go on, and have that section of your Bible available as you read. May the Lord enable you to be the spiritual leader He has called you to be, and may He use you to be a part of the process that brings freedom to your ministry.

THE PASTOR AS SAINT

For a life that counts for time and eternity, nothing beats the ministry. It is a great life; one that is full of joys, challenges and rewards. Pastors, missionaries, church planters, professors, counselors, church staff members and career Christian workers are the most fortunate of all people. No one denies the crucial role of the laity. Nevertheless, the career ministry has some special joys. Think of some of the benefits.

Significance: What counts more than leading people to a saving knowledge of our Lord Jesus Christ? What changes lives more than helping them to grow in Him? For significant impact on people's deepest values and their eternal destiny, the ministry is the premium of ways to invest one's life.

Blessings: In the Lord's economy, it is simply impossible to give without receiving in return. Give love and you will be loved. Give encouragement and you will be encouraged. Give as unto the Lord and the Lord will give back to you in abundance. Although this is true for all Christians, we who serve in the full-time ministry have more time and more opportunities to give. The result is that we receive more as well.

Friendship: Good friends are by no means the exclusive right of ministers and career Christian workers. But it is next to impossible to serve well in the ministry without developing many friends—loyal, caring, genuine friends. They are a treasure beyond compare.

Belonging: The church is a great place to belong, and few others find themselves more a part of the church family than pastors, staff members and missionaries. Counselors, professors and Christ's servants in parachurch ministries likewise experience wider communities who love and accept them as one of their own.

Satisfaction: It is a documented fact that pastors have a longer life expectancy than people in most other professions, yet their work hours are longer than most and the stresses never stop. What accounts for the longevity? Maybe it is clean living coming through, but more likely the inner peace and satisfaction make the big difference. Those who feel good on the inside enjoy greater health and longer life than those who do not.

Joy: What is more joyous than a life connected to Christ? What is more uplifting than prayer partners who regularly bring you before God's throne of grace? What is more fun than using spiritual gifts and watching them build up other people? What is more fulfilling than watching lives change for the better right before your eyes?

Add to this list the power that flows from the gospel, the freedom that comes with truth, the maturity that results from living in the Spirit, the confidence that builds with answered prayer. All these benefits are, in fact, available to every Christian. But pastors can seize the opportunity to experience these benefits in even greater measure.

Thank God for Pastors

As a superintendent of churches, I (Chuck) love pastors. I thank God for them.

- They preach and teach us the Word of God with diligence and joy.
- They love us and stand by us in our hour of greatest need.
- They lead, plan, coach in all kinds of ministries and church activities.

- They model the life they teach through example.
- They manage their own weaknesses and call on us to do the same.

Knowing pastors as I do, let me tell you that today they face incredible pressure. Life in the ministry is more like a battlefield than a playground. If the truth were known, most pastors battle with discouragement. Some feel it only once in a while, but others struggle with it almost all of the time. I am not criticizing pastors for feeling discouraged, because I have been there myself. I know, as they do, that it is a reflection of how much pastors care. Leaders never feel discouraged about churches they do not love. Think of a few of the more common pressure points of pastors today.

Pastors confront the disintegrating moral fiber of our culture. Constantly exposed to the worst of people's hurts in counseling and crisis, pastors live on the raw edge of life. They counsel abandoned spouses whose marriages fell apart because of adulterous affairs. They agonize with parents whose children start using drugs. They stand at the bedsides of the dying because of attempted suicide or self-exposure to AIDS. Pastors anguish about apathy toward God. It hurts to see decent, upstanding people caught in the materialism and selfishness of "me and mine." Pastors exhort, correct and discipline, most of which goes on in private, few others ever knowing.

Pastors feel the need to succeed or sometimes simply to survive. It is easy for their churches to move into a damaging, downward spiral of too little powerful prayer, shortage of workers, declining attendance, financial shortfall and feelings of failure. Like dominoes, each one leads to the next. Also like dominoes, the defeating cycle can start at any point, but can be reversed only by returning to the point of original failure. The fact is that it is much harder and more painful to turn this downward spiral around than most people ever dream.

The more effective the pastor, the more time drain is a major problem, especially if dysfunctional people are sapping energy. All pastors walk the tightrope between working too hard and neglecting family, or not working hard enough and neglecting ministry. Some manage both family and ministry fairly well; others fall off the tightrope to certain disaster.

Pastors smart under the sting of gossip and criticism. Most spouses feel it more intensely than the pastors themselves. In many churches, one or two critics can give the pastor fits. Church bullies, whiners, rumormongers, slanderers, tattlers and prattlers all burn pastors' emotional fuel. Their families suffer the most of all. Most pastors are people persons, so they thrive on good relationships, warm words and encouraging, handwritten notes. When they receive criticism instead, they wilt on the inside.

Pastors as Targets

Pastors sense a spiritual struggle is going on and discern that they themselves are the target of the archenemy. Unexplained hassles, marriage pressures, physical illness, conflicts with close associates and feelings of inadequacy often plague pastors. What is scary is that these things defy rational explanation, occurring far too often and for no apparent reason.

Play a biblical mental game with me. This is not too serious, just enough to make a point. Suppose for a moment that you are Satan. As the opposite of an archangel (not the opposite of God), you are not omnipresent. You cannot be everywhere at the same time, so you must deploy the fallen angels under your command to carry out your ugly purposes. Your mission statement reads that you intend to blind people to God's glory and the free offer of salvation. Your goals are to prevent people from coming to Christ, disrupt God's work in the world and, in general, make people as bad and miserable as possible. Where would you assign your demonic troops?

Would you assign some to keep unbelievers blind so they cannot see the light of the gospel? Would you assign some to stir up wars and rumors of wars? Would you assign some to governments, to education, to false religions, to economic systems, to the media? Would you assign some to Christians to keep them apathetic or rebellious or compromising? Would you bring persecution on the Church? Go ahead and think biblically and creatively.

As you finish up this biblical mental game, please recall that, although the prince of this world has lost the war because of Christ's conquest in the cross and resurrection, the battles are not over. The devil's strategy may be far better than the one you imagined. It is doubtful, however, that the adversary bypasses attempts to defeat or deter Christians and their leaders. Satan knows who to hit to stop the Church's progress.

Three Ministry Skills

In a later chapter we will return to the subject of Satan's attacks on churches and Christian leaders. At this point, think about three ministry skills that all pastors need. It helps to recall them by thinking of the three offices held by our Lord Jesus—Prophet, Priest and King (see chapter 3). Please understand that we are using these simply as reminders and not drawing a comparison of pastors with Jesus Himself. As *prophet*, pastors fill the role of God's *communicator*—preacher, teacher, public evangelist and worship leader. Communicating for Christ is the most visible of pastors' roles, and for many the most valued.

Pastor as Communicator

Some of the greatest preachers of all times communicated profound Bible truths in simple, colorful language. Martin Luther, scholar, pastor and reformer, not only preached this way, but also understood exactly what he was doing. Listen to his own comments: "When I preach I regard neither doctors nor magistrates, of whom I have above forty in the congregation; I have all my eyes on the servant maids and on the children. And if the learned men are not well pleased with what they hear, well, the door is open."[1] The challenge to every Spirit-filled communicator of the Scripture is to teach and preach with accuracy and authority, with laughter and tears, with encouragement, conviction and joy.

Pastor as Caregiver

As *priest*, pastors fill the role of *caregiver*—people builder, discipler, personal evangelist and counselor. People skills and relationship-building qualities flowing from our loving Lord Jesus are needed here. As caregivers, pastors minister best one-on-one or in small groups. Whether it is in a home visit, over lunch, at a hospital bedside, before a wedding or funeral, in a counseling session, or in an unplanned conversation, pastors are friends in times of need. Long after people can no longer remember the sermons, they will remember the personal moments of crisis when the pastor stood by them.

Sometimes caregivers must learn to receive love from fellow Christians as well as give love. At age 30 and pregnant for the first time, my friend Linda LeFeuvre was the picture of health. For a few days she had headaches, but they did not seem too severe. Then her left side began feeling numb. Within hours, her vision blurred and she lost the use of her left hand and left leg. The doctors feared it might be a malignant tumor but emergency surgery revealed it was an abscess in her brain. She made some progress during the next four weeks, but then the old symptoms began to return. A second surgery removed another abscess, larger than the first.

Day after day during the five weeks of her hospital stay, her pastors, family and friends visited. They prayed, talked, laughed, hurt and shared progress and setbacks. Other Christian friends phoned, sent flowers and cards, and kept showering her with love. What was special was that Linda was a caregiver herself. She was the kind of person who was always putting her arms around other people. Now she found herself in a place where she was vulnerable. Her God-given assignment was to *receive* care as well as give it. She described it this way:

> At the time I could think of nothing more distressing than paralysis and being all hooked up to tubes. Those seemingly endless days and nights in that hospital bed fostered bitterness toward this unsolicited helplessness. Gradually, the Lord taught me to allow Him to comfort and reassure me through Christian friends and family. I wouldn't have learned this lesson had anything less debilitating happened to me.

As a significant leader of International Friends Fellowship, an inner-city ministry, Linda learned what many pastors must also learn: The role of caregiver includes both giving and receiving.

Pastor as Leader

Pastors serve not only as communicators and caregivers, prophets and priests, but also as *king* or *leader*. Just as Jesus led with excellence, so pastors in this role move God's people forward. God's leaders come in two varieties: motivators and organizers. Motivational leaders cast a vision, stir up the people for action and excite others to carry out the details. Organizers, on the other hand, are capable administrators. They follow through on plans, make contacts, offer training and communicate thoroughly. They keep projects moving and on target.

Gifted motivators and talented organizers lead the church well. Little wonder that the Bible exhorts, "If a man's gift is...leadership, let him govern diligently" (Rom. 12:6,8). Those who are task oriented often need to work on nourishing the people who work with them. Those who are people oriented often need to focus on a clear vision and reachable goals, while doing the tasks necessary to finish the job. What works best is to have both motivators and organizers teamed up together in harmony. Then the church really moves forward.

The Weakest Role Is the Snag

Here is the catch: Few pastors have it all. Only superstars excel in all three ministry skills of prophet, priest and king (or communicator, caregiver and leader). Jesus never called us to be superstars; He called us to be servants. Living with limitations and weaknesses provides an opportunity for God to perfect His grace in our lives (see 2 Cor. 12:9). Most pastors are gifted in one skill, do well in the second and struggle in the third. Pastors who have strengths in only one of the three skills seldom succeed in local church ministry, no matter how much they excel in the one skill. One-skill specialists may be superb at teaching in a Christian college, engaging in a counseling ministry, leading a parachurch organization or possibly working on a large church staff. The principle still stands, however. Local church ministry most often demands expertise in two of the three roles.

Some well-intentioned pastors spend most of their time trying to take care of their weakest role. For example, those with poor administrative skills may spend endless hours preparing the bulletin and midweek paper, running errands, taking care of the facility and doing detail work. Weak in delegation and follow-through, these poor stewards find it easier to do it all themselves. Gifted in communication and people skills, they get by in their areas of strength, but never have enough time left to excel. Foolish!

A wiser course of action is for pastors to specialize in their strongest role, developing its full potential. They will also want to excel in their second role, using it for the glory of God. The weakest role is the snag. It takes two kinds of action to compensate. One is to improve it enough to stay out of trouble and avoid a trail of damage. The second is to find other people who will compensate for the weakness because it is their role of strength. All the people in the congregation are also gifted. Their spiritual gifts all fit at least one of the three roles, and some excel in more than one.

A word to the wise in every congregation: Most pastors have one weak role, so the lay leaders also need to take the initiative to compensate. If the pulpit is weak, find some gifted teachers to lead adult Sunday School classes and Bible studies. If the one-on-one ministry is lacking, look for lay counselors and small-group leaders. If the leadership is poor, look for people who are gifted motivators or experienced administrators. Never, never attack a pastor because only one role is lacking. Pastors, also, must never give up the ministry because of a weakness in just one area.

Wise are the pastors who delegate their weakest ministry skills to others. Wise also are the people in the churches who assume that role as a God-given ministry. Working together, the Body of Christ functions amazingly well. Solo performances in ministry that eliminate the need for others violate the way Christ designed His Body. The ways that a ministry can become dysfunctional are legion. But they all have one thing in common: The Lord Jesus Christ is not being fully heard and obeyed.

Dysfunctional Ministry

Pastoral skills certainly include communication, caregiving and leadership. But ministry skills alone are not enough. In fact, it is not uncommon for a pastor to excel in all three ministry skills and yet have a dysfunctional ministry. One of the major reasons is that many pastors themselves are not experiencing freedom in Christ. Their own lives are plagued by lust, fear, anger, resentment or unforgiveness. Some feel driven to succeed; others fear failure. Some also succumb to the temptation of inappropriate sexual behavior.

The headlines scream scandal as high-profile Christian leaders fall into sexual immorality. If it were only the famous, the situation might not be so tragic. But every denominational leader knows, just as I do, that the plague of sexual immorality reaches pastors and Christian workers as well. It crosses all denominational and theological lines and most age brackets. When those who fall immorally are trusted colleagues and friends, or youth pastors whose example affects our children, the pain becomes intense.

In Neil's book *Released from Bondage,* "Doug" tells how he grew up having the self-image of a bastard.[2] His mother was not married when he was born. In his early childhood and even into adolescence, he was often abused by others. He pursued sexual encounters as a way of gaining acceptance. Eventually he moved into homosexual behavior. At age 16 he felt suicidal. Then someone invited him to summer camp and he accepted Jesus Christ as his Savior. For him it was a new lease on life, spiritually and physically.

Doug did well in school, trained for the ministry and threw himself into serving Christ. He married a wonderful Christian wife, but his thought life was still a mess. The old perversions and invasive thoughts of male images wracked his brain. Needless to say, they fouled up his sexual relationship with his wife, too. He turned to masturbation as a protected environment. He felt such shame about his bisexual tendencies that he began mentally making plans to end his life.

A therapy group using some hypnosis caused him to disclose something of his past. The group encouraged him but he left in a cloud of regret for having said too much. On the way home he kept looking for a semitruck to ram into, hoping to cause a head-on collision and kill himself. For some sovereign reason, no semis were on the road that night. Arriving home, his children ran to meet him with the love only children can give. He snapped back to reality.

After attending Neil's "Resolving Personal and Spiritual Conflicts" conference, Doug found genuine freedom in Christ. His sexual bondage was broken. His ministry took on fresh power and new fruitfulness as he shared how he found freedom. Then the adversary hit with a major counterattack of flashbacks to perverted behavior and tidal waves of perverse thoughts that almost sent Doug back into the old life. Once again he felt suicidal. However, he called on his prayer partners and the men's group. Their intercession broke the attack and freed him up for ministry.

Doug's self-image changed from bastard to a new creation—holy, beloved and chosen in Christ (see Col. 3:12). His marriage improved. On the inside he knew who he was in Christ. He was a growing Christian, not perfect, but growing.

Living by Principles

Pastors, like others, feel the pressures of a morally decaying culture. They are not exempt from the trends in our society. Just a few years ago people lived more by principles than rules. Back then people did not ask, "Is this legal?" or "Is there a law against it?" or "Can we get away with it?" Instead they asked, "Is this right?" or "Is this fair?" or "Will this help the most people?" or "Is this honest?"

Moral decline, self-interest and materialistic greed is so obvious around us, most people have abandoned principles as their governing pattern for all kinds of relationships. Life must go on, however, and have some sense of order, decency and honesty, or our whole system breaks down. So as people abandon principles, they rely more and more upon the government that substitutes laws, regulations and rules. Honest people then have to spend more time and money-changing procedures, filling out reports, paying added taxes, fulfilling new requirements and conforming to rules.

How did we get into this mess? We moved from living by principles to endless laws and regulations by quietly moving away from God. We kept up the appearances, but at work, in our marriage relationships, in our businesses and in social contacts we made little compromises with His principles. Like Martha, we became distracted and felt worried and upset about so many things. We needed instead to choose what is better, as Mary did (see Luke 10:38-42). Our culture offers plenty of ways to distract us. Unfortunately, they are more lethal than Martha's worries were. Our distractions—namely me, my money and my morality—actually oppose God and His kingdom.

What Is Killing Us?

Let's start with the first distraction—*me*. Radical individualism pervades our thinking today. We elevate the individual above marriage, family, church, community or nation. The result is a shameless self-interest and self-indulgence that destroys everything it touches. Me-ism, at heart, is selfish and sinful. It leads to satanic influence and, if not checked, satanic control.

My money is a second distraction. As a nation we have made the pursuit of money (i.e., a "healthy economy") our first priority. Materialism reigns supreme. Jesus said, "You cannot serve both God and Money" (Matt. 6:24). The Bible teaches we are to be generous, caring for others, supporting God's work. Money is to be our servant, not our master.

My morality is a third mark of the current world system in our culture. This is relativism in truth, values and ethics. "What's true for you may not be true for me." "Things aren't black and white; they are differing shades of gray." This nonsense rejects the Bible, the Ten Commandments and the Sermon on the Mount as idealistic. We are left with few moral restraints and end up lying, cheating, stealing, committing adultery and killing unborn babies.

The false trinity of me, my money and my morality is eroding our moral character and our nation. "Do not be deceived: God cannot be mocked. A man [or a nation] reaps what he sows" (Gal. 6:7). We can and should turn back (even one person at a time) to God's principles. The Bible makes it more than clear that this kind of change does not come naturally. It requires the inner transformation of Jesus Christ (see Eph. 2:8-10).

The Missing Role

Pastors, however, know about the trends in our society and preach and teach about them with accuracy and skill. So what is wrong? How does the devil get a foothold in the lives of those who fall? What is missing? The missing role in pastoral ministry is that of *saint*. We are not talking about superstar Christians, ancient relics or old people who wear halos. We will stand by the biblical definition of saints as God's called and holy people, redeemed by Christ and set apart for His purposes (see 1 Cor. 1:2). By filling the role of saint, we mean that our Lord Himself expects all biblical pastors and elders to model life in Christ. They serve as examples of lives filled with the Holy Spirit and constantly connected to Christ.

It is no accident that the requirements for elders and deacons in 1 Timothy 3 and Titus 1 focus on character qualities rather than on spiritual gifts or ministry skills. Godly character qualities are not personality traits nor the result of growing up in an emotionally healthy family. They are the clothing of Christ, the fruit of the Spirit, the full armor of God (see Rom. 13:14; Col. 3:12; Gal. 5:22,23). The examples pastors and elders set by living in freedom in Christ and moving toward maturity in Christ are crucial.

Most people in the Church believe that godliness goes with the territory of being pastors. *After all,* the thinking goes, *pastors study the Bible, pray with people and lead the way in the church. Certainly, they must live closer to God than the people they serve.* It is true that these activities give pastors the opportunity for increased knowledge and growth. It is also true that these activities are special objects of attack, temptation, accusation, deception and discouragement from the evil one. Subtle compromises can remain hidden for years. Spiritual gifts and ministry skills function quite well, even when some hidden conduct is out of control and displeasing to Christ. Let's consider time spent in prayer as an example.

Secrets of Pastors' Prayer Lives

In his excellent book *Prayer Shield,* C. Peter Wagner writes a chapter with the intriguing title "Secrets of Pastors' Prayer Lives."[3] His personal survey of 572 American pastors revealed the following data. (Incidentally, he measured only time spent in actual prayer; not Bible study, listening to praise tapes or reading devotional books.) Here is what Wagner found:

- 57 percent pray less than 20 minutes a day.
- 34 percent pray between 20 minutes and one hour a day.
- 9 percent pray one hour or more a day.
- The average prayer time was 22 minutes daily.

The shocker in Wagner's study is that 28 percent spent 10 minutes or less a day in prayer. That is more than one pastor out of every four who has an anemic personal prayer life. Just how much do pastors in other countries pray? Wagner polled four other places and found significant variations:

- Australia   23 minutes a day
- New Zealand   30 minutes a day
- Japan   44 minutes a day
- Korea   90 minutes a day

According to a *Leadership Journal* survey, most pastors feel totally unsupported in their efforts to maintain an effective prayer life.[4] Their survey also revealed that the average time pastors spent in prayer daily was about 22 minutes. Some pastors feel content praying 22 minutes a day; most do not. Many feel frustrated and wonder why they struggle so much in what should be so basic. The truth is that intimacy with Christ comes no easier for pastors than for anyone else.

Spiritual Abuse

When pastors and church leaders fail in the role of saint, they may subtly become false examples of true Christianity. In fact, some churches and Christian organizations fall into patterns of spiritual abuse. In their revealing book, *The Subtle Power of Spiritual Abuse,* David Johnson and Jeff VanVonderen point out seven marks of spiritually abusive systems. They list these danger signs: (1) power posturing; (2) performance preoccupation; (3) unspoken rules; (4) lack of balance; (5) paranoia; (6) misplaced loyalty; and (7) code of silence.[5] A church or a ministry that is struggling with corporate bondage (i.e., bondage resulting from patterns of behavior in a church that are displeasing to God and contrary to His revealed will) is vulnerable to becoming abusive.

Spiritual abuse can sometimes be subtle, one distortion in an otherwise healthy ministry. However, sometimes the church itself can become abusive, inflicting incredible damage upon people for time and eternity. At other times church leaders can become abusive of their pastors. The abusive church most often harbors abusive people—pastors or lay leaders—who are themselves deceived by the evil one. Some are totally unaware of the trap they are in. Others hear the warnings but for some reason ignore them. When the role of saint is neglected, then the example of living free in Christ becomes distorted. What is taught from Scripture and what is practiced in the church are far from the same truth.

Abusive leaders are often more concerned with their image than with an authentic closeness to Christ. Their identity is more in performance and appearance than in Christ who called them to serve as true shepherds of God's people (see 1 Pet. 5:1-5). Johnson and VanVonderen warn us to watch for these marks of image-oriented leaders:

- They operate from a false basis of authority;
- They lack integrity;
- They wear their spirituality on the outside;
- Spirituality is a put-on performance, an image they project;
- They require the recognition of people, calling it respect;
- They point to themselves as the primary source of knowledge, direction, authority and life.[6]

It is possible, however, for healthy, nonabusive pastors to believe some lies from the adversary. When Jesus said one of His chosen Twelve would betray Him, Judas responded, "Surely not I, Rabbi?" (Matt. 26:25). Satan can work his way into the highest levels of leadership if we let him. Even good people can be deceived.

A pastor shared with Neil how a board member in his church was doing everything he could to destroy the reputation of the previous pastor before him. Not content with the past, the leader was trying to run the current pastor out of the church as well. When confronted with his malicious actions, the board member said he had no choice; the voice of God Himself told him to do it. Assuming he truly believed what he was saying, this man was paying attention to a deceiving spirit (see 1 Tim. 4:1). How could the voice of God contradict His own word (see Heb. 13:17)? The Holy Spirit is not schizophrenic.

Trusting and Training

The evil one specializes in putting excuses into the minds of God's people. For example, too many American pastors believe a lie about who gets the work done. Dr. Timothy Warner, vice president of Freedom in Christ International Ministries, is the one who first pointed this out in our hearing: Those who believe that people get the work done will either become workaholics, or give up and begin to coast. Those who really believe the Holy Spirit gets the work done will pray and pray until God empowers their ministries.

Spiritual disciplines such as Bible meditation and memorization, fasting and prayer, silence and solitude are training exercises to put us in shape spiritually. Attaining freedom in Christ is a matter of trusting Christ. Moving toward maturity in Christ is a matter of training. Many Christians, pastors included, fall into the trap of sin, confess; sin, sin, confess; sin, sin, sin, confess; sin, sin, sin, sin, give up. It is trying and failing, trying and failing, trying and failing.

The missing step between trusting and trying is training. That is what the role of saint is all about—training in godliness. Paul wrote to Timothy, "Train yourself to be godly. For physical training is of some value, but godliness has value for all things, holding promise for both the present life and the life to come" (1 Tim. 4:7,8). More and more seminaries and Bible schools are offering courses in biblical spirituality. Along with the recent breakthroughs on knowing our identity in Christ and experiencing freedom in Christ, we believe this is a much-needed trend. May God forbid that it ever turns into a program or academic exercise that misses Christ!

Self-Defeating Neglect

Let's say it again: A model of ministry that includes prophet, priest and king but leaves out saint is dysfunctional. For pastors to serve as communicators, leaders and people helpers while neglecting intimacy with Christ is ultimately self-defeating. The basic problem is that it leaves Satan and his demons a place to attack. The attack is not just upon the pastor and leaders but also upon the local church.

Here are some symptoms that surface when pastors neglect prayer time, spiritual disciplines and character development, giving inadequate attention to the role of saint:

- Much work but little lasting progress;
- Good growth in the church for a while, followed by devastating conflict;
- Apparent progress, but in time it fades away and nothing much lasts;
- People become like their leaders—good workers but not pray-ers;
- The church maintains its functions but shows little power.

Unfortunately, these symptoms sound much like what is ailing the Church in America today. Does it sound like your church?

Accountability

The tragedy is that so few church leaders hold their pastors accountable for fulfilling the role of saint. What is more, I doubt that this will change. I believe that pastors themselves must take responsibility for the crucial role of saint, which they can only do as they discover their own identities in Christ rather than in performance. Then the personal "Steps to Freedom in Christ" (see appendix C) provide a searching moral inventory and a helpful guide to personal freedom in Christ.

A close prayer partner and an intercessory prayer team can make a marked difference, especially if pastors request prayer for their own growth in grace and knowledge of our Lord. Add accountability groups, preferably outside the local church, with whom pastors can be open, honest and vulnerable, and major progress toward fulfilling the role of saint is well under way.

Recently I met with a pastors' prayer group. It was a good time of sharing both ministry and personal needs. Afterward one of the pastors approached me. "Chuck, promise me that whenever you see me you will ask me two questions. One is whether I'm thinking about anyone other than my wife. The other is how much time I've spent in prayer in the last 24 hours." It was a great offer, just the kind that will keep both of us more accountable to the Lord and to each other.

Recovering the Role of Saint

The Bible is explicit in its call to Christian leaders to serve as examples, to model the life of Christ that they proclaim to others. In short, God calls on pastors and all Christian leaders to fulfill the role of saint. The apostle Paul is the most bold. In his farewell address to the Ephesian elders, his primary appeal emerges from his own personal role of saint. The starting point for his exhortation was for them to live as he had lived in Christ.

You know how I lived the whole time I was with you, from the first day I came into the province of Asia. I served the Lord with great humility and with tears, although I was severely tested by the plots of the Jews. You know that I have not hesitated to preach anything that would be helpful to you but have taught you publicly and from house to house. I have declared to both Jews and Greeks that they must turn to God in repentance and have faith in our Lord Jesus (Acts 20:18-21).

Later, when Paul was on trial before Felix, he appealed again to his role as saint as evidenced by his attempts to live with a clear conscience: "So I strive always to keep my conscience clear before God and man" (Acts 24:16).

Paul understood that his life communicated the gospel as well as his words did. Today, many observers report a growing hostility toward biblical Christianity as a by-product of our culture's moral decline. In fact, it appears that our society is coming closer and closer to the Gentile lifestyles in New Testament times. Although we decry the moral decay, we can rejoice in the opportunities for biblical Christianity to flourish. The darker the night, the brighter "the light of the knowledge of the glory of God in the face of Christ" (2 Cor. 4:6). In such a degraded moral climate, example becomes essential.

Follow my example, as I follow the example of Christ (1 Cor. 11:1).

Join with others in following my example, brothers, and take note of those who live according to the pattern we gave you (Phil. 3:17).

Whatever you have learned or received or heard from me, or seen in me—put it into practice. And the God of peace will be with you (Phil. 4:9).

For you yourselves know how you ought to follow our example (2 Thess. 3:7).

Someone might object, "This is normal for an apostle, but what about an ordinary pastor like me? I'm far from perfect." Wait a minute. You have access to the same Christ you preach. You are united with Christ in your salvation.

From His riches He has already given you grace, truth, love, power and right-eousness. You can keep on growing, just as you hope your people will mature in Christ. Your Lord does not expect absolute perfection in you, but He does expect you to be responding to Him with faith, hope and love. It is not too much for His people to expect their undershepherd to model a lifestyle of biblical obedience and holy living.

A life that fulfills the role of saint means modeling growth, not absolute perfection. No one likes a phony! People need to see how we handle mistakes and failures more than they need to see our successes. Then they will know what to do when they fail or blunder or foul up. Our children, especially, need to see how we handle our flaws. It never undermines leadership to own up to our weaknesses if we are humble and honest in the process.

Paul exhorted Timothy and Titus, who were not apostles, to make the role of saint, namely their personal example, a central part of their ministries:

> Don't let anyone look down on you because you are young, but set an example for the believers in speech, in life, in love, in faith and in purity (1 Tim. 4:12).

> In everything set them an example by doing what is good (Titus 2:7).

What is clear in these verses and their contexts is that the role of saint is more than having a good daily devotional time. It is a way of life, a pattern of godliness, a daily conduct that results from living in union with our Lord Jesus Christ. To put it in modern terms, pastors must become examples of life in Christ, communicators, caregivers and leaders.

- The saint, the example, is the godly pastor.
- The prophet, the communicator, is the teaching pastor.
- The priest, the caregiver, is the encouraging pastor.
- The king, the leader, is the motivating or organizing pastor.

All effective ministry calls for using strengths and compensating for weaknesses. To emphasize the role of saint and leave out prophet, priest or king will also lead to a weakened ministry. Pastors and churches who have poor leadership, for example, will not thrive no matter how godly their personal example or intense their prayer lives. The same can be said for poor preaching or poor pastoral care. It takes all three ministry skills and the one crucial role of saint to build a strong, healthy, Christ-glorifying church.

Suffering Saints

For most pastors, learning to excel in the role of saint does not come easily. It helps to know that all of us Christians, including pastors, are already identified with Christ. We are crucified, buried, made alive, raised up and seated with Christ in the heavenlies (see Gal. 2:20; Rom. 6:4; Eph. 2:4-6). Once we know who we are in Christ, then we can live up to our true identity. So we run with perseverance the race marked out for us, fixing our eyes on Jesus (see Heb. 12:1,2). It helps to understand that we are already seated with Christ in the heavenly realms, even while running hard toward Him in this world.

It is smack dab in the middle of pain and suffering that the role of saint really has the light of heaven thrown on it. When things are not going well, and when the influencers of the church criticize the pastor, all eyes in the congregation watch for the response. When the ministry is discouraging, so very discouraging, everyone looks to see if the pastor's confidence is in Christ or in circumstances. It is in the dark hour of trial that the people sense the pastor's integrity, character and true identity. It is when the weaknesses are exposed, when pain and suffering strike hard, when circumstances move beyond control that real life in Christ is brought to light. In these circumstances, Christ both reveals and builds genuine character.

In those times, pastors cry out in pain and in faith with the apostle Paul: "We are hard pressed on every side, *but not crushed;* perplexed, *but not in despair;* persecuted, *but not abandoned;* struck down, *but not destroyed"* (2 Cor. 4:8,9, italics added). Suffering with Jesus under the disciplining hand of God is part of what it takes to fulfill the role of saint. There are no shortcuts, no easy answers, no instant maturity—not even for pastors.

Jesus said it best: "For whoever wants to save his life will lose it, but whoever loses his life for me will find it" (Matt. 16:25). Pastors who lay down their lives for Christ find resurrection life. They find it full of living hope, fresh with the newness of life. They find it fully identified with Christ in their own experience. They find it as a life that is crucified, risen and reigning with Him.

Pastors, pursue your calling as a communicator, as prophet. Pursue it as a caregiver, as priest. Pursue it as a leader, as king. But most of all pursue your calling as an example of life in Christ, as saint. You will use the skills of prophet, priest and king for a long time—all the rest of your ministry. But you will use the crucial role of saint for all time and for all eternity. The role of saint comes only through clothing yourself with Christ, finding your identity in Him and living in constant communion with the Lord Jesus.

Notes

1. Frank S. Mead, ed., *The Encyclopedia of Religious Quotations* (Grand Rapids, MI: Fleming H. Revell Company, 1965), p. 353.
2. Neil T. Anderson, *Released from Bondage* (Nashville, TN: Thomas Nelson Publishers, 1991), pp. 113-119.
3. C. Peter Wagner, *Prayer Shield* (Ventura, CA: Regal Books, 1992), pp. 77-93.
4. Terry C. Muck, "10 Questions About the Devotional Life," *Leadership, A Practical Journal for Church Leaders,* Winter Quarter, 1982, p. 37.
5. David Johnson and Jeff VanVonderen, *The Subtle Power of Spiritual Abuse* (Minneapolis, MN: Bethany House Publishers, 1991), pp. 63-79; for a summary chart see pp. 187,188.
6. Ibid., p. 136.

THE CHURCH IN COMMUNION

One of the more creative and colorful speakers about the church today is Jim Dethmer, former teaching pastor at Willow Creek Community Church in South Barrington, Illinois. In an insightful article in *Leadership Journal*, Dethmer describes the church as three interlocking circles or functions.[1] His terms are *Cause*, *Community* and *Corporation*. He finds a biblical basis for each role of the church, and using an intriguing style describes its major characteristics. Let us paraphrase and summarize.

The *Cause* of the church is its mission—fulfilling its vision. The biblical image is an army. The key person in the army is the most highly committed, the one who sacrifices most, the martyr. An army succeeds when it advances, capturing people or territory for its commander. Recruits enter the army by being enlisted or drafted. If battles are raging, they can leave the army only when the war ends or when they become casualties. The paybacks are glory and special honors. The "cause people" in the church sacrifice themselves to spread the gospel, win people to Christ, plant churches, launch mission efforts and take new ground for Christ. The role of communicator (prophet) fits well in the Cause circle.

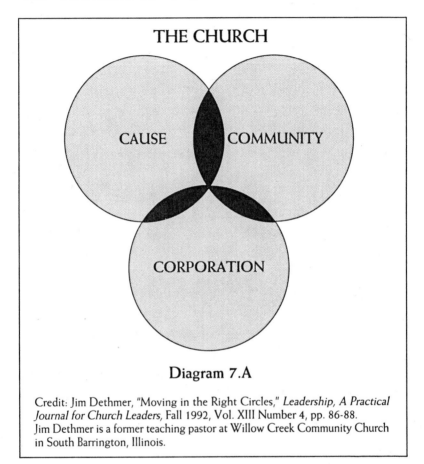

THE CHURCH

CAUSE   COMMUNITY

CORPORATION

Diagram 7.A

Credit: Jim Dethmer, "Moving in the Right Circles," *Leadership, A Practical Journal for Church Leaders,* Fall 1992, Vol. XIII Number 4, pp. 86-88. Jim Dethmer is a former teaching pastor at Willow Creek Community Church in South Barrington, Illinois.

The *Community* of the church is the fellowship of the people of God who love one another. The biblical image is the family, the household of faith. At any given moment the most important person in the family is the weakest or the one with the greatest need. A new baby or the family member who undergoes surgery rightly receives the greatest care. A family succeeds when it nourishes and provides for all its members according to their needs. Family members are born or adopted into it, and they never really leave it. They may divorce, disown or change names, but the social and psychological imprint always remains. The payback in family life is security, love and belonging. The "community people" in the church put their arms around the hurting and the needy. The role of caregiver (priest) fits well in the Community circle.

The *Corporation* of the church is its organization. Finances and facilities, boards and procedures, progress and expansion are its interests. The best image is a business. Although the Bible does not compare the church to a business, it does speak of official elders, deacons and overseers. It calls for everything to be done decently and in order. It speaks of gifted leaders and administrators who organize God's people for their progress and well-being. The key person in a business is the one who produces the most. Business people enter the ranks by being hired, and leave by quitting or being fired. The paybacks are pay increases and promotions to greater responsibility and privileges. The "corporation people" in the church motivate and organize to reach its common goals, whether facilities, finances or services. The role of leader (king) fits well in the Corporation circle.

Improved Communication

Dethmer's view of the local church is practical and helpful. For example, it helps in communicating to let others know which hat you are wearing. A pastor might have a talk with the part-time youth leader who is also going to seminary. "Joe, I need to have a talk with you, in private. Let me put my corporate hat on for a moment. It seems that things are not going as well as we expected. Some of the high schoolers are unhappy and the parents are complaining loudly. It seems that many of the activities lack organization, some kids find out too late about special events, and the behavior is too often out of control. If we do not see some changes for the better in the next six months, we are going to have to take more serious action." (Translation: Joe is told to shape up or look for a new position).

"Now, Joe, let me take off my corporate hat and put on my community hat. It seems to me that you are living with far too much stress. Your wife gave me permission to let you know that she has been in to talk with me. She feels abandoned at home alone with the preschoolers while you are always gone to church or school or busy studying.

"Joe, here's what we're going to do. We're going to cut back your time

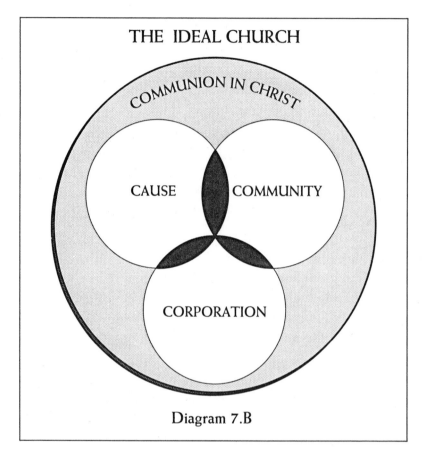

THE IDEAL CHURCH

COMMUNION IN CHRIST

CAUSE   COMMUNITY

CORPORATION

Diagram 7.B

requirements here at church by five hours per week, but we are not going to cut your pay. In addition, I've arranged for the church to pay for some counseling for you and your wife over the next six to eight weeks. I'll make some personal appeals for some capable adults to volunteer for your youth staff. We'll look for individuals with good organizational and promotional skills. You have a lot to offer, Joe, and I'm for you. I'm convinced you have a wonderful ministry ahead of you and that God's call and gifts are evident in your life."

Benefits of Dethmer's helpful paradigm in this case include identifying what kind of communication is going on and understanding the major motivation of the pastor. In thinking through the paradigm and teasing it out, benefits abound. It gives a realistic way of viewing the church. It provides a grid for evaluating personal action and ministry. It is a contemporary way of showing how the functional roles of prophet, priest and king work in a practical way.

Dethmer names three circles, and his insights are helpful. A secular person, however, conceivably could apply Dethmer's ministry model to any social organization, as well as a cult group. So I would like to suggest a fourth circle. It includes what makes the Church unique, namely, constant communion with the crucified, risen and reigning Lord Jesus Christ. Without Christ as Head of the Body, no social organism is really a church. Consider this fourth circle that

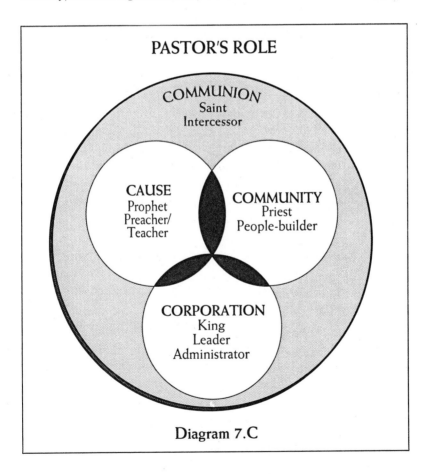

Diagram 7.C

encompasses the other three. It is larger and surrounds the three functions Dethmer describes.

The Missing Circle

Call this fourth circle "Communion in Christ." The communion of the Church is its living union and communication with Christ. It includes submission and obedience to its Head. It means living in intimacy with Christ and practicing His presence. The biblical image is the Body. The most important part of a human body is the head. In a similar way, the most important part of the Church Body is our Head, the Lord Jesus Christ. The formation of a human body begins with conception. The only way a member is severed from the body is by death or by being cut off. The paybacks of close connection with the Head are life, energy and direction. The "communion people" pray and praise and worship until the whole Body experiences the near presence of their Lord. The role of example (saint) fits well in the Communion circle, as you can see from Diagram 7.C, the Expanded Dethmer Ministry Model.

In the ideal church, the Communion circle is primary. Our Lord Jesus Christ is both the Circumference and the Center of the Church. He is alive, present, active and, through prayer, often consulted for direction and decisions. He encompasses every other circle.

- For the Cause, Jesus is the Message and the Messenger—the Prophet.
- For the Community, Jesus is the Counselor, Helper, Healer— the Priest.
- For the Corporation, Jesus is the CEO, President, Commander— the King.

The Dysfunctional Church

No church is perfect and few seem close to the ideal. Like people, churches all have strengths and weaknesses, good memories and painful ones. Most, if not

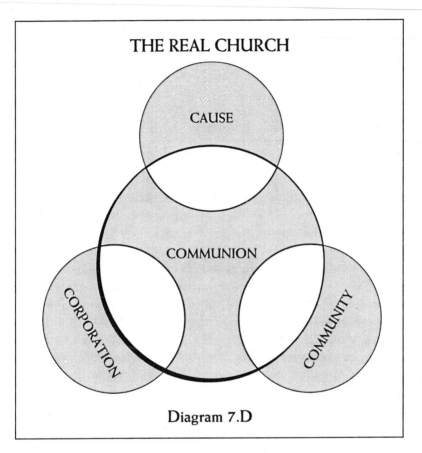

Diagram 7.D

all, tolerate or take part in corporate sins. All of the Lord's churches have an evil enemy who fires flaming arrows aimed to inflict damage. All the members and attenders of churches are themselves imperfect people. They find themselves vulnerable, at least to some degree, to the world, the flesh and the devil.

What is truly scary is that it is possible to "do church" without the big circle of Communion in Christ. A church can proclaim a sound biblical message, care for its own and keep its organization and finances in order (Cause, Community and Corporation) without much if any help from its Head. Using a distorted message, cults and false religions do it all the time. Good churches can also fall into this trap, and hardly notice.

A church can proclaim its cause, socialize in its community and direct its corporation without constant communion with Christ Himself. Any or all of the three functions can bypass His presence, direction and counsel. A reality check would indicate that some people in the church do maintain constant communion with Christ, but others do not. Some are keenly aware of Christ's presence and power while carrying out their functions of cause, community or corporation—but others are not. Some are ministering in Christ, others are not. (See Diagram 7.D)

Who among us is always conscious of Christ's presence and continually praying and praising? Thank God for those who do, but unfortunately, many committed Christians fit Diagram 7.D, at least part of the time. Sometimes we feel in tune with Christ; at other times our hearts are far from Him. Think of a few specifics. Some Cause functions—teaching, evangelizing, serving—are done in living union with Christ; others are not. Some Community functions—counseling, caring, helping—are offered with Christ's love; others fall short of His felt presence. Some Corporation functions—raising funds, making decisions, hiring or firing—are done listening to His direction; others come off as merely human efforts. (You understand, of course, that this is someone else in your church, never you!)

The subtle danger in any church body is to miss the constant communion, inspiration, and direction from its Head. What a deception to assume that Christ is central while all the time ignoring Him! Ask yourself a penetrating question: "Where is Christ—really, not theoretically—in relationship to my church?" Is He the unseen Chairman of our committees? Is He the unseen Teacher in our classrooms? Is He the unseen Counselor as we seek to help people? Or are we serving Him in our own strength, in reality leaving Him just outside our ministry functions?

A Balanced Purpose

Let's tease out the Ministry Model even further. To be fair, let's assume the best about your church. Let's suppose your people understand the four basic functions of Communion, Cause, Community and Corporation. Let's surmise that they practice each function reasonably well, but would like to improve.

One of the first steps might be to write a balanced purpose statement. Many churches find it helpful to put into words why they exist. The Ministry Model gives balance to the process.

In a Doctor of Ministry class, Neil and I asked the students to write a purpose statement that fit their own church. One of the pastors in the class submitted a colorful one:

> As people of faith, we seek to center our lives on Christ as we take the good news to people in our local and worldwide community and celebrate our relationship as God's children while carefully administering the resources God has bestowed on us.

Here is a more generic model:

Communion	As (church name) in living communion with Christ we exist to fulfill
Cause	the Great Commission and
Community	the Great Commandment
Corporation	as biblical stewards of our resources
All four	to the glory of God.

Take a second look at the more colorful Purpose Statement. Note how it fits the Ministry Model:

Communion	As people of faith, we seek to center our lives on Christ
Cause	as we take the good news to people in our local and worldwide community
Community	and celebrate our relationship as God's children
Corporation	while carefully administering the resources God has bestowed on us.

Some churches will want to write a more specific Mission Statement or Vision Statement just for the Cause function. Here is an example from Friends Church Southwest, my denomination. Remember, this is only Cause and not any of the other functions:

We exist to make more friends, and deeper, better friends of our Lord Jesus Christ. Our passion is for everyone in every culture to know Jesus and to know Him better. Our intent is to penetrate the culture around us, whether at home or abroad, with the life-changing gospel and loving acts of service in the name of our Lord Jesus Christ.

Incidentally, for those who prefer 15 words or less, the first 15 words will stand alone!

Crucial Problems

Having a comprehensive purpose and specific mission in mind, let's apply the Ministry Model even further. Each ministry function—Communion, Cause, Community and Corporation—holds a special problem for the local church. If resolved, it propels the congregation to greater health and growth. If neglected, however, the problem turns into a painful pitfall.

The crucial problem in the Communion function is to resolve spiritual conflicts and set people free in Christ. This comes faster and easier when Christ's people know their identity in Christ. What a freeing truth to answer the identity question "Who am I?" with the biblical truth, "In Christ I am a child of God" (see John 1:12). Clinton E. Arnold, associate professor of New Testament at Talbot School of Theology, Biola University, makes a fascinating observation about the Christian's identity:

We cannot forget that our new identity as Christians is not only individual but also corporate. We have been joined to fellow Christians in the solidarity of a corporate body. Christ has created the church as the primary vehicle for his grace to resist and overcome the powers of darkness.[2]

Knowing one's identity in Christ, both personally and corporately, is a good foundation for winning the battle for the mind. The personal "Steps to Freedom" (see appendix C) are helping thousands to win these battles. We believe these steps are so important that we insist every pastor, elder and board member process them personally before attempting the "Steps Toward Setting Your Church Free" (see appendix B) described in the remainder of this book.

Leadership

Move in your thinking from the Communion to the Cause function of your church. The crying need in any great cause is for leadership. It is also the great need of your church. If your church is growing, you need more and better leaders just to keep up. If your church is plateaued, you need good leadership to inspire, plan, motivate, enlist and mobilize people to fulfill your purpose. If your church is declining, you need leaders to replace those who are leaving and to reverse the downhill slide.

Attendance and Finances

In creating Community, attendance is the common shortage. Without people there is no Community. When the Community expands, we call it church growth. More services, more classes and groups, more new churches and more mission outreaches all expand the Community.

When it comes to the quality of Community, regular attendance in groups is crucial. If people come together only occasionally, the Community becomes weak. Church health calls for meaningful interaction among people who care enough to show up and be there week after week. Personal friendships and spontaneous activities seem to occur most often in churches when people participate fully in church activities. Deepening relationships simply do not happen if people do not attend.

In the Corporation function, the plaguing problem is finances. Only endowed churches, usually older, have too much money. (And they do not know it!) It is a fact that churches who hoard money instead of giving it away most often decline, become ineffective or sometimes turn heretical.

It is no secret that most churches have too little money. A few live from financial crisis to crisis. It is also no secret that, if well managed, church finances can become an incredible strength. These finances provide staff, programs and facilities. A church that is faithful in its stewardship and wise in its money management will have stability and longevity. The church that neglects its finances will severely limit its potential for ministry. Space problems, staff shortages and general unhappiness among the people most often result.

Great Opportunities

Most of us tend to value one or two of the ministry functions more highly than the others. Community people tend to cluster together while the Corporation people are meeting in committees and the Cause people are busy serving in activities. Meanwhile the Communion people are praying that God will bless all of them. We hope the Ministry Model makes good sense to you by now. If so, you can more readily appreciate the spiritual passion of someone who is gifted for a different function in the church from the one you prefer. When we catch the big picture of all four functions, we appreciate one another more. With a dash of humility we "look not only to your own interests, but also to the interests of others" (Phil. 2:4).

What are the greatest opportunities of the church? Here are some starter lists. Why not add or subtract to fit your church—and what your church might become.

In a day when denominations are often derided or considered outdated, it is good to take a fresh look through the eyes of this Ministry Model. The results can be enlightening. Allow us once again to comment briefly on some items that occurred to us. They may start you thinking and praying about possibilities for your denomination or grouping of churches. For me, it greatly clarified what our ministry was really about on the district or denominational level.

The Denomination's Role

The Corporation functions of the denomination are possibly the best established, but the most criticized. Yet, considering all the talk about the day of

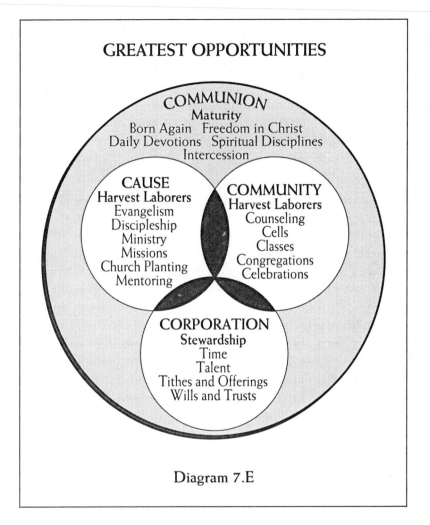

Diagram 7.E

the denomination being over, these functions are not yet being picked up by any parachurch organization. Some independent or community churches must incorporate these functions on the local church level. Even then the independent churches tend to cluster in "families" and follow the organizational patterns of churches in a similar movement. Although I see denominations and families of churches changing in some ways, I firmly believe denominations are here to stay.

In the Corporation function, the district or denomination provides an organized society and an accepted form of church government. In technical terms this is called "church polity." Policies, traditions, precedents and procedures all help form a denomination or church movement's polity. Another Corporation activity often carried out by districts is church discipline. Often disciplinary procedures and restoration processes are supervised by denominational officials. This may well be because the government still looks to denominations to grant ordination, commissioning, licensing or in some way recording the official status of pastors. The right to give credentials, as well as take them away, is a Corporation function not duplicated by parachurch organizations.

Standards for ministerial service, conduct and competence are sometimes set by denominations. When a church is unhappy about any of these items and releases the pastor, denominational executives move into action. Most often they give guidance on pastoral searches to both churches and candidates. This is only one of a multitude of services. Curriculum, audiovisuals, bookkeeping, insurance coverage, church building loans, printing and legal matters all fall into the Corporation function for districts and denominations. This is not to say that the local church cannot carry out these functions; many do. Nevertheless, these are common responsibilities of the Corporation where denominations do exist.

Communication is a big item for all Christian movements. Almost all denominational leaders find themselves accused (and probably guilty) of not communicating well enough or often enough or about the right things. Unlike local church pastors, denominational leaders do not have weekly face-to-face contact with their people. They must depend upon the printed page, the video, the annual conference, the board meetings and an occasional personal appearance. Real communication then often depends upon the loyalty and desires of the pastors and local church leaders.

Corporate Culture
Creating, shaping or changing corporate culture is a delicate function for denominational executives. Many components shaped this common culture

from its inception. Even today, sharing the church's history and formative stories gives color, uniqueness and anchor points to a denomination or movement. Doing things in the traditional way lessens controversy and promotes harmony. Family histories sometimes intertwine with denominational backgrounds, adding to loyalty. Distinctive doctrines and points of emphasis often serve as teaching tools to other movements. The truest and best of any movement can be adapted and used by others.

On the down side, every movement that has enough history behind it holds sacred boundary markers. Often appearing superficial to outsiders, these traditions are held with fierce loyalty by some. The simple reason is that unique, observable practices set a people apart from other social groups, other denominations and other churches. Sometimes these distinctives hold little relevance for life today, except to make us different from others. When someone challenges these shared practices or beliefs, the cry often comes back, "If we give this up, why should we exist as a denomination?"

One helpful insight about denominational distinctives is the importance of our focus. It is vital to keep our focus on the Center rather than on the boundaries. The Center is the Lord Jesus Christ. God's Spirit, God's Word and God's works are all consistent with what God revealed in Jesus. When the focus is on Christ, the Center, then the crucial question is whether an individual, church or denomination is moving closer to the Center or away from it. Are the unique beliefs and practices of this movement drawing people closer to Christ or moving them further away?

When the focus is on boundaries, we see the past workings of God and the present traditions of imperfect people. Lyle Schaller writes, "As the decades turn into centuries, each of the Protestant denominations in North America gradually evolves into a different institution from what it was in its early days. That can be seen by tracing the history of that particular religious tradition."[3]

Sometimes, not always, denominations find nonbiblical, highly observable ways such as vocabulary, customs and social fit to judge whether or not their members "really belong." We can so easily fall into the trap of the Pharisees whom Jesus criticized: "You have let go of the commands of God and are holding on to the traditions of men....You have a fine way of setting aside the commands of God in order to observe your own traditions!" (Mark 7:8,9).

The balance in this delicate matter is first to focus on Christ and then to remain firm on helpful boundaries. Authentic boundaries are always consistent with Scripture and usually edifying for people today. Simply destroying old boundary markers without any replacement is often a futile exercise. New boundaries will inevitably emerge. Wise leaders will listen to the Holy Spirit for guidance in bringing Christians to focus on Christ. The Lord is pleased when Christians come closer to one another across denominational lines without destroying the best that the Holy Spirit continues to teach through each historical Christian movement. Every denomination has something valuable to offer all the others.

Denominations and Community
Interchurch conferences, conventions, annual sessions, seminars and rallies all build a sense of community. So do work projects, sports leagues, summer camps, annual conferences and almost any activity that draws people together across local church lines. Both denominational and parachurch groupings are active in these ways. High profile events, such as the great festivals of the Old Testament, build an intense sense of belonging.

What is more, denominations are still giving the personal touch to missionaries, church planters, pastors and spouses. District superintendents and their associates care and laugh and cry with the local church pastor. Often pastors minister to one another in special ways, too. This mutual, one-to-one caring often crosses denominational lines and has great benefit, although it is usually haphazard. Organized efforts to provide support systems and ongoing nurture most often come through denominations and movements. When asked, "Who pastors the pastor?" the ones who are trying are most often denominational leaders.

Reaching the World
Denominations have a mixed record on evangelism, church planting and missions. Almost every one has glorious stories to tell from their past. Many have marginal records of growth, or even decline, to report in the United States today. For most denominations, the third world is leading the way. In virtually every continent, except North America and Western Europe, the Church of Jesus Christ is growing.

When it comes to the Cause—namely, fulfilling a specialized vision such as the Great Commission—missions and parachurch organizations often excel. The same can be said for camping, theological education, Bible translation and a host of other specialties. However, many interdenominational mission efforts contribute directly or indirectly toward forming new denominations among the people they serve. Others specialize in nourishing people within present movements or denominations. For fulfilling the Great Commandment, nothing replaces the local church. The interaction between mission and church is healthy and essential for reaching the world.

The Missing Denominational Circle

What is most often missing in denominational efforts is the Communion function. Whether paid executives or unpaid board members, few in leadership positions see this function as top priority. We are talking about creating a Christ-centered, biblical, spiritual climate. We are advocating learning how to set a district or denomination free from Satan's advantage. We mean connecting with all of God's resources. We certainly include the discerning of Christ's unique vision and direction. The goal of every denomination should be the same as the apostle Paul's: "Christ in you, the hope of glory. We proclaim him, admonishing and teaching everyone with all wisdom, so that we may present everyone perfect in Christ. To this end I labor, struggling with all his energy, which so powerfully works in me" (Col. 1:27-29).

I shared a visual display of a generic denomination's role, using the Ministry Model as a guide. I asked several boards on the district level to locate their special place among the four functions. Each one did it well, finding more than one function for themselves. What was fascinating to me, however, is that, as a general rule, the board members did not primarily see their responsibilities in the Communion circle. With one notable exception, they moved instinctively to Cause, Community or Corporation.

Does this suggest that no one is taking responsibility for the primary function of the church—namely, the Communion role? I hope not! Can we "do church" without the active awareness of Jesus Christ, our Head? Can we carry out a cause, strive to build a caring community or manage our corporate

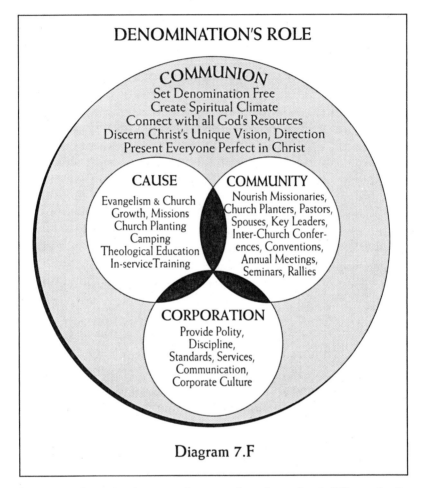

Diagram 7.F

business without the direct involvement of our living Lord? What a deadly danger if, in fact, we can!

What is the solution? What can be done? How can we improve in the Communion function? How can we stay connected to the Hub, to Christ Himself, in our church activities and functions? How can we become more intentional about making Communion with Christ our first priority? We do not pretend to have all the answers, but here are a few suggestions that relate to freedom in Christ for your church or denomination:

- Hold worship services that focus on Christ more than the performance of the musicians and preacher. God is the audience, not the congregation.
- Preach and teach the Christian's true identity in Christ. When we know who we are in Christ, we hold a biblical basis to value others and rightly esteem our own lives.
- Guide the people in your church or denomination to personal freedom in Christ. The "Freedom in Christ" video or audio series, complete with workbooks, is available for this purpose.
- Name a Prayer Coordinator for every board, committee or ministry staff member. The task is to stimulate prayer before, during and after meetings or ministry events. Ask these intercessors to become creative.
- Find a wise, godly Christian leader who will lead your pastors, elders and governing board through the "Seven Steps Toward Setting Your Church Free." The rest of this book explains this process in detail.
- Follow through with diligence on the last two steps of the "Setting Your Church Free" event. Pray consistently and faithfully the Prayer Action Plan (see chapter 12), and carry it out!

A Fictional Illustration

Some churches have, in fact, pursued putting the Communion function first. They are learning how Christ sets first their people, then their churches free, and what their responsibility is in the process. Consider Pastor Brent King (a fictional name), who serves as minister of First Church. Although this particular church does not exist, it will illustrate good ideas actually put into practice in various churches.

Pastor King understood well the four functions of First Church—Communion, Cause, Community and Corporation. He was a systematic thinker and used the Ministry Model for both strengthening his ministry and building up the people in the church. He also grasped the corresponding functions of Saint, Prophet, Priest and King.

- Model it as an example (saint).
  Demonstrate it in the church's Communion.
- Preach and teach it as a communicator (prophet).
  Make it the church's Cause.
- Coach and encourage it as a caregiver (priest).
  Build it into the church's Community.
- Motivate and organize it as a leader (king).
  Develop it in the church's Corporation.

As an example, Brent King began to model freedom in Christ in his own life. He attended a "Resolving Personal and Spiritual Conflicts" seminar. This seminar, taught by Neil, is a comprehensive, 18-hour event that helps people find their true identity in Christ and break out of bondages that inhibit them from fully experiencing the Christian life.

Then, along with a fellow pastor, Brent processed the personal "Steps to Freedom." These seven steps seek to help people resolve the critical issues in their relationship with God. Brent found the steps soul-searching, uplifting and helpful. With fresh freedom in his own soul, he wanted to share these truths with his congregation. He fervently longed for personal freedom for his people and corporate freedom for the church. He became an example of the believer for the Communion function of the church.

Pastor King loved to preach and he was good at it. He soon launched into a sermon series on finding identity in Christ, winning the battle for the mind and discovering personal freedom in Christ. He understood that any breakthrough in Bible application needs more than one voice. Calling on the best Sunday School teachers, he introduced them to the *Breaking Through to Spiritual Maturity* curriculum, a comprehensive guide for teaching through the material in Neil's first two books on personal and spiritual freedom, *Victory over the Darkness* and *The Bondage Breaker.* The Sunday School teachers, too, discovered a wonderful responsiveness. Pastor King communicated the message as part of the Cause of First Church.

Maybe it is the honesty of students today. Maybe it is their idealism. Whatever the reason, the youth leaders found that students caught the message of *Stomping Out the Darkness* (the youth version of *Victory over the Darkness)* and *Bondage Breaker—Youth Edition* with amazing enthusiasm.

They applied it with the eagerness reserved for the young. Many were excited, and some were radically transformed.

In his counseling, Pastor King began to take others through the "Steps to Freedom." Those who sincerely wanted help found amazing breakthroughs. In time he began to notice a pattern. People who saw it as a shortcut or a pat-answer formula received little lasting help. Those who saw it as a way to seek God with all their hearts moved rapidly toward a renewed mind and a transformed heart.

Seeing the value in people's lives, Pastor King began to use the "Steps to Freedom" in both the membership class and the new believers class. He exposed the elders and deacons to the steps through a Freedom in Christ Ministries video seminar on "Resolving Personal and Spiritual Conflicts and Counseling." Premarital lay counselors and support group leaders also took the training. A support group on depression used the "Steps to Freedom" with every participant. It greatly aided their ministry. Pastor King used his counseling and discipleship ministries as a capable caregiver. The Community function of the church took on a spiritual depth in Christ that was refreshing.

Pastor King almost did handstands when he read that Neil Anderson was coming to his city for a live conference. He promoted it as well as he could. Knowing that this was the weak area in his own ministry capabilities, he called on the best motivators and organizers in the church to take over. They were creative and effective in their publicity and recruitment efforts.

Notices appeared in every church publication for 10 weeks in advance. Several people who had already found their freedom shared testimonies about their release from bondage. Every other week a brand-new display went up just outside the sanctuary, visually presenting the conference. A letter to the congregation and a follow-up phone call to every attender clinched it. One half of the youth and adults of the church actually attended. With lots of prayer power, the personal results were extremely gratifying.

The enthusiasm was contagious for weeks after the conference. Several people began taking friends and family members through the "Steps to Freedom." The church library could not keep up with the demand to check out the video and audiotapes. Several families bought their own sets. One of the most popular items was the self-directed video in which Dr. Anderson took a group through the steps. It was designed with shut-off points and special instructions so a person could work through the steps alone or with a trusted friend.

In time, however, Pastor King began to notice that his church still showed signs of spiritual bondage. The old patterns were ever present. Few gave more than lip service to evangelism. The gossip lines of communication were wide open, as destructive as ever. The marriage hassles in his own home and among many of the church leaders seemed beyond rational explanation. What became clear was that spiritual warfare was more than a hot topic for popular books; the battle was up close and personal.

About this time, Pastor King heard from a fellow minister about Freedom in Christ's "Setting Your Church Free" seminar. The major requirement of 100 percent of the pastors and board members in attendance almost scared him off. In these time-greedy days it seemed impossible to secure 100 percent attendance to anything. Nevertheless, he talked it over with the elders (who in his church were the same as board members). They liked the idea, and with much effort found a mutually satisfactory date when they could all attend. Just before the date, however, one elder had to go out of town. The seminar leader refused to budge. They rescheduled.

On the designated Saturday, they were all present—not one was missing. All had previously processed the "Steps to Freedom" themselves—a few were active in leading others through them. The seminar took about seven hours; the time flew by. The interaction, prayers and insights were eye-opening. With the Holy Spirit's guidance, when the day was over the group had identified five strengths and seven corporate sins. Actually, some of the "sins" were more accurately weaknesses, but they still needed correction.

Two things amazed Pastor King. One was the accuracy of insight into the real spiritual condition of the church. He knew some of these problems were around but now they were out in the open. The other was the incredible sense of unity about what the problems were and what to do about them. It was almost as if Jesus had written something similar to the seven letters of the Revelation (see Rev. 2,3) exclusively for First Church. It was exactly what they needed to begin turning things around.

Shifting Gears

Chapters 8 through 13 intend to give you the hands-on application of the
"Setting Your Church Free" process. They will spell out the specific procedures
for the approximately seven-hour event for pastors, elders and members of
the governing board of your church. The practical whats, whys and hows
show up here. This section will also give the biblical basis, especially from
Revelation 1–3, for corporate freedom for your church.

After reading chapters 8 through 13, you should understand the specifics
of "Setting Your Church Free." Appendix B will be your guide when you actually meet together for the one-day event. The "Setting Your Church Free"
process is only one part of a larger whole. Detached from the biblical view of
leadership and ministry in your church, "Setting Your Church Free" is not
enough by itself. You may simply find your church cleaner and healthier for a
while, but still weak and unable to move forward. Apart from Christ you can
do nothing; you must stay connected to the Hub.

Before proceeding further in the book, take a few moments and read carefully Revelation 1–3. Let its truths and its message sink deep into your being.
We will take a careful look at these letters from Jesus and their application to
us in the next few chapters.

Each chapter deals with a specific step in the "Setting Your Church Free"
event. Why is this process so important? Because our churches are not going
to experience all God intends unless we break out of our corporate bondages.
It is essential for us to discern the ways Satan may have gained an advantage
over our church. Once the adversary's deceptions are exposed, we will take
specific steps to bring our weaknesses back under the full Lordship of Christ.

Let's turn our attention now to each of the steps in "Setting Your Church
Free." In case we have not made our point before, please remember, your leaders can participate in the "Setting Your Church Free" event if they have already
been through the "Personal Steps to Freedom" (found in appendix C).

Notes

1. Jim Dethmer, "Moving in the Right Circles," *Leadership, A Practical Journal for Church Leaders,* Fall Quarter, 1992, pp. 86-91.

2. Clinton E. Arnold, *Powers of Darkness, Principalities and Powers in Paul's Letters* (Downers Grove, IL: InterVarsity Press, 1992), p. 213.

3. Lyle E. Schaller, "What Is the Future of Your Denomination?" *The Parish Paper,* Yokefellow Institute, Richmond, IN, 1992, p. 1.

PART TWO

This section will walk you through each of the seven steps involved in bringing freedom to your church.

8

LOOKING AT YOUR CHURCH'S STRENGTHS AND WEAKNESSES

(Steps One and Two in the "Setting Your Church Free" Event)

What if Jesus wrote a letter to your church? What do you think He would say? What would He commend? What would He compliment you on? What would He take pride in? What would He praise you for? What would He describe as your greatest strengths?

On the other hand, what would He rebuke? What would He ask you to correct? What would He hold against you? What faults would He expose? What sins would He uncover?

What promises would He give you? What warnings of judgment would He issue if you did not obey Him?

Although no church today can have a letter from Jesus having the authority of Scripture, no one needs to remain ignorant of His will. Jesus already dictated seven letters to the seven churches of Asia, and He wants to help you discern His view of your church (see Rev. 1–3).

Jesus Knows

Why did Jesus write to His churches, seven of whom were representative of all the rest? Because He knew what was going on. He knew they were in bondage. He knew they were indulging in corporate sins. He knew they were under attack. He knew they needed encouragement. He knew they needed tough love.

Our Lord Jesus Christ was, and is, walking among His churches. He knows everything—all the strengths and all the weaknesses. Most often He starts His letters by mentioning their strengths, unless they seem proud. Then He begins with their weaknesses. Always, then as now, the risen Jesus knows each of His churches intimately. To every one of the seven He said, "I know."

I know your deeds, your hard work and your perseverance. I know that you cannot tolerate wicked men (to Ephesus, Rev. 2:2).

I know your afflictions and your poverty—yet you are rich! I know the slander (to Smyrna, Rev. 2:9).

I know where you live—where Satan has his throne. Yet you remain true to my name (to Pergamum, Rev. 2:13).

I know your deeds, your love and faith, your service and perseverance, and that you are now doing more than you did at first (to Thyatira, Rev. 2:19).

I know your deeds; you have a reputation of being alive, but you are dead (to Sardis, Rev. 3:1).

I know your deeds....I know that you have little strength, yet you have kept my word and have not denied my name (to Philadelphia, Rev. 3:8).

I know your deeds, that you are neither cold nor hot (to Laodicea, Rev. 3:14).

What is gripping in Jesus' letters is His near presence. More than 50 times in these seven short letters in Revelation Jesus says, "I," referring to Himself. He is alive, powerful, caring. He is not stuck somewhere far away in a remote heaven. He is not absent. He is present, involved, active.

Jesus feels:	"I hold this against you: You have forsaken your first love" (2:4; also see 3:15).
Jesus threatens:	"If you do not repent, I will come to you and remove your lampstand from its place" (2:5; also see 2:21,22; 3:3).
Jesus promises:	"To him who overcomes, I will give" (2:7; also see each of the letters).
Jesus predicts:	"I tell you, the devil will put some of you in prison" (2:10).
Jesus rebukes:	"I have a few things against you: You have people there who hold to the teaching of Baalam" (2:14).
Jesus judges:	"I am he who searches hearts and minds, and I will repay each of you according to your deeds" (2:23).
Jesus acts:	"I have placed before you an open door that no one can shut....I will make them come and fall down at your feet and acknowledge" (3:8,9).
Jesus prophesied:	"I am coming soon" (3:11).
Jesus counsels:	"I counsel you to buy from me gold refined in the fire, so you can become rich" (3:18).
Jesus loves:	"Those whom I love" (3:19).
Jesus disciplines:	"I rebuke and discipline" (3:19).
Jesus is here:	"Here I am! I stand at the door and knock. If anyone hears my voice and opens the door, I will come in and eat with him, and he with me" (3:20).

When you go to church next Sunday, when you meet with your Christian friends during the week, when you talk with another believer, when you think no one notices, when God seems far away...Jesus is there. When you meet for the "Setting Your Church Free" day, the risen Lord Jesus will move among you. He is present and, by His written Word and by His Holy Spirit, He wants to help you discern His message to your church.

During the "Setting Your Church Free" event, each person needs to be sensitive to God's leading. To each of the churches in Revelation 2,3, Jesus writes through John: "He who has an ear, let him hear what the Spirit says to the churches." In the Hebrew way of understanding, to hear meant not only to listen but also to obey. It meant to respond and to do what was heard. If the Lord Jesus wrote a letter to your church, would you obey Him? If He allowed the leaders in your church to agree on their discernment of what Jesus would say, would you treat it as a letter from Jesus?

A Vivid Vision

Before we turn to the specifics of the process of setting your church free, we need to examine the biblical basis. The seven letters from Jesus in Revelation are built upon the insights and truths from a vivid vision given to the apostle John on the island of Patmos. John was in exile on this rock quarry island "because of the word of God and the testimony of Jesus" (Rev. 1:9). As the *Contemporary English Version* puts it, "We all suffer because Jesus is our king, but he gives us the strength to endure. I was sent to Patmos Island, because I had preached God's message and had told about Jesus."

In Revelation 1:9-20, John received a vision from an angel (see 1:1) of the resurrected and ruling Christ. The symbolism seems strange to us but the overall meaning is clear to careful Bible scholars who compare this vision with earlier ones given in the Old Testament. Bible expositor, Earl F. Palmer, writes:

John's vision brings to mind many Old Testament messianic phrases and images: *"Son of Man"* is a messianic phrase from Daniel (7:13); the white wool is found in Daniel 7:9 and the flame of fire in Daniel 10:6; the sound of water is from Ezekiel 43:2 and the sword from Isaiah 49:2.

Though the name of our Lord does not appear in this description, it is clear that Jesus is the One whom John has seen. "...I died, and behold I am alive for evermore..." (Rev. 1:18 RSV). In the vision, John is assured of the reign of Jesus Christ, even over death and the place of death (Hades).[1]

In simple terms, the vision tells us that Jesus is alive and exalted to the highest place of authority. He has conquered His enemies, including the evil powers of darkness. The goddess *Hekate,* according to the pagans, was said to hold "the keys to Hades."[2] Because Jesus now holds them in His hand, He is the Conqueror of the evil powers.

Jesus is pure, powerful, full of radiant glory and possesses the very attributes of God. Yet He is present with His people and closely attentive to His churches. Bible teacher, G. Campbell Morgan, gives us a colorful word picture of what the vision teaches about the risen Lord Jesus:

Take this picture and look at it again and again until the vision holds you in its marvellous power. His head and His hair white like wool, His purity and His eternity; His eyes like a flame of fire, His intimate knowledge, penetrating and piercing; His feet like burnished brass, signifying the procedure of strength and purity; His voice like the voice of many waters, a concord of perfect tones; in His hand seven stars, His administrative right, power and protection; from His mouth a sharp two-edged sword, keen and accurate verdicts concerning His people; His whole countenance as the sun, creating day, flashing light, bathing all the landscape with beauty.[3]

The Seven Lampstands

The vision of the glorified Christ, once crucified but now resurrected and reigning, full of purity and power, includes two more symbols that the Lord Himself singles out for special attention. John's first glimpse in his vision was of the "seven golden lampstands, and among the lampstands was someone 'like a son of man'" (Rev. 1:12,13). At the end of the vision the meaning is given: "The seven lampstands are the seven churches" (Rev. 1:20). Jesus, the Son of Man, "walks among the seven golden lampstands" (Rev. 2:1).

The risen Jesus Christ is moving among His churches. In the Bible study portion of the "Setting Your Church Free" seminar, we find it helpful to assign one letter of the seven to each person. If more than seven people are present, we ask them to work in twos or threes or small groups. Each person counts the number of times Jesus says "I" when referring to Himself in their assigned letter. The results are astonishing! Although it varies according to Bible translation, the count in the *New International Version* ranges from a low of four for Smyrna to a high of 14 for Thyatira. As already mentioned, the total is more than 50.

Here is the point: The same Jesus who is revealed in the vision as awesome in power, and the Conqueror of death and Hades, is carefully inspecting His churches. We believe the all-powerful, glorious Jesus is walking up and down the aisles of your church. He is observing, encouraging, rebuking, asking for change, motivating, promising rewards and warning of judgments.

When churches die or lapse into ineffectiveness, we tend to think in terms of poor attendance and financial problems, lack of leadership or dysfunctional patterns of infighting. We seldom speak of the biblical truth that the living Christ may be carrying out His judgments. "If you do not repent, I will come to you and remove your lampstand from its place" (Rev. 2:5). When churches flourish and launch effective ministries that bring many to Christ, build up their people in Christ and serve the needy in Christ's name, we tend to praise the pastor for outstanding leadership and good preaching. We look to committed lay leaders in these churches with respect and admiration. We seldom say that Christ is the One who is rewarding them for obeying His Word. Yet, in every one of the seven letters of Revelation Jesus says, "To him who overcomes" and then He promises a great reward, usually an eternal one.

The Seven Stars

Another symbol that the Lord Jesus singles out for special attention is the seven stars. Jesus Himself explains it like this: "The seven stars are the angels of the seven churches" (Rev. 1:20). Please make a mental note here that the angels are just as literal as the churches. In others words, just as the lamp-stands represent churches, so the stars represent angels. The angels are not the symbols but rather the explanation of the symbols. It is our belief that they are real angels, not symbols for human messengers.

Angels Are Really There

Most Christians believe in guardian angels for children based on Jesus' statement in Matthew 18:10. Every Christmas we read about the angel Gabriel appearing to Mary, and every Easter about the angels at the empty tomb. Jesus spoke often about angels; the New Testament is full of references to angels. A quick check of a concordance reveals that angels appear 51 times in the Synoptic Gospels, 21 times in Acts and 67 times in Revelation. Combined with other New Testament references to angels, the total is 175; including the Old Testament, the total is almost 300. That is a lot! Always, always in Scripture, the Son of God stands above the angels (see Mark 13:27; Heb. 1:4-14; Phil. 2:9-11).

In more recent times, Billy Graham wrote a book entitled *Angels*. Although the famous evangelist reports that he had never heard a sermon on the subject, his book sold more than one million copies. The Gallup poll reveals that 50 percent of the population in the United States believes in angels. In a well-written article in *Christianity Today* magazine, Timothy Jones reports that among the young, the percentage who believe in angels is even higher.

> Gallup polls reveal that teen belief in angels has increased steadily from 64 percent in 1978 to 76 percent in 1992. That three out of four young Americans now believe in angels says something about a coming generation and its search for something beyond self to believe in.[4]

New Age practitioners promote contact with angels as spiritual mentors. Undoubtedly these are the fallen kind of angels the Bible warns against. A book such as *Ask Your Angels,* promoted by Ballantine, one of New York's biggest publishers, is immersed in the occult and New Age.

The authors present the channeled wisdom of Abigrael, a genderless being they claim was sent to instruct them. They also lead New Age-flavored workshops on getting in touch with "celestials" and aligning with "angelic energy fields." Conversing with angels, they write, is another "divination tool." Knowing that many readers face major decisions, the authors give instructions on making a deck of "Angel Oracle" cards.[5]

The apostle Paul warned the Corinthians about "a different spirit from the one you received" and stated flatly that "Satan himself masquerades as an angel of light" (2 Cor. 11:4,14). As mentioned earlier, the Bible also warns about demons who teach. "The Spirit clearly says that in later times some will abandon the faith and follow deceiving spirits and things taught by demons" (1 Tim. 4:1). The part about abandoning the faith ought to cause sober reflection on the part of every Christian and every church. This is a clear and present danger! It is all the more so in an age that is actively promoting New Age and occultic themes in medicine, education, business and children's entertainment.

Neil and I agree that deception is the adversary's primary strategy. Unfortunately, the adversary is good at it. In the book of Revelation, words such as "deceive," "deceives" and "deceived" occur often in relationship to Satan's activity (see Rev. 12:9; 13:14; 19:20; 20:3,8,10). Sometimes the *New International Version* translates the original Greek word into "led astray" or "deluded," but the meaning is the same. Twice in the book of Revelation holy angels insist that John should not worship them but only God (see Rev. 19:10; 22:9). Paul also goes so far as to say that anyone who delights in the worship of angels is disqualified from God's prize and has lost connection with the Head—namely, Christ (see Col. 2:18,19). Watch out!

Holy Angels

What is the job description for holy angels? Andrew J. Bandstra, professor emeritus of New Testament at Calvin Theological Seminary, Grand Rapids, Michigan, summarizes five ways the Bible describes the work of angels:

- Angels are God's messengers;
- Angels praise God;
- Angels exercise God's providential care;
- Angels encourage Christian obedience;
- Angels carry out God's justice.[6]

The Angels of the Churches

All of the letters from Jesus to the churches of Revelation (and to us) are addressed to the angels of the churches. For example, the first letter begins: "To the angel of the church in Ephesus" (2:1), and all the others have similar headings. The angels are not mentioned in any other way in the seven letters. Further, it is clear that the letters are written to the churches from the risen Christ who is identified with the Holy Spirit. Every one of the letters also contains the phrase, "He who has an ear, let him hear what the Spirit says to the churches." So why do we believe that the angels mentioned in Revelation 2 and 3 are real angels assigned to the churches, supernatural beings of the same nature as the holy angels that have appeared throughout Scripture?

In the original Greek language of the New Testament, the word "angel" can be translated either "messenger" or "angel." Some have thought that each letter was addressed to an overseer, the human messenger of the Church. This is a possible interpretation, but does not fit the context of the book of Revelation. Throughout Revelation, angels are always real angels, and never symbols for human messengers.

The best test of a text is its context. Good exegesis that rightly interprets Scripture would indicate that the use of the word "angel" here and its use in the rest of the book of Revelation would be consistent. "Probably 'the angels of the churches' (Rev. 1:20; 2:1, etc.) are really angels and not pastors," writes Hans Bietenhard in the scholarly *New International Dictionary of New Testament Theology.*[7]

Another theory is that "angel" means the personification of the prevailing spirit of the church people.[8] This interpretation fits neither the context nor the statement in Revelation 1:16 that Jesus holds the stars (angels) in His right hand. In the imagery of Scripture, the right hand is the sign of authority and power. God uses it to take action. When Jesus holds the angels in His right hand, it indicates that they are His executive agents or heavenly soldiers, ready to carry out His orders. This truth affects your church with awesome power.

The risen and reigning Lord Jesus has already issued orders to His heavenly hosts, His angels, concerning His churches, including yours. They are poised, ready to carry out the orders of their Commander-in-Chief. They will administer rewards or judgments in light of His Word. At the time of this writing, the United States and the United Nations have peacekeeping forces in Somalia. Picture your church's angel as a huge United States soldier in that African nation. He is armed to the teeth with weaponry capable of destroying any opposition. He already has orders to shoot, even to kill, under certain conditions spelled out by the Commander. Yet he is escorting a truck loaded with food, clothes and the essentials of life. He comes to bring life, not death. His mission is to save lives, not destroy them.

So it is with the angels of the churches. No angel takes the place of the Commander, Jesus. The Lord Himself moves among His churches. He initiates. He is at work in your church. He knows everything that is happening, all that is tolerated and every attitude that is displayed. He encourages and warns His churches. When a church obeys Him, its angel hands out Christ's rewards. When a church disobeys Him, its angel metes out Christ's judgments. We dare not play church or simply have a nice time socially. Jesus will not put up with continued indulgence in either personal or corporate sins.

Your church's angel in Christ's right hand is ready to be released upon your church with rewards or punishments. It all depends on your church's response to Christ's Word. His Word is indeed a two-edged sword, bringing blessing or cursing, life or death. He provides everything needed for obedience, including His own powerful and compassionate presence. Yet He expects human leaders to deal with false teachers, resist the infiltration of the adversary and obey their Lord, no matter the cost.

The risen Christ is still moving among His churches and He still holds their angels in His right hand. What is true for the seven churches of Revelation is true for all of Christ's churches in all of time. So today, based on Revelation 1–3, we can see that every local church might well have an angel assigned to it by our sovereign Lord Jesus. That is encouraging!

The angels of the churches are only one means by which the Lord Jesus Christ and the Holy Spirit work within your congregation. God also uses His Word and His people and His works. In light of Jesus' close involvement in our churches, it is time to take action. It is time for each of our churches to seek God's specific will for their local body of believers. Then our assignment is to respond in faith and reap Christ's rewards. The grave danger is to ignore our living Lord. If we neglect and disobey, we can expect only to reap His judgments.

Preparing for the Process

We will return to the study of Revelation 2,3 and other passages as they give biblical background for the various steps. At this point, turn your attention to the process for discerning your "letter from Jesus." Although it will not be in letter form, the goal is to discern your church's strengths, weaknesses, memories that bless or bind, corporate sins and attacks from the evil one. Then a Prayer Action Plan (see chapter 12) gives direction for the church leadership.

Who should participate in the "Setting Your Church Free" day? This process is for the leaders of the church, not all of the people. We recommend participation by all of the pastoral staff and the members of the governing board or its equivalent. For some churches this may include the elders and deacons. For some it may include the pastoral staff and all the key lay leaders that hold elected positions. It helps in follow-through if the group has the primary role of leadership and already meets together on a regular basis. However, if one or two key decision makers do not now hold office but should be included, please invite them.

It is essential that 100 percent of the elders or board members and all the ordained pastors be present. Please postpone the event if even one member cannot attend. It is critical that all the designated leaders participate in these steps. The process works best when every member is present, and is greatly weakened if only one is missing. When every leader participates, incredible unity and ownership of the outcome builds. Misunderstandings and criticism of the "Setting Your Church Free" process seem to disappear. At key points in the process, confession and forgiveness take place. Every church leader needs to experience this corporate cleansing.

We recommend that an unbiased outside facilitator lead your church leadership through these steps. It might be a retired pastor, a denominational official or a capable leader from a nearby church. The senior pastor should be part of the process, not the facilitator. Qualifications for the facilitator include the biblical requirements for elders and deacons (see 1 Tim. 3:1-13; Titus 1:6-9).

The facilitator will want to process the personal "Steps to Freedom" and be aware of the basics of resolving spiritual conflicts. If possible, find someone who understands group dynamics and has experience in working with church leaders. Although this is the ideal, let us be quick to add that the process almost carries itself and is not especially difficult to facilitate. The spiritual qualifications are the most vital.

Prayer Power
Each participant must experience personal freedom in Christ before engaging in the corporate event. We also recommend a day of fasting and prayer by pastors, elders and anyone else who is willing to seek God's best before the "Setting Your Church Free" retreat. Some may want to meet together the evening before the event for prayer. Do not hesitate to ask for prayer partners to intercede for this time together. Nearly every church has one or two faithful intercessors. Ask these prayer warriors to seek the Lord's face for this day together. The greater the prayer power, the more lasting the benefits. Nearly all churches find the process helpful, but eternal results come when faithful people pray.

Scheduling
Schedule the event following a time of teaching about resolving personal and spiritual conflicts. Take as many of the people of your church as possible, including the leaders, through the "Steps to Freedom." All of the pastors and elders must have gone through the steps recently. Personal freedom is an essential foundation for corporate freedom. A Friday evening and all-day Saturday format is the ideal schedule. Friday evening can be used for worship and prayer. If any of the leaders have not yet gone through the "Steps to Freedom," then Friday evening is the time to do so.

Another scheduling option is Sunday afternoon and evening. Please allow a minimum of seven hours for the event. Remind all the participants not to schedule anything immediately following the event on Saturday or Sunday evening. The event sometimes goes longer than anticipated and it is harmful to the process when leaders leave early. Some groups enjoy a fellowship meal together at the close of this time. Plan in advance what you will do to celebrate.

Preparing the Room
Select a comfortable room that has restrooms nearby, and especially lots of open wall space. Check to see that heating or cooling keeps the room pleasant. The room will need to be large enough for tables and chairs. The ideal setting is for the participants to be seated on three sides of a large table, hav-

ing the open side toward a blank wall. Tape several large pieces of poster paper or butcher paper on the front wall—masking tape works well. During breaks some of the members can add more sheets as the process continues. You will probably need a total of 15 or 16 sheets of paper. Bring a supply of fresh marker pens; new ones are first choice. Try them out to make sure they are not bleeding through the paper and onto the wall.

Poster or butcher paper is preferable to overhead projectors or chalkboards. Paper and marker pens leave a permanent record (in case the recorder missed something, abbreviated or paraphrased items). The facilitator can also write large enough for everyone to see easily. If enough wall space is not available up front, some of the sheets can be moved to another part of the room until they are needed at the close of the process.

Food for the Hungry

It is often wise to begin the actual "Setting Your Church Free" process after a simple but healthy breakfast on Saturday morning or a lunch on Sunday. Avoid the trap of taking too long with the meal or making it a social event. Most groups will want to have light refreshments available for breaks, although some have maintained a fast for the seven to nine hours of the process and then enjoyed a meal together afterward. If a Saturday lunch is served, keep it light and as short as possible. Some simply bring in sandwiches or a salad. Trying to discern God's will after a big meal in the middle of the day is like fighting a much-needed nap during a boring sermon.

Day of the Event

When the group gathers for the "Setting Your Church Free" event, it is wise to begin with prayer and Bible study. Follow the prayers and suggestions in appendix B. During the initial prayer time we find it helpful to begin with a renewal prayer. The participants pray it once silently and then out loud together:

Dear heavenly Father,
Open my eyes to see Your truth. Give me ears to hear and a compelling desire to respond in faith to what the Lord Jesus Christ has already done for me.
I confess Jesus Christ—crucified, risen and reigning—as my one and

184 LOOKING AT YOUR CHURCH'S STRENGTHS AND WEAKNESSES

only Lord and Savior. I renounce any past involvement with non-Christian religions or experiences. I announce that Christ died on the cross for me and for my sins and rose again bodily from the dead for my justification.

I confess that the Lord Jesus Christ rescued me from the dominion of darkness and transferred me into His kingdom of light. I renounce Satan in all his works and all his ways. I announce that Jesus Christ is my Lord, Savior, Teacher and Friend. I give myself to obey everything that He commanded. I yield myself fully to Christ to do whatever He wants me to do, to be whatever He wants me to be, to give up whatever He wants me to give up, to give away whatever He wants me to give away, to become whatever He wants me to become.

I confess, reject, renounce and utterly disown every sin in which I have ever been involved. I announce that in Christ I have received redemption, the forgiveness of sins. I accept His reconciliation to the heavenly Father and welcome peace with God.

As an expression of my faith of Christ's forgiveness of me, I forgive every person who has ever hurt, abused or taken advantage of me. I let them off my hook and let God settle the score as the final Judge who metes out perfect justice.

I open all the doors of my life to the Lord Jesus Christ and ask Him to take control of every part of my being. I gladly accept the filling of the Holy Spirit into every part of my life. I surrender myself to live in union with the Lord Jesus Christ from this moment until I stand before the Judgment Seat of Christ and hear my name read from the Lamb's Book of Life.

Thank You, heavenly Father, for uniting me with the Lord Jesus Christ and with all those who truly belong to You and live under Your gracious reign.

In Jesus' powerful name,
Amen.

We find that this printed prayer is a simple yet powerful way to begin. It leads the participants to renew their commitment to Christ. It contains many of the essential elements of the personal "Steps to Freedom." If church leaders have been well taught on these issues, they feel comfortable with this prayer. If they have not, it introduces them to some needed biblical concepts. Processing the corporate steps to freedom is not business as usual, however, nor can you allow yourselves to settle into routine patterns of behavior. To move out of your comfort zone in a meaningful way, take the next step in prayer. Engage in a form of prayer that is not your church's usual custom. For instance, in many countries Christians pray out loud, all together, at the same time. If you have not done this before, stand in a circle holding hands, praying aloud at the same time. Ask the Lord to fill you personally with His Holy Spirit, guide you and your church and protect you from the evil one. Claim Christ's resources against Satan and his evil forces. Conclude this time with the Lord's Prayer. If this is customary for your group, find a way to pray that is not your usual practice. If the facilitator is at ease in leading the group into another style of praying, the participants will find it interesting and faith stretching. Praying to God in a new style may well open your hearts and minds to look for new insights from God later on.

Discerning the Lord's View

We will consider the Bible study section of the procedure as it corresponds with each of the steps described in the following chapters. At this point, turn your attention to the process itself. The facilitator leads the group with wisdom, sensitivity and enthusiasm. Explaining the process as it goes along is important but not really difficult. It helps greatly if the elders have read this book. A video/audio series on "Setting Your Church Free" is also available from Freedom in Christ Ministries. Appendix B serves as a guide for each participant during the day itself. Each person needs an individual copy of the guidelines in appendix B. The facilitator simply points out where the group is in the process and guides them through it. For example, at the close of the Bible study it is time for the first break of about 10 minutes.

When the participants gather again, appoint a recorder for the group. This person jots down on notebook paper exactly what appears on the poster sheets up front. This saves much time later on, as well as possible misunderstanding. The facilitator writes on the sheets on the wall. A good tip in writing down the lists under each step is to use the actual words of the person who made the suggestion. People feel heard when their thoughts are not paraphrased but rather stated in their own words. If their description is too wordy to write out, the facilitator simply requests, "Say that for me in a few words so I can jot it down." In the first three of the seven steps, list making is the needed activity. Every suggestion is okay. The facilitator will let the group know that no judgmental comments or disagreements are acceptable. The process itself will weed out what is not necessary or helpful. In the last four steps, however, the group needs to come to consensus. Appendix B alerts the group to which activity is needed and when.

Praying and Listening

Each step begins with a group prayer written out in appendix B. It focuses on what the step is about and asks the Lord to reveal it. For example, in Step One here is the group prayer:

Dear heavenly Father,
    Thank You for calling and choosing us as shepherds of the flock and servant leaders in Your Church. Thank You for this church and what You have done through it. Thank You for the people who worship and serve You here.
    Show us what the living Lord Jesus commends in our church. Remind us of what we are doing right and the strengths You have given to our church. As we wait silently before You, show us our good works that glorify our Father in heaven (Matt. 5:16).

    After repeating this written prayer out loud together, spend a few moments in silent prayer. All the participants should be asking the Lord to impress upon their minds the strengths of the church, those things you are doing right. After two or three minutes of silence, the facilitator closes the time by praying audibly. In later steps, it adds participation and variety to name two people to close the time in prayer. Always ask in advance if some participants prefer not to pray out loud, then honor their requests. When both people have prayed, the group knows that it is time to begin listing what the Lord impressed on their minds and hearts. Each of the steps follows a similar process.

Listing Strengths

Step One has two parts. In the first part, the facilitator asks the group to list the church's strengths as the Holy Spirit brings them to mind. No church is doing everything right nor everything well. Yet every church that calls upon the name of the Lord is doing many things right. It is a fact of life that most church leaders will not feel right about facing their weaknesses and corporate sins until they have talked about their strengths. Encourage all the participants to identify as many strengths of the church as possible.

A small church came up with this short list of strengths:

- Pastor;
- Worship;
- Desire to do what's right;
- Feeling of togetherness;
- Adaptable, flexible;
- Committed to having church;
- Loving fellowship;
- Truth;
- Intolerance of false teaching;
- Intolerance of sexual immorality;
- Music;
- Children's sermons;
- Sense of family;
- Dedicated core group;
- Current leadership;
- Denominational support;
- Openness;
- God's Spirit.

Some churches will fill two or three poster sheets with strengths. When the group begins to fall silent because of no more ideas, the facilitator can say, "What else do you think of?" "What other strengths has God given us?" "What are we doing right?" The additional questions encourage the timid to speak and satisfy the whole group that most of the strengths are listed. The facilitator can also tell the group that it is fine to add other items to the strengths list if they come to mind later on during the day.

Greatest Strengths

The second part of Step One takes place after all of the strengths are listed. The facilitator asks the group to summarize the greatest strengths God has given to the church. Good questions to ask here are: "What are the things we always do best?" "What works for us every time?" "How has God uniquely gifted us as a church body?" Keep this list short and have only the greatest strengths identified. The list will often be about five to seven items.

The facilitator writes on the poster or butcher paper the greatest strengths, beginning each one with, "We thank God for..." State them in complete sentences and save the statements for the final summary in the Prayer Action Plan (Step Six). Here is a typical list drawn from several actual churches:

1. We thank God for a dedicated pastoral staff and other servant leaders.
2. We thank God for meaningful worship through fine music, the power of prayer, and good preaching.
3. We thank God for a strong unity in Christ that creates a close family feeling and loving relationships.
4. We thank God for a strong and active children's ministry.
5. We thank God for a fine facility in a good location that gives us great potential.
6. We thank God for a core group of people who are faithful and dedicated to service.
7. We thank God that Christ is put first and the Bible is taught.

Each step concludes by praying in unison a written prayer. As an example, here is the group prayer for Step One:

Dear heavenly Father,
Thank You for the strengths You have given to us and to our church. Thank You for gracing us with Your presence and for working through the gifts, talents and service of Your people. We bow in grati-

tude for the ways that You have ministered through our church. We know that apart from Christ we can do nothing. So we gladly acknowledge that every good and perfect gift is from above. Continue to equip us to be good stewards of these strengths as well as responsible managers of all the relationships and all of the resources You have given us. In Jesus Christ our Lord we pray. Amen.

Listing Weaknesses

Step Two begins the process of identifying the church's weaknesses. Patterns will emerge after looking at painful memories and corporate sins, so the goal for this step is not to determine the greatest weaknesses as was done with the strengths. Instead the objective is simply to let everyone state what they sense from the Lord, what they feel and see.

The procedure follows the same format as Step One. The group prays together the printed prayer in appendix B. Then they spend a couple of minutes in silent prayer, asking the Lord to impress upon their hearts the weaknesses of the church. Two of the participants, or the facilitator, can close this time with a spoken prayer.

The facilitator will encourage everyone to express an opinion. This is not a time for any objection or defensiveness from others. Absolute accuracy is not essential this early in the process. It is at this point that the first signs of discomfort begin with the group. The "Setting Your Church Free" process may be emotionally draining and spiritually taxing at times. If some of the contributions feel like criticisms, try not to become defensive. The facilitator, of course, will make sure that everyone focuses on issues, not personalities. Some may experience ill feelings toward others who state weaknesses that seem to point a finger at them. Some may sense mental disturbances or a desire to leave. This type of interference is common in personal counseling, although it seems more rare among groups of leaders who have already experienced their own freedom in Christ.

The facilitator can alert the group to the possibility of internal interference and encourage them to share it. Usually, simply exposing such thoughts and feelings to the group will move them out of hiding and into the light of disclosure. Most often the honesty and openness will put a stop to the internal interference. If not, the facilitator may need to stop and pray against such opposition.

Few groups have a problem coming up with a list of weaknesses. In most groups, the list will be somewhat longer than the list of strengths. If some member of the group mentions this fact, which is not uncommon, the facilitator simply asks, "Have we overlooked any strengths?" It is sometimes reassuring to tell the participants that most groups of church leaders see more weaknesses than strengths. This church is not abnormal for taking an honest look at its shortcomings, faults and flaws.

If the pace is normal, the group is now ready for their second break. The fellowship time is important for a relief in the concentration. When the strengths and weaknesses of the church are listed for all to see, the stage is set to dig deeper. We will focus more and more on Christ as the process continues. Church memories, both good and painful, come next in chapter 9.

Notes

1. Earl F. Palmer, *1, 2, 3 John, Revelation*, Lloyd J. Ogilvie, General Editor, *The Communicator's Commentary* (Dallas, TX: WORD Inc., 1982), p. 122.
2. Clinton E. Arnold, *Powers of Darkness, Principalities and Power in Paul's Letters* (Downers Grove, IL: InterVarsity Press, 1992), p. 108.
3. G. Campbell Morgan, *The Letters of Our Lord, A First Century Message to Twentieth Century Christians* (London, England: Pickering & Inglis Ltd., n.d.), p. 18.
4. Timothy Jones, "Rumors of Angels," *Christianity Today,* April 5, 1993, p. 18.
5. Ibid.
6. Andrew J. Bandstra, "A Job Description for Angels," *Christianity Today,* April 5, 1993, p. 21.
7. Hans Bietenhard, "Angel," *The New International Dictionary of New Testament Theology, Vol. 1,* (Grand Rapids, MI: Zondervan Publishing House, 1975), p. 103.
8. Robert H. Mounce, *The Book of Revelation, The New International Commentary on the New Testament* (Grand Rapids, MI: Wm. Eerdmans Publishing Co., 1977), pp. 82, 85.

For a full treatment of angels as impersonal entities that are the prevailing spirits of the churches, see the trilogy of books by Walter Wink, *Naming the Powers, Unmasking the Powers* and *Engaging the Powers,* published by Fortress Press (Minneapolis, MN). For a scholarly answer to his major thesis, see Clinton E. Arnold, *Powers of Darkness,* cited earlier.

DEALING WITH THE POWER OF MEMORIES

(Step Three in the "Setting Your Church Free" Event)

Memory is a powerful force for good or for evil—and sometimes for both. Good memories bring joy to the heart and delight to the mind. God often commands us to remember His mighty acts, His gracious mercy and His compassion for our weakness. But painful memories nudge us toward regret and resentment—unless we forgive and find freedom in Christ.

My computer dictionary defines memory as: "The mental capacity to retain and recall past experiences." It is, as Oscar Wilde called it, "the diary we all carry around with us." It conditions our attitudes and our prejudices, our hopes and our dreams.

Appealing to the corporate memory of Israel, Ezra recounted in prayer God's powerful acts and loving forgiveness. The people turned back to God in great revival. The joy of the Lord became their strength (see Neh. 9). Stephen recalled a similar listing of good memories from God's mighty hand (see Acts 7). He proclaimed how God's sovereign action, memories engraved in Scripture, set the stage for the Lord's greatest gift of Jesus. Sadly, Stephen was speaking to the Sanhedrin, the ruling council of men who sent Jesus to Pilate and the cross. They responded to Stephen's pricking their conscience by stoning him to death.

Memories of better days in times past can cause us to turn a corner. The prodigal son recalled the food and fare in his father's house, and turned homeward in brokenness and humility. Jesus used the parable to teach how the heavenly Father receives each sinner who genuinely repents and turns his heart toward home (see Luke 15:11-32).

Recall some of your good memories. Turn back in your mind's eye to the time when you first received Christ Jesus as your own Lord and Savior. Scroll back in your memory to the emotions, the humility, the relief, the joy, the relationship. If you do not remember, then think back to the first time Christ was meaningful to you. Remind yourself of some holy-ground experience with Christ, some time when He was really special to you. Then thank Him, praise Him, worship Him.

Try another kind of warm memory. Recapture from the recesses of your mind one of the best experiences of your church. Reflect on a time when God moved among the people in a remarkable way. Think about the joy of Christ's people at Easter, Christmas or some special occasion. Remember the achievement of a great goal accomplished by everyone working together. Think about the fun of a social time together as a church family. Thank God for the good memories from your church life.

Painful memories have their place, too. Remind yourself of a painful memory from your church experience. Did someone you loved and admired change churches or move away? Did someone criticize you, belittle you, oppose your ideas? Were you abused, taken advantage of, used for someone else's purpose? What is the most painful memory from your experience with the church?

Church Memories

Every church has memories. These memories are not neutral. They hold hidden power. They shape a church's sense of worth. They help build or destroy morale. They become foundations for more faith or reasons for more fear.

They color how the leaders see the pastor, view church conflicts or approach fresh goals. These past events affect the present and the future of the church.

Memories are recalled in stories and rumors, buried in emotional joys and pain, lived out in spiritual victory and deadening defeat. They are sources of pride and shame, happiness and sadness, health and disease. They provide us with opportunities or dangers. They serve as a shield against the enemy or as an open door for the adversary. They turn us toward God or away from Him.

The memories themselves are important, but not nearly as important as how well the church leaders respond to them. If a church's leaders rejoice in God and His goodness, recalling specific ways He intervened on their behalf, the church thrives. If the leaders recall their Lord and gladly obey Him in simple trust, the church prospers. If the leaders forgive those who hurt them and pray for God's blessing on them, the church flourishes. Such a church is on the way to health and freedom.

One pastor called the "Setting Your Church Free" event "a new window into the memories of the church." Another church had completed most of the Memories section (Step Three) and then gave a chance for the participants to pray in their own words. It was refreshing to hear the spontaneous prayers of forgiveness. The leaders named specific people as they prayed, knowing that everything would be kept in the strictest confidence. One woman began to weep. The others surrounded her, hugged her and stood by her as she released her resentment and regret. Just the day before she had gone through forgiveness in the personal "Steps to Freedom." But this church-related problem had not come to mind. Like peeling another layer off of an onion, the Lord Jesus gently uncovered this painful memory and resolved it.

Resolving Differences

Memories, both those that bless and those that bind, can be abused as well as used positively. If church leaders take credit for what God did, they rob Him of glory and become preoccupied with themselves. If the leaders criticize former pastors, they build resentment into the congregation. If the leaders bury the painful past and refuse to discuss it, they cut themselves off from God's blessings for today and tomorrow. On the other hand, if they resolve differences, even among participants in the group, it can transform relationships within a church.

Those who do not understand forgiveness and the power of praying for past offenders sometimes refuse to face old painful memories. They delude themselves and fall into the devil's trap. Some of Satan's favorite deceptions are that darkness is safer than light, that things hidden are better not discussed, that pain has no permanent resolution. Misguided leaders see painful church memories as something embarrassing that will damage rather than heal. But covering up old sins is what Jesus warned against. "Be on your guard against the yeast of the Pharisees, which is hypocrisy. There is nothing concealed that will not be disclosed, or hidden that will not be made known" (Luke 12:1,2).

Wise church leaders bring everything into the light. They expect neither themselves nor their churches to be perfect. They claim God's grace to release them from the bondage of the past. They feel the pain, release it through the forgiveness of Christ, and bless those who curse them. What results is freedom and joy. Peace replaces pain. Wisdom grows from poor judgment. People, even people in their church, have permission to fail if they are attempting great things for Christ. Love, laughter and a sense of life mark these churches. High morale is their hallmark.

Good church memories will always bless, if God receives the glory. Painful church memories will always bind, unless leaders and people alike forgive as Christ forgave them. But painful memories can become good memories if they are redeemed by being released from the dark shadows of denial and used as teaching tools for the future. David Seamands, in his balanced, biblical book *Healing of Memories,* shares some commonsense wisdom: "We cannot change the facts we remember, but we can change their meanings and the power they have over our present way of living."[1]

Turning away from the damage of sinful memories and turning back to God changes the meaning of our memories. Forgiving old offenders, including in our church, and doing good to those who hate us breaks the power that crippling memories have over us. Forgiveness of offenders, however, does not turn church leaders into wimps. In a certain church, the leaders graciously forgave someone with a strong personality who tended to dominate people in their fellowship. But they also committed themselves in the Prayer Action Plan (Step Six) to confront with love. Forgiveness prepares the way for tough love. If leaders sweep repeated offenses under the rug, they will soon trip over them.

Let's consider our primary Bible passage once again, Revelation 2,3. In these chapters, we find a few instances of both good and painful memories. Jesus commands the churches at Ephesus and Sardis to *remember.* He also reminds Pergamum of a painful memory.

Lost Love

Turn to the letter to the church at Ephesus (see Rev. 2:1-7). After bragging on many of their strengths, Jesus says: "Yet I hold this against you: You have forsaken your first love. *Remember* the height from which you have fallen! Repent and do the things you did at first" (Rev. 2:4,5, italics added).

Jesus tells them to jog their memory, to recall the times when their love flowed back and forth from God and encouraged and built up one another. In spite of their hard work, doctrinal purity and dogged perseverance, their love had grown cold.

The greatest danger to the Church today is not that it will deny the deity of Christ or the authority of Scripture. The greatest danger lies in the warning of Jesus' prophecy in Matthew 24:12: "Because of the increase of wickedness, the love of most will grow cold." When evil spreads, people defend themselves or stick up for their rights. But in the process they stop loving each other and do not have as much love toward God as they used to.

It is painful for people to recall their first love and face up to the fact that they tumbled down the slippery slope. *"Remember* the height from which you have fallen!" (Rev. 2:5, italics added). Recalling the fact of their fall is not enough by itself. They are to change their ways and do the loving things they used to do. That is what "repent" means for them, as well as for us.

Have you ever tried to start "feeling love" again? Have you ever fallen out of love and then tried to will the old feelings back again? It does not work. Jesus does not tell us to feel love. What does work? Start doing the loving things you did when you were in love. If it is your wife, start dating again. If it is your God, start praising and thanking, believing and trusting, rejoicing and worshiping. You can behave your way into feeling much faster than you can feel your way into behaving.

When it comes to recovering your first love, it always helps to remind yourself who you really are in Christ. In Christ you are loving because God is love. What is more, the fruit of the Spirit is love. Taking time for God, practicing the spiritual disciplines and living up to your true identity are probably the things you did when you felt that first love. Start climbing back up the mountain you slid down.

Begin to act like the person, or the church, that you really are in Christ. Do the loving things you used to do. Climbing back up always seems tougher and takes longer than falling down from a height. The progress comes one step at a time, one loving act at a time. Perseverance pays. Each step brings you closer to the time when you, or your church, will regain the height of your "first love."

Pain of Loss

To the church at Pergamum Jesus reminds them of a bittersweet memory. He recalls "the days of Antipas, my faithful witness, who was put to death in your city" (Rev. 2:13). Antipas was a martyr, a victim, a soldier of Christ slain in spiritual combat. The church in Pergamum kept true to Christ's name and did not give up their faith in Him. But the loss of the faithful witness, Antipas, left an indelible mark on their corporate memory. It was the most traumatic event in the history of their church, and their troubles were not over.

Pergamum was the city where Satan had his throne. The temples built to two of the Roman emperors and several false gods were outward evidence of a spiritual reality. Satan headquartered here. In this city, people followed his demonic orders. Antipas may have been their first martyr but he was not to be the last. History records that later on in Pergamum, men named Carpus, Papylus and Agathonike also shed their blood as martyrs for Christ.[2]

Your church may not have physical martyrs for Christ, but it may well have people who have burned out, given up or been blown away. Your leaders may ache over good people who chose to go to another church and left the burdens of ministry to an overworked few. It may have sorrowful memories of accidents or death that took out an effective leader just when things seemed to be moving in the right direction. Or it may have painful memories of a more destructive kind—false teachers, selfish controllers, power-hungry leaders, immoral hypocrites or critical gossips.

A healthy, growing church was going through the "Setting Your Church Free" process. The participants were praying individually, forgiving those who hurt their church. During the silence between spoken prayers, a man began to shake and weep. This man was a leader, a supporter, a server, a teacher, a pillar. But deep inside his soul, old hurts festered like open sores. Strong personalities in the past abused their power and influence in the church. He was among those who dealt with the offenders, but it was never easy.

For a minute or two, he quietly sobbed. This was not a cry of regret nor the tears of confession, but simply a time of release. It was a tender moment as the pain of church leadership surfaced, perhaps for the first time in years. The pain ebbed away. The rest of the group simply waited silently and prayerfully. It was a healing moment.

Church in a Coma

The church in Sardis was dead (see Rev. 3:1-6). It looked alive but Jesus said it was dead. However, He also commanded it to wake up, saying it had a little strength left. Maybe it was in a coma. This church had a great reputation. Others thought it was alive, and it was vibrant at one time. But now most of the people had dirtied their clothes with sin. What little strength it had left was almost gone. It was in a coma and its life was slipping away.

The Lord Jesus writes to the church at Sardis, recalling a good memory, a memory of the gospel that brings life to the dead, alertness to the sleeping, consciousness to the comatose:

> *Remember,* therefore, what you have received and heard; obey it and repent (Rev. 3:3, italics added).

> *Remember* the teaching that you were given, and that you heard. Hold firmly to it and turn from your sins (Rev. 3:3, *CEV,* italics added).

Some of the best memories of a church are of the gospel being preached and taught. When the whole counsel of God is proclaimed, believed and obeyed, sometimes those in a coma come to life!

David A. Seamands gives some helpful insight into what the Bible means when it calls us to remember:

> Memories include feelings, concepts, patterns, attitudes, and tendencies toward actions which accompany the pictures on the screen of the

mind. This is the way the Bible uses the concept of remembrance, or stirring us up to remember something. When Scripture commands us to "remember the Lord," it does not mean to simply have a mental picture of God. It is a command to whole persons to orient all our thoughts and actions around God.[3]

You can't fix the past, but you can free yourselves from it by facing it, forgiving and seeking forgiveness. Keeping this biblical background in mind, let's focus on the actual procedure for the next step of "Setting Your Church Free."

Dealing with Memories

In Step Three you are asking the Lord to remind you of the best memories as well as the traumatic events in your church's past. Make two lists for Step Three, one titled "Good Memories" and the other titled "Painful Memories."

Good Memories
List all of the good memories first. They provide an occasion for thanksgiving to God for His blessings upon your church over the years. The participants enjoy this step, and the emotional tone of the group sometimes lifts noticeably. This is good in itself, and it also provides a cushion of support for the pain that goes with the second part of this step.

If yours is an older church, consider it decade by decade, beginning in the earliest recalled past. What happened in the 1930s, '40s, '50s, '60s, '70s, '80s, '90s? Some churches may want to do some research or talk with long-time attenders. If anyone in the congregation has written a history for a major church anniversary, read it and, if possible, talk with the author. The patterns that emerge are often eye-opening to the participants.

If yours is a younger church, you may want to divide its history in half or into thirds. What happened in the first five years, the last five years? Although the lists may be shorter for a younger church or especially a brand-new church, both good and painful memories exist. This is a good time to capture them.

The written procedure in appendix B gives a printed prayer for good memories. Some people object to written prayers, but this process moves us out of the ordinary for a distinct purpose. When in fresh ways we seek the Lord, Who never changes, we sometimes catch fresh glimpses of His goodness and then we are changed. As one participant commented, "The 'Set Your Church Free' seminar requires you to open your heart and let go of painful memories, but then this allows more room to let Jesus *completely* into your heart!"

Once again follow the group prayer with a time of silent prayer. The facilitator will ask two of the participants to close the time of silence with spoken prayer. The facilitator and recorder once more move into action. The oldest members of the group often do most of the sharing for the earliest decades because they are the only ones who remember.

A good opening question from the facilitator is, "Who remembers the furthest back? Was anyone here during the (1930s or whatever decade seems to fit the age of the participants)?" Other questions might include, "Did anyone do any reading or research on this church's early history? What did you find?" To keep the process from bogging down, the facilitator needs simply to list memories in a few words. Beware of storytellers who want to reminisce in detail.

Typical good memories participants may list might include all-church activities and social events, youth groups that were strong and helpful, the tenure of an outstanding pastor, special meetings in which fresh commitments to God were made, major programs that required teamwork, people accepting Christ, periods of growth and building, sports teams, musical groups and much more. When the list of good memories is complete, the facilitator will ask the participants to lift them before the Lord in thanksgiving and praise. Encourage everyone to pray aloud, beginning with the words, "Lord I thank you for (name the good memory)."

Painful Memories
After thanking the Lord for the good memories throughout the church's past, make another list; this time of painful memories. Every church has its own history of pain, although some more than others. If not addressed, these painful memories will continue to have a choke hold on those who felt the pain as well as upon the church's present ministry. Again, use the decade by decade method of recalling. This allows the participants who have the most

longevity in the group to speak first, a disarming move. Their sharing will drop defenses and give permission for others to talk about the pain of more recent years. The more recent the conflict, the more apt it is to be a point of tension between members of the group.

One board came to a point of tension that led to a confrontation. Both of those who disagreed were mature in the Lord and respected by the group. It was a healthy time of asking one another "Why?" without anger or accusations. The issue was resolved and the two felt greater respect and closeness to one another. The one who first challenged the other later wrote:

> The personal relationship that became more open has become one of the important blessings in my life. Without the seminar, that relationship would likely still be closed. This openness has led to more cooperation and greater good for our movement.

Real Names

The facilitator will ask the group to use real names of those involved in painful memories. It is nearly impossible to get in touch with the inner emotional core of pain without using people's names. In order for the participants to feel comfortable in using actual names, absolute confidentiality must be assured. No person will be permitted to share this confidential information outside the group. The facilitator may want to say, "This is the leadership of the church. Everything said here must be kept with the strictest confidentiality. This information is not even to be shared with husbands or wives who are not here today. Let's be careful in this section not to place blame or make disparaging remarks. We're here to heal the pain, not spread the gangrene."

The recorder is not to write down the painful memories section. After the process is finished you will want to destroy the large sheet up front. The group will then pray together, following a similar procedure as before. Then the list making begins. Focus on what was done rather than analyze why it was done. Analysis only leads to rationalizations, verbal excursions or problem solving. You are not trying to solve problems in this step. This is a freeing time. You will have plenty of time to solve problems later.

Problem Solving

Whenever anyone in this "Setting Your Church Free" event begins problem solving (which almost always happens), the facilitator must address it. Here is an example:

> "The problem with elders (board members, pastors) is that they keep acting like elders." (Laugh)

> "Every time we get together we solve problems. This is not a problem-solving time. We are simply identifying them in this step. We will have plenty of time in future meetings to work on solving problems."

Once again the group interacts and the facilitator writes the list on the sheets up front. Then each person is to lift the painful memories before the Lord, asking for courage to face the pain honestly and for grace to forgive fully. Releasing the offenses results in relieving the pain.

Silent Forgiveness

Begin by individually and silently forgiving each person who has ever hurt you or your church (when you were involved), then release the offenses. The facilitator suggests a similar prayer to the one used in the personal "Steps to Freedom":

> Lord, I forgive (name the person) for (specifically name every painful memory).

Do not hurry through this time of individual silent prayer. It helps to ask the participants to review the list, bow their heads and lift them only when they are finished forgiving those who hurt them. This lets the facilitator know when everyone has processed this personal forgiveness. Often it takes longer than expected.

During the time of silent forgiveness, prayerfully focus on each person until every remembered pain surfaces. What is to be gained is freedom, not necessarily reconciliation. Principal people on the list may be dead. Some who are presently alive may not be willing to reconcile. Neither your freedom nor your church's can depend on what you have no right or ability to control. Paul writes, "If it is possible, as far as it depends on you, live at peace with everyone" (Rom. 12:18). But let's face it, sometimes it does not depend on us.

If, during this process, you recall that someone has something against you, then commit yourself to go and ask forgiveness at your earliest opportunity. If it is someone in the group, then take advantage of the next break to go to the person and ask their forgiveness. Not to do so would hinder the Lord's leading in your life and the freedom of your church.

> Therefore, if you are offering your gift at the altar and there remember that your brother has something against you, leave your gift there in front of the altar. First go and be reconciled to your brother; then come and offer your gift (Matt. 5:23,24).

The Joy of Reconciliation

One church finished the memories section and took a break. The pastor's wife, whom we will call Renea, and her former close friend Shirlee began talking while everyone else vacated the room. (Some churches invite spouses to participate in this process; some do not.) The other leaders did not hurry back because they suspected what was going on.

The pastor had come under heavy criticism from Bev, a mutual friend of both Shirlee and Renea. It all started because Bev felt offended over a conflict between her husband and the pastor. What began as a misunderstanding escalated into criticism, charges and church meetings in private and public. The person Bev confided in most was Shirlee, a good friend of Renea's. Shirlee loved the pastor and his wife. She also loved Bev, and her heart went out to her because of the misunderstandings and the pain. But the more she listened to Bev's complaints and criticisms, the more estranged she felt from Renea. A distance and coolness soon developed in their friendship.

Renea sensed the rift of tension between herself and Shirlee. She felt shunned. She felt like the innocent victim who was attacked for no good reason. She felt like she was dying on the inside. By the time of this meeting, Bev had left the church with her husband, but Shirlee and Renea were both in the room. The church leaders had done their best in the process of resolving the church issue, but not the personal one between these two.

At the break time Renea and Shirlee began talking, working out their misunderstandings, asking forgiveness of one another. When they finally showed up for refreshments and had tears in their eyes and their faces were beaming, the other members of the group were ready to go back to work! It had been worth every minute of the wait. Months later the pastor, a capable and godly man, reported that this healing of old hurts by the Lord was the highlight of the event for his family.

Blessing Enemies

Returning to the process of Step Three, we move on past the silent time of forgiveness. The group now prays together following the printed guideline (see appendix B). The facilitator will alert the group to what is coming next. After praying the written prayer together, but before saying the "Amen," all the participants are encouraged to pray individually and audibly. One at a time they lift spontaneous prayers before the Lord, beginning with, "We forgive..." "We release..." or "We bless..."

One church had a capable former pastor who fell into sexual immorality. His sin had a delayed effect upon the church. After the initial shock, the church seemed to recover well. But soon deep pain and disillusionment began to set in. Those who trusted him most felt the deepest sense of betrayal. After the former pastor's divorce, his tardiness in paying child support aggravated their feelings. Conflicts with his former wife, whom they also loved, intensified their pain. Their anger was deep and certainly seemed justified. If there is such a thing as righteous indignation, this was a case in point.

Forgiveness, however, was not the toughest issue. Most of these church leaders had responded to the message to forgive. But to obey the teaching of Jesus—"Love your enemies, do good to those who hate you, bless those who curse you, pray for those who mistreat you" (Luke 6:27,28)—seemed far more difficult. As we approached the "We bless...," "We release...," "We forgive..." prayers, the feeling of pain in the room was intense. One godly Christian woman prayed with shocking honesty: "Lord, I can't pray to bless him by myself. I'm not even sure I forgive him. But by faith I ask you to bless him, and I release him." Her honesty blasted a big hole in the resistance and others soon joined in with similar prayers of forgiveness and blessing.

Months later another elder who was present that day reported that the most helpful part of the session for their church was "coming face-to-face with the issue caused by the former pastor. Some of our people have been healed."

Corporate Forgiveness

Although we will not put all the prayers in appendix B in the text of the book, this one on corporate forgiveness needs your prayerful understanding:

Dear heavenly Father,

We forgive each and every person who has hurt us or our church. We forgive as the Lord forgave us.

We release our resentments and regrets into Your hands. You alone can heal our broken hearts and bind up our wounds. We ask You to heal the pain in our hearts and in the corporate memory of our church. We ask for Your forgiveness for allowing a root of bitterness to spring up and defile many. We also ask You to forgive us for the times we did not seek to resolve these painful memories according to Your Word.

We commit ourselves to think of these memories, whenever we may happen to recall them, from the vantage point of our union with Christ. We will recall our forgiveness and Your healing. May Your grace and mercy guide us as we seek to live out our calling as spiritual leaders. By the authority of the Lord Jesus Christ, Who is seated at Your right hand, we assume our responsibility to resist the devil. In Jesus' all-powerful name we retake any ground that Satan may have gained in our lives and in our church through these painful memories. Because we are seated with Christ in the heavenly realms, we command Satan to leave our presence, our ministries and our church. We ask You, heavenly Father, to fill us with Your Holy Spirit. We surrender full control of our church body to our crucified, risen and reigning Head.

We ask You to bring healing to those who have hurt us. Also bring healing to those who may have been hurt by us. Bless those who curse us and give rich and satisfying ministries to all who belong to You but

have gone away from us. We bless them all in the name of our Lord
Jesus Christ, Who taught us, "Love your enemies, do good to those
who hate you, bless those who curse you, pray for those who mistreat
you" (Luke 6:27,28). According to Your Word, we pray for those who
have hurt us:

> We forgive...   (Individually, as the Lord
> We release...   leads, pray for people and
> We bless...   situations, beginning with
> these phrases.)
> In Jesus' name we pray. Amen.

Satan's Advantage

Is it really possible that Satan can take advantage of a church corporately
because of painful memories? Can the evil one exploit pain or divisions or
misunderstandings to create more strife and problems? Can the accuser of the
brethren misuse the memory of church conflicts to stir up more trouble in a
church? We believe he can. However, our position needs a bit of clarifica-
tion when it comes to memories. It is not the memory itself that gives the
enemy an advantage over us, but rather how we respond to the memory.

The church in Corinth was tolerating a man among them who was living
in incest. He was sleeping with his father's wife (i.e., stepmother), a scandal
even among the pagans. Paul wrote to them in 1 Corinthians 5 to expel the
immoral brother—and they did (see 1 Cor. 5:1-13; 2 Cor. 2:1-11). After his
expulsion from the church, apparently the man broke off his sexual immorality and repented of his sin. The apostle then writes again that the church
should engage in corporate forgiveness, comfort and love:

> The punishment inflicted on him by the majority is sufficient for him.
> Now instead, you ought to forgive and comfort him, so that he will
> not be overwhelmed by excessive sorrow. I urge you, therefore, to reaf-
> firm your love for him (2 Cor. 2:6-8).

Of special interest to us is the spiritual reason Paul gives for both personal and corporate forgiveness:

> But whom you forgive anything, I forgive also; for indeed what I have forgiven, if I have forgiven anything, I did it for your sakes in the presence of Christ, in order that no advantage be taken of us by Satan; for we are not ignorant of his schemes (2 Cor. 2:10,11, *NASB).*

Forgiveness is not simply for the good of the offender, nor is it simply for the good of the people who forgive. It is especially important because refusing corporate forgiveness allows Satan to outwit a church. It allows the evil one to defraud a church of its rightful riches in Christ. Like a hungry lion stalking prey, Satan pounces on its corporate sin (in this case, unforgiveness). Gaining an advantage over a church and getting the better of it is one of Satan's schemes.

If we disobey the clear teachings of Jesus to love, do good, bless and pray for our enemies, including any who caused painful memories in our church, then we give the devil ground. The painful memories will bind us if we do not deliberately take action to obey our Lord. But these truths have not been taught to churches, indeed they are recent insights to us. We believe all churches need to examine their corporate life together and take action to free themselves from the past and from the enemy's cunning devices.

Past Patterns

The memories step has other benefits as well. Working through it is sometimes insightful for church leaders to see patterns emerging from the past. One church discovered a repeated pattern of strong personalities joining their fellowship. Because of their natural forcefulness and personal ego strength, they were soon put up front or given responsible positions. However, they had character flaws that caused severe problems. Dealing with the strong personalities was painful and sometimes damaging to the church.

This happened not once but several times during different eras of the church's history. Believing that the evil one may instill a strong spirit of independence, the leadership at this church now takes more precautions in selecting their leaders. They have become alert to their tendency to put strong, outgoing personalities up front before proven character from Christ is evident. The pastors and elders talk openly about this tendency when they see a problem coming. In some cases, they deal with a problem before it becomes severe. They are on alert to where their church is vulnerable. We wonder how many churches do not have the foggiest idea about what patterns from the past might be repeated in the future. They are ignorant of Satan's schemes and so he easily takes advantage of them.

Some months after the "Setting Your Church Free" retreat, one pastor wrote, "Sometimes we really don't know what our church may be facing. At those times it certainly is good to do something like this to see if our apathy, pain, anxiety or whatever is caused by giving footholds to Satan." For those who sense a reluctance to give credit for anything—even bad things—to the devil, let us reassure you that this process is psychologically healthy. It would work on a human level even if there were no demonic activity in a church. However, it is more powerful when the church leaders know that Christ's kingdom of light is crushing Satan's kingdom of darkness. As my friend Corrie ten Boom used to say so often, "Jesus is Victor!"

After working through the first three steps, the participants need a break. When they come back, they will be ready to consider corporate sins and their effects on the church, which is the topic of the next chapter.

Notes

1. David A. Seamands, *Healing of Memories* (Wheaton, IL: Victor Books, 1985), p. 186.
2. Robert H. Mounce, *The Book of Revelation, The New International Commentary on the New Testament* (Grand Rapids, MI: Wm. B. Eerdmans Publishing Co., 1977), p. 97, citing Eusebius, *Hist. Eccl.* iv. 15. F. F. Bruce is general editor of the *New International Commentary on the New Testament* series.
3. Seamands, *Healing of Memories*, p. 15.

DEALING WITH CORPORATE SINS

(Step Four in the "Setting Your Church Free" Event)

A friend of mine tells of his summer in China. When people asked him about crime and divorce rates in the United States, he admitted the press reports were true. The Chinese people replied that such terrible things were not allowed in their country. My friend felt ashamed for "Christian America."

I recall the astonishment of some Japanese students of mine at the H. P. Haggard School of Theology at Azusa Pacific University. The counseling course was addressing the problem of sexual abuse of children. The students were aghast and said such things did not happen in Japan. Their explanation was simple— adults are never alone with children. Everyone lives so close together that privacy is unknown and children are protected. I felt ashamed for our culture.

Think of the discomfort and dismay we feel when we learn about other cultures' corporate sins. Abortion for the sole reason of gender selection is common in India. That is abhorrent. A few years ago I visited in Thailand. In the beautiful city of Bangkok, the guides pointed out to us the "spirit houses" outside of the homes and as well as hotels. They look like ornate bird houses. Some are also fairly elaborate. The people place offerings and sacrifices in them to appease the spirits. My soul felt grieved. Any institution or social organization can, and probably does, have corporate sins—churches included.

What Are Corporate Sins?

By corporate sins we mean patterns of behavior in a church that are displeasing to our God and contrary to His revealed will. They do not differ from individual sins in nature. Sin is still sin whether practiced by an individual or a group. What sets corporate sins apart from individual sins is their being held in common by the whole church or by a significant group within it. This pattern of sinfulness within the group life of the church calls for corporate action on the part of its leaders in order to deal with it.

"Lord, you are righteous, but this day we are covered with shame" (Dan. 9:7). As strange as it sounds to our ears, Daniel was confessing corporate sins. He felt shame for the wickedness, rebelliousness and disobedience of "all Israel" (see Dan. 9:7,11). When is the last time you heard someone confess the sins of "all America" or "all of our church"? What Daniel knew, and what we seemingly do not, is the power of confessing corporate sins—feeling the shame that goes with them. But along with godly sorrow comes confidence in the power of Christ to forgive, cleanse and heal (see 2 Chron. 7:14; 2 Cor. 7:10).

If praying for the whole nation or all of Western culture seems too much, how about confessing the corporate sins of your family or your church? It is easy to blame our disintegrating culture for what is wrong and then forget that corporate sins may touch our own families, churches and denominations. Let's take churches as an example. Just what are their corporate sins? For starters, look once again at the letters from the risen Jesus to the seven churches of Revelation 2,3. Five of the seven churches were guilty of corporate sins.

Ephesus	Forsaking their first love.
Pergamum	Tolerating false teaching that approved of participation in non-Christian religious rituals, and committing sexual immorality.

Thyatira	Ditto to Pergamum, plus tolerating people within the church who committed adultery with a false teacher.
Sardis	Deadness and incomplete works.
Laodicea	Lukewarmness and finding security in material things.

Corporate sins and the shame that goes with them are not limited to Bible times. Congregations today, maybe even yours, often fall into sinful patterns practiced by a church as a whole or a significant group within it. After many "Setting Your Church Free" seminars, we are acutely aware that nearly all churches tolerate corporate sins. These sinful patterns in our group life cause incredible pain and damage. Worse yet, they hold us back from good progress and Christ's full blessing. Let's take gossip as an example.

Digging Up Dirt

Something within us revels in finding dirt about someone else. Gossip columns are always well read. Scandal magazines sell by the millions. Prominent personalities constantly face not only criticism, but also scandalous accusations based on little or no evidence. Local schools, service clubs, sports leagues and, yes, churches as well do not fare much better. The gossip communication channels are well established. Digging up dirt is a way of life—not a healthy one, but certainly an entrenched pattern.

Why? Why do so many people like to know about others' dirty laundry? We do not have all the answers, of course, but one thought might help. All of us have a God-given longing to feel good about ourselves. We were made in the image of God—healthy, complete, whole and very good. Through the Fall and our own sinful acts, God's image within us is flawed, distorted and broken. But the longing to feel good about ourselves remains.

One counterfeit way to heighten our sense of worth is by comparing. When we learn something bad, dirty or gossipy about a prominent personality or a personal acquaintance, we stand back in self-righteous horror, thinking, *I may have problems but I'm not that bad!* At the same time, we may feel tempted by their kind of sin, or feel that it excuses our weakness. *If the circumstances were right,* we think, *I just might...* A common defense mechanism for almost everyone is comparing. Sometimes we compare our strengths with others' weaknesses, which is a substitute satisfaction for genuine character building, giving a false sense of feeling better. The Bible warns against this kind of comparing (see 2 Cor. 10:12).

If we feel depressed, we may take the opposite tack and compare our weaknesses with others' strengths. Self-pity thrives on this negative mind game. At heart, of course, is the flesh with its corrupted and evil desires. Something about digging up dirt, or any kind of evil for that matter, has a strange attraction. The Bible warns us about our subtle hunger for gossip. "The words of a gossip are like choice morsels; they go down to a man's inmost parts" (Prov. 26:22).

The only safe comparison is between ourselves and Jesus Christ. At first it humbles us, but then, as we enter deeply into Christ, He becomes our new focus, our Savior, Lord, Teacher, Friend and Hope. In the process, He restores a healthy self-image as we "put on the new self, which is being renewed in knowledge in the image of its Creator" (Col. 3:10). One practical result is that our words change. Instead of digging up dirt we mine for gold in other people. "Therefore encourage one another and build each other up, just as in fact you are doing" (1 Thess. 5:11).

In his conferences, Neil often says that if we would memorize Ephesians 4:29 and put it into practice, half of our problems would disappear overnight: "Do not let any unwholesome talk come out of your mouths, but only what is helpful for building others up according to their needs, that it may benefit those who listen." When we build others up according to their needs, we never grieve the Holy Spirit, as the next verse warns against (see Eph. 4:30). Instead, we speak the words of comfort, counsel, teaching, encouragement or just good, Christian fun that lift people's spirits and build them up in Christ. How much better than putting others down!

Poison in the Body

Suspicion, gossip, dissension, divisiveness, rebellion—these corporate sins are garbage. Neil said earlier that demons are like flies. They feed on garbage. And this kind of fodder they like better than dessert. The devil constantly stirs up a spirit of independence that causes division. It happens in churches, and it is poison in the Body.

People question the motives of those in authority. The gossip mill begins to churn. Some are sowing seeds of dissension. Before long, leaders and people are not really trusting each other. Divisiveness shows up in business and committee meetings. The next thing you know, hurt feelings are leading some to leave the church. What is dangerous at this point is that the focus can turn away from the issue. Winning, coming out on top, restoring or maintaining self-image, and other beneath-the-surface desires wrongly seem far more important than discerning God's will. Good food and garbage neither look alike nor taste alike. Let's avoid the poison.

The sins we have named and discussed so far are not the only corporate sins. What about prayerlessness, apathy, disobeying the Great Commission? What about church leaders who look the other way when scandalous sins occur among their members? What about those who ignore it when their members violate biblical standards regarding fornication, adultery, divorce and remarriage, abortion and homosexual behavior? What about leaders who lie, misuse finances or cover up their own scandalous sins? What about those who conceal the sexual sins of church leaders?

If you ask the Lord to show you the corporate sins of your church, be ready for Him to open your eyes. When He does, it is time to renounce them, confess them and forsake them. Then remind yourselves of your unlimited resources in Christ and give yourselves afresh to obedience. "Remember, therefore, what you have received and heard; obey it, and repent" (Rev. 3:3).

The Bible and Corporate Sins

In one seminar a man commented, "I don't believe in corporate sins. I believe we are each responsible for our own sins." However, after a time of Bible study he was convinced. Let's look into the written Word of God, beginning with Daniel. The people of Judah were in exile, captive in Babylon for nearly 70 years. Upon learning that Jeremiah the prophet had prophesied 70 years of captivity, Daniel recognized from the Scriptures that God's time for deliverance was at hand. Soon Israel was going to become eligible for parole from their captivity and return to their homeland in Judah. What they lacked at that point was good behavior.

Daniel's Confession

Daniel interceded before God and confessed their corporate sins and the sins
of their ancestors. He confessed the wickedness, rebelliousness and disobedience of "all Israel." His prayer is recorded for us in Daniel 9:4-19. We reprint
it here with certain words and phrases highlighted to reveal the corporate
nature of their sins:

O Lord, the great and awesome God, who keeps his covenant of love
with all who love him and obey his commands, we have sinned and
done wrong. We have been wicked and have rebelled; we have turned
away from your commands and laws. We have not listened to your servants the prophets, who spoke in your name to our kings, our princes
and our fathers, and to all the people of the land.

Lord, you are righteous, but this day *we are covered with shame*—
the men of Judah and people of Jerusalem and *all Israel,* both near and
far, in all the countries where you have scattered us because of *our
unfaithfulness* to you. O Lord, *we and our kings, our princes and our
fathers are covered with shame because we have sinned against you.*
The Lord our God is merciful and forgiving, even though *we have
rebelled* against him; *we have not obeyed* the Lord our God or kept
the laws he gave us through his servants the prophets. *All Israel has
transgressed your law and turned away, refusing to obey you.*

Therefore the curses and sworn judgments written in the law of
Moses, the servant of God, have been poured out *on us,* because *we
have sinned* against you. You have fulfilled the words spoken against us
and against our rulers by bringing upon us great disaster. Under the
whole heaven nothing has ever been done like what has been done to
Jerusalem. Just as it is written in the law of Moses, all this disaster has
come *upon us, yet we have not sought the favor of the Lord our God by
turning from our sins and giving attention to your truth.* The Lord did
not hesitate to bring the disaster *upon us,* for the Lord our God is righteous in everything he does; yet *we have not obeyed him.*

Now, O Lord our God, who brought your people out of Egypt with
a mighty hand and who made for yourself a name that endures to this day,
we have sinned, we have done wrong. O Lord, in keeping with all your

righteous acts, turn away your anger and your wrath from Jerusalem, your city, your holy hill. Our sins and the iniquities of our fathers have made Jerusalem and your people an object of scorn to all those around us.

Now, our God, hear the prayers and petitions of your servant. For your sake, O Lord, look with favor on your desolate sanctuary. Give ear, O God, and hear; open your eyes and see the desolation of the city that bears your name. We do not make requests of you because we are righteous, but because of your great mercy. O Lord, listen! O Lord, forgive! O Lord, hear and act! For your sake, O my God, do not delay, because your city and your people bear your name.

Please note carefully the major point we are making. Daniel is confessing the corporate sins of his people and of his ancestors. He is not confessing his own personal sins, although he includes himself in the group prayer. Also note that Daniel wrote this prayer down. (Sometimes written prayers are extremely important.) Corporate sins do exist and responsible, godly leaders can seize the initiative and confess them to the Lord on behalf of themselves and all their people. The Lord heard and answered Daniel's prayer. In three waves of immigrants, a remnant of the people of Israel returned from Babylon to Judah.

Nehemiah's Confession

Just before the third immigration, Nehemiah called out to God, confessing his own sins and the corporate sins of his people:

O Lord, God of heaven, the great and awesome God, who keeps his covenant of love with those who love him and obey his commands, let your ear be attentive and your eyes open to hear the prayer your servant is praying before you day and night for your servants, the people of Israel. *I confess the sins we Israelites, including myself and my father's house, have committed against you. We have acted very wickedly toward you. We have not obeyed the commands, decrees and laws you gave your servant Moses* (Neh. 1:5-7, italics added).

Nehemiah acknowledged God's justice in scattering them among the nations for their sins. He also appealed to God's promises in Scripture to gather them back from the farthest horizons of exile if they returned to Him and obeyed His commands. He claimed their true identity as the redeemed people of God. Then he wrapped his prayer up for favor before the king (see Neh. 1:8-11).

Because he was the king's cupbearer, he planned to make an appeal to lead the third wave of immigrants back to Jerusalem (see Neh. 2:1-9). The king heard his surprise request and granted it. In time, Nehemiah became governor of Judah. He is famous for his leadership in rebuilding the wall of Jerusalem with a volunteer crew in a mere 52 days (see Neh. 6:15). The next task took a little longer. It was to rebuild the people.

The people assembled together and asked Ezra, the leading priest, to read from the book of the Law of Moses (see Neh. 8:1). As the people heard God's Word read and expounded, intense conviction of sin came upon them. They repented and abandoned their sins. What followed was rejoicing in the Lord and significant changes in their lifestyle. They gave themselves to obey God's Word (see Neh. 9:2).

Ezra's Confession

The fires of confession and revival spread, it appears, because on the twenty-fourth day of the same month they assembled together again (see Neh. 9:1). It is possible that many more gathered this time, including many who were not present the first time. Once more they heard God's law read and confessed their sins, both individual and corporate, including the sins of their ancestors. "They stood in their places and confessed their sins and the wickedness of their fathers" (Neh. 9:2). Some of these corporate sins included some painful memories.

But they, our forefathers, became arrogant and stiff-necked, and did not obey your commands. They refused to listen and failed to remember the miracles you performed among them. They became stiff-necked and in their rebellion appointed a leader in order to return to their slavery. But you are a forgiving God, gracious and compassionate, slow to anger and abounding in love. Therefore you did not desert them (Neh. 9:16,17).

But they were disobedient and rebelled against you; they put your law behind their backs. They killed your prophets, who had admonished them in order to turn them back to you; they committed awful blasphemies (Neh. 9:26).

But as soon as they were at rest, they again did what was evil in your sight. Then you abandoned them to the hand of their enemies so that they ruled over them. And when they cried out to you again, you heard from heaven, and in your compassion you delivered them time after time. You warned them to return to your law, but they became arrogant and disobeyed your commands. They sinned against your ordinances, by which a man will live if he obeys them. Stubbornly they turned their backs on you, became stiff-necked and refused to listen. For many years you were patient with them. By your Spirit you admonished them through your prophets. Yet they paid no attention, so you handed them over to the neighboring peoples (Neh. 9:28-30).

In all that has happened to us, you have been just; you have acted faithfully, while we did wrong. Our kings, our leaders, our priests and our fathers did not follow your law; they did not pay attention to your commands or the warnings you gave them. Even while they were in their kingdom, enjoying your great goodness to them in the spacious and fertile land you gave them, they did not serve you or turn from their evil ways (Neh. 9:33-35).

Like Daniel and Nehemiah before him, Ezra confessed the corporate sins of Israel, especially concentrating on the sins of their ancestors. The elders and people were with him in this case. However, they did more than point the finger of blame at past generations. They also confessed their own sins:

Because of *our sins*, its abundant harvest goes to the kings you have placed over us. They rule over our bodies and our cattle as they please. We are in great distress (Neh. 9:37, italics added).

The people, including their leaders, Levites, priests and Nehemiah the governor, then made a binding agreement with God. This document committed them to strict obedience to the law of Moses and its practical appli-

Jesus - "Go, show yourself to the priest
and fulfill the law of Moses

cations for their day. You might even call it something of a Prayer Action Plan (Step Six). Our point here, however, is that corporate sins do exist, that they invite God's judgment, and that leaders and people can confess them and turn away from them. This pleases God and brings His blessings upon leaders and people alike. These Old Testament examples were written for our good and the principles apply to us as well as them (see 1 Cor. 10:11; 2 Tim. 3:16; 2 Pet. 1:20,21).

The Day of Atonement

Daniel and Ezra did not dream up the concept of corporate sins. God built it into the sacrifices of Israel as He prescribed in Leviticus. The Lord designed the Day of Atonement specifically for the corporate sins of Israel (see Lev. 16). Individual sins had precise sacrifices that were required by the person who committed the transgression. But confession of individual sins alone was not enough. "Make atonement for the sons of Israel *for all their sins* once every year" (Lev. 16:34, italics added, *NASB*). On the annual Day of Atonement, "Aaron [the high priest] is to offer the bull *for his own sin offering* to make atonement for himself and his household....*He shall then slaughter the goat for the sin offering for the people*" (Lev. 16:6,15, italics added). The purpose of the Day of Atonement was not for individual transgressions but for the uncleanness, rebellion and wickedness of all Israel (see Lev. 16:15,16, 21,24,30,34).

The good news is that our Lord Jesus Christ has made a better sacrifice than the blood of bulls and goats. He is the Atoning Sacrifice for both individual and corporate sins (see Heb. 9:22-28). Because of His grace and kindness expressed to us in the perfect sacrifice of the Cross, our task is to respond to Him with repentance and faith. In Revelation 2,3, Jesus gave sharp commands to His churches in regard to their corporate sins:

Ephesus	Remember, repent.
Pergamum	Repent.
Thyatira	Hold on.
Sardis	Wake up! Strengthen what remains remember, obey, repent.
Laodicea	Be earnest, repent.

Renounce and Announce

A helpful word that summarizes what Jesus commanded His churches to do about corporate sins is "renounce." It is close to "repent," but for most people today it carries a greater sense of completely rejecting and disowning a sin (or any kind of demonic activity). "Renounce" means, according to Webster's dictionary, "to give up, especially by formal announcement." When a church renounces its corporate sins, it gives them up as their possession. It rejects and disowns them. It signs a quitclaim deed, handing them over to our Lord Jesus Christ, who died and rose to put away all sins, personal and corporate.

In the "Setting Your Church Free" process, the participants renounce the sins of Revelation 2,3, paraphrased and applied to life today. They then announce the positive biblical opposite. For the theologically minded, this amounts to repentance and faith, our biblical response to any kind of sin. Because renounce and announce will be important concepts later on, take a look at this list.

Church Renunciations

We renounce...
We renounce forsaking our first love.

We announce...
We announce that Christ is our first love because He first loved us and gave Himself an atoning sacrifice for our sins (see Rev. 2:4; 1 John 2:2; 4:10).

We renounce tolerating false teaching.

We announce that God's truth is revealed to us through the living and written Word of God (see John 17:17; Heb. 4:12; 2 Tim. 3:15,16).

We renounce overlooking non-Christian beliefs and practices among our members.

We announce that Christ is our true identity and the only way to salvation and fellowship with God (see 2 Cor. 5:17; John 14:6).

We renounce tolerating sexual immorality among some of our members.

We announce that our sexuality is God's gift, and that sexual inter-course is to be enjoyed only within the marriage of one man and one woman (see 1 Cor. 6:18-20; 2 Thess. 4:3-8; Gen. 2:24).

We renounce our reputation of being alive when we are dead.
We renounce our incomplete deeds, starting to do God's will and then not following through.

We announce that Christ alone is our Resurrection and our Life (see John 11:25,26).
We announce that Christ is the Head of His Body, the Church, and that as His members we find freedom and strength to finish the work He has given us to do (see Eph. 1:19-23; 2:10; Phil. 4:13).

We renounce disobedience to God's Word, including the Great Commandment and the Great Commission.

We announce that God energizes us to desire and to do His will so that we can obey Christ (see Phil. 2:13).

We renounce our lukewarmness, being neither hot nor cold for Christ.

We announce that Christ is our refining fire Who disciplines us for our own good so that our faith may prove genuine (see Mal. 3:1-3; Heb. 12:10,29).

We renounce our false pride in financial "security" that blinds us to our actual spiritual needs.

We announce that Christ is our true wealth, purity and insight— and outside of Him we are wretched, pitiful, poor, blind and naked (see Col. 2:1-3; Rev. 3:17,18).

Corporate Sins Today

Corporate sins are no more limited to Bible times than are personal ones. Congregations today often fall into sinful practices. Every church needs to examine its spiritual health in response to the living Christ. In my tradition, the Friends Church, we have a practice called a "Meeting for Clearness." It is a time set aside with significant leaders to discern God's will on a matter through prayer, discussion and seeking the will of the Holy Spirit. In one such meeting on a denominational level, the subject of corporate sins was explored. Among many possibilities, three seemed to stand out as especially applicable to us: rebellion, arrogance and self-righteousness. Those who know Friends history will recognize that these corporate sins lie embedded in our genes. These sins are our heredity handed down from our spiritual ancestors. What is fascinating is that each is the demonic opposite of one of our greatest strengths.

Rebellion, for example, is the flip side of the strength of standing up for truth and speaking that truth with power to those in authority. Friends, sometimes called Quakers, were among the first to win the right of religious freedom in both England and the American Colonies. It did not come easy. Many of our forefathers and foremothers were imprisoned; some were martyred. (Three men and one woman were hanged in Boston Common for preaching the Friends' understanding of the gospel.)

Arrogance, as another example, is the exact opposite of the Christlike humility that cannot tolerate sin. Friends, led by John Woolman, was the first Christian movement to free their slaves in America, nearly 100 years before the Civil War. Separated from Christ, however, humility vanishes and intolerance for God's truth, when it differs from our perception of it, becomes a real temptation.

In a similar way, self-righteousness is a distorted form of true righteousness. It is no accident that Friends, motivated by a true righteousness, produced several classics of devotion. Those who enjoy the devotional masters may recognize names such as George Fox, John Woolman, Stephen Grellet, Hannah

Whithall Smith, Thomas Kelly, Douglas V. Steere and Richard J. Foster.

Renouncing Rebellion

How does a movement or any given church renounce corporate sins such as rebellion, arrogance and self-righteousness, replacing them with their positive biblical opposite? One way is to do it in prayer, preferably in public. The following three declarations or prayers are useful for making such a break with our old sins. They also serve as illustrations of what corporate sins might look like today. In the "Setting Your Church Free" seminars, we use these as both strong prayers and as teaching tools.

> *We renounce rebellion as one of our corporate sins.* We have so often rejected authority from any source that displeases us—government, church officials, Scripture, critics of other theological persuasions, and especially our own chosen leaders. We have so often given responsibility without authority. We have so often set ourselves up as judges of the actions and attitudes of our pastors, elders and leaders. At times we have valued our own traditions above God's truth, rebelling against the very Holy Spirit we profess to obey. We rebel against evangelism because it embarrasses us. We rebel against holiness because it makes us distinct from the world around us. We blindly deny the works of Satan and his demonic forces, clearly taught in Scripture, because they do not neatly fit into our own understanding of reality. We admit that we are guilty and we repent of our rebellion.
>
> *We announce that in Christ we have godly submission to our living Lord and His called and gifted human leaders.* In Christ we submit ourselves to every authority He has placed over us—government, church officials, Scripture, whatever is true from critics of other theological persuasions, and especially our own chosen leaders. We submit to the spiritual authority of our pastors, elders and leaders, especially in the responsibilities we have given to them.
>
> We submit ourselves to the Holy Spirit and the Scriptures, including the clear commands regarding evangelism, holy living and continuous prayer. We humbly ask for the renewing, reviving work of the Holy Spirit as we love, trust and obey the Word of God.

Renouncing Arrogance

We renounce arrogance as one of our corporate sins. Pride in ourselves and in our past spiritual insights and achievements has become an idol in our hearts. We have wrongly believed that the distinctives the Holy Spirit revealed to us were superior to the distinctives the Holy Spirit revealed to others. Some of us have prided ourselves more on belonging to our denomination than on belonging to Jesus Christ. We have even taught that what we emphasize is so special that it comes across as spiritually superior—as if somehow we were God's ultimate work, His pet project, His specially chosen vessel of truth above and beyond His other children. In our arrogance we believe that we are better than others, that we have a corner on knowing God in the most intimate way. We admit that we have been deceived and we repent of our arrogance.

We announce that we have authentic humility in living union with our Lord Jesus Christ. We humbly confess that Jesus Christ is the only way to salvation and fellowship with God. Our confidence is in Him and in Him alone. We cherish what the living Christ has revealed to us through God's Spirit, God's Word, God's works and God's people. Yet we humbly declare ourselves needy of His searching light in our lives today. We gladly acknowledge that the same Lord Jesus—crucified, risen and reigning—Who gave insights to our founders is present to teach us Himself. We humble ourselves before God—heavenly Father, Lord Jesus Christ and Holy Spirit—Who alone teaches us to understand and practice His truth unveiled to us through Scripture, sound reason and the spiritual gifts of His people.

Renouncing Self-righteousness

We renounce self-righteousness as one of our corporate sins. Many of us have believed that "what's right for me" is okay, even if it contradicts the clear teaching of Scripture. Many of us consider satisfying our own needs as more important than obeying God's Word. Many of us have made up our own rules and feel content in our self-made righteousness.

As a corporate body, and as individuals, we so often tolerate these false ideas in one another and refuse to confront nonscriptural behavior, especially if we are comfortable with it.

While ignoring biblical righteousness we too quickly judge one another for not conforming to the nonscriptural expectations of our group such as appearance, social fit and religious vocabulary. We too easily believe gossip and rumor about people instead of loving and forgiving them in Christ.

We excuse ourselves and judge others, which is the heart of self-righteousness. We admit that we are guilty of setting up our own rules instead of God's, and we repent of our self-righteousness.

We announce that in Christ we have the righteousness of God that comes by faith alone. We gladly acknowledge His righteousness as a free gift of grace, which we can never earn or deserve. We announce that in Christ we increasingly are made right before God in our daily conduct. We affirm that being a Christian includes a way of life intent on obeying all that Christ commands us in His written and living Word.

We announce that in Christ we have genuine love for all people, even if they do not seem to fit into our group. Among our own members we announce the gracious accountability that encourages one another to love, to do good deeds and to practice biblical, holy living.

These examples apply to more than one denomination or grouping of churches. Parts of them, at least, fit others as well. Wherever they fit you, please use them. More important for our purpose in this book is that you understand what corporate sins are really like. If you are not yet convinced that corporate sins really exist for churches, consider one more point: Corporate sins include tolerating open sins within the church, and neglecting to do anything about them.

To Thyatira Jesus wrote, "Nevertheless, I have this against you: You tolerate that woman Jezebel, who calls herself a prophetess. By her teaching she misleads my servants into sexual immorality and the eating of food sacrificed to idols" (Rev. 2:20). Current equivalents of Thyatira's problems might be tolerating false teachers, sexual immorality by leaders or non-Christian rituals such as the New Age use of crystals or channeling. Tolerating sins, we say, can only be done by those in authority, even if they themselves are not involved. This clearly is a corporate sin distinct from an individual sin.

Procedure for Step Four

The procedure for Step Four (dealing with corporate sins) in the "Setting Your Church Free" process follows a similar format to the other steps. The participants pray a group prayer and then follow with a few moments of silent prayer. They ask the Lord to help them discern all sins of commission and omission by present and past leadership, as well as the church as a whole. This is necessary because spiritual leaders represent the body of believers, and their decisions affect the whole church. Then the facilitator asks the group to share the church's corporate sins.

One major change occurs from this point onward. Unlike the first steps, the facilitator will seek discernment from the group. From this step onward, group discernment is vital, rather than only listing each person's ideas. This builds unity and ownership. It creates balance, sharpens discernment and removes a major cause of criticism. By this time, the trust level in the group is usually high and the communication open. Because of the strangeness of the concept of corporate sins, however, this step starts slowly, gradually gaining momentum. Be patient and wait for general agreement.

The actual list will vary from church to church, but all groups so far have come up with an agreed-upon list of corporate sins. Here are actual examples compiled from several different churches, using their own words:

- Complacency and passivity;
- Apathy;
- Critical spirit;
- Self-pride ("My way is best," not humbling before the Lord);
- Unwillingness to forgive;
- Poor stewardship;
- Believing gossip and rumor;
- Power struggles;
- Allowing sins to continue, unwilling to confront;

- Accepting of unacceptable behaviors—not challenging each other, not keeping each other accountable;
- Unwillingness to evangelize.

In this step, and again in the next one, an opportunity is given to pray together against each specific sin. The suggested prayer is as follows.

Heavenly Father,
    We confess (specifically name each corporate sin) as sinful and displeasing to our Lord Jesus Christ. We turn from it, forsake it and renounce it. We thank You for Your forgiveness and purifying of our lives and our church.

In the case of our example church, this short prayer is prayed through once with "complacency and passivity" filling the blank. Then it is prayed through again, out loud and together, for "apathy," and so on through the corporate sins. Repeat it again for each item on the list. Although this sounds redundant, in practice it is quite powerful for the leaders to renounce, one by one, the corporate sins of their own church. Then they join together in a group prayer that biblically deals with corporate sins and their consequences. It also calls upon God to give His cleansing, renewal and filling. The spiritual warfare is obvious in this prayer (see appendix B).

At this point, the facilitator will invite everyone to search their own hearts. Ask for the Holy Spirit to reveal each one's participation in the church's corporate sins. Each person, as directed by the Holy Spirit, should then pray out loud, confessing personal involvement in these corporate sins. Alert everyone that it is off-limits to confess someone else's sins. (The participants will usually laugh when the facilitator says this, but it prevents a big mistake from happening.)

It is not uncommon for nearly all the participants to confess out loud in spontaneous prayer their own personal involvement in the corporate sins of the church. The sense of sincerity is transparently clear to all who are present. The moving of the Holy Spirit in the leaders' hearts and minds is evident as His cleansing takes place. Their ownership of the church's corporate sins, and then confessing them openly, seals the unity of the group as few other things will. The facilitator may want to encourage people to talk during the break with anyone in the room with whom they need to reconcile, make amends or ask forgiveness.

In one church, an older gentleman had never prayed out loud in a spontaneous way in front of any group in the church. He passed on praying anything aloud with this group except repeating the printed prayers. But during this step, he too prayed out loud in front of the group. He confessed his own sins, just as the others were doing. The Holy Spirit works in marvelous ways when we become biblically obedient in confessing corporate and personal sins.

Sense of Release

The sense of release that comes from honest confession and "letting the cat out of the bag" can be incredibly refreshing. Some were not aware of all of the corporate sins. Others had felt one or two of these sins weighing on their conscience. Although every church is different, many have left board meetings feeling spiritually defeated. They may have struggled with guilty thoughts such as, *We covered over it again,* or *I didn't want to be a troublemaker by bringing it up,* or *I must be the only one feeling this way.* Their spirit was troubled but they did not want to be negative. In some cases, they lacked the leadership or the understanding to resolve the problem.

The "Setting Your Church Free" process has created an environment where it is safe and acceptable to name corporate sins and to let Christ resolve them. The church leaders have acknowledged their corporate sins and confessed them to God. Further, the participants have acknowledged their own personal involvement and repented. These are the first steps toward setting your church free in Christ. But the process is not yet complete. In chapter 11, the group will discern the attacks of the evil one, and find out what to do about them.

DEFEATING SATAN'S ATTACKS

(Step Five in the "Setting Your Church Free" Event)

A hazy idea that Satan might put a corporate church body into bondage began coming to me in the strangest way. I had served as a denominational leader for several years, and observed many churches firsthand. Some were healthy and happy; others were diseased and unhappy. Many seemed simply to hold their own, serving quietly and well. But in a couple of churches I saw strange patterns that defied rational explanation.

Main Street Church (not its real name) was one of these two congregations. For 40 long years the people in this church have fought with each other. Their fights did not seem to occur over any one issue or between two groupings of people. But they did follow a predictable pattern, distorted though it was.

Their syndrome of conflict went something like this: An issue arose, big or small, and people chose up sides for the church fight. They inflicted verbal and emotional pain on each other. In time the winning side ran the "problem person"—the one who led the losing opposition—right out of the church.

Everyone breathed a sigh of relief that, with the problem producer gone, everything would be better. After all, the rest of that person's group remained in the church and life seemed to be getting back to normal.

A new problem soon emerged, however. Instead of returning to the same groupings as the last church fight, new coalitions formed. Former enemies became allies and former friends became foes. When it was all over, another problem person had been run off. (The church attendance kept slowly declining for years.) The time of peace did not last long until yet another conflict popped up. The same pattern repeated itself again and again, having still new groupings of good guys and bad guys. What was going on here?

Denominational Rebellion

Consider another congregation that had a different scenario. Small Town Church—again, a fictitious name—had a repeated pattern of rebellion against denominational leaders over a period of 80 years or more. Then came an interesting turn of events. An aggressive new pastor came to Small Town Church. He was brash, sometimes unwise, but too quick for the leaders to nail him to a wall. Talk about fireworks! It went from light show to light show or, to change the analogy, from Round 9 to Round 10. Anyway, within a few years almost all new attenders replaced the original members of the church. The total attendance, however, was somewhat larger than when the pastor came.

In time, this pastor accepted a call to serve in another church more than a thousand miles away. His replacement came from a different denominational background in another state and knew nothing about the history of this church. Both the new pastor and the church were doing well, when a denominational issue arose. It stirred up some heated controversy in many congregations, as these sorts of things often do. The other churches in the district seemed to take it in stride, but not Small Town Church. The pastor gave me a phone call. "Our people are talking about leaving the denomination," he reported.

I about dropped my teeth! How could a church that had a new pastor and almost 100 percent different people fall right back into their historic pattern of rebellion against denominational authority? How could they so overreact to this issue when they handled other kinds of problems in a more normal way? This pattern went way beyond any predictable group behavior a sociologist might analyze. Nor did it fit any group pathology a psychologist might describe. What was going on here?

Possible Relationship Between Fallen Angels and Churches

An unconventional thesis began to form in my mind. I began to suspect that Satan may target a church with a fallen, evil angel. If the leaders indulged in gross personal sins and the church put up with corporate sins, I might expect the demonic forces to take advantage of their vulnerability. Angels, both good and bad, are personal beings and may well have their own preferred ways of doing things. If an evil power followed predictable patterns in causing trouble in a congregation, it would repeat itself over and over. Even an outsider like myself could observe it. It would last as long as the church existed, and sometimes would defy the tenets of group psychology. Interesting theory.

Having inner feelings of "I'm on to something," mixed with understandable fear that colleagues might think I am someone who sees demons as the cause of everything, I began to share my findings with other denominational officials. They were in a position to observe many churches firsthand and were often involved in problem solving. So both within our denomination and outside of it, I shared my observations and tentative theory. To my surprise, I found a sweeping sense of agreement. Others also had observed irrational patterns that repeated themselves in the same churches. Most of my colleagues believed these patterns were more than social psychology or group dynamics could explain. Real evil was involved, and many believed as I did that it was spiritual and demonic.

Whenever Neil and I do conferences, we ask an unusual question: "How many here have been awakened, either terrorized or alertly awake, at precisely 3:00 A.M.?" At least one-third of the audience will respond that they have. Chances are they are being targeted. Just as the Lord sends angels as messengers and guardians, Satan sends demons to terrorize and harass. It is part of satanic worship to summon and send demons. Neil once asked a couple who were brought up in satanism, "What is going on at 3:00 A.M.?" They replied that it was like "prime time" spiritually.

Before you dismiss this proposition as ridiculous and unbiblical, at least think through a few questions. Is it not a fact revealed in Scripture that Satan

234 DEFEATING SATAN'S ATTACKS

exists? Doesn't the Bible say, "Our struggle is not against flesh and blood, but against the rulers, against the authorities, against the powers of this dark world and against the spiritual forces of evil in the heavenly realms" (Eph. 6:12)? Is it not true that these evil powers in the heavenly realms are fallen angels under Satan's command? Is it possible, even theoretically possible, that Satan might target Christians and churches with some of his fallen angels?

The Bible does not tell us with any precision how Satan organizes his kingdom of darkness. Some passages clearly give different names and titles to evil powers. Some suggest ranks and assignments. Some appear to teach something of a hierarchy. But all in all, we have to admit that our biblical knowledge of Satan's organization is pretty sketchy—and for good reason. If God told us precisely how Satan organized his troops, the tricky schemer would change it. Then the Bible would be full of errors. God is not stupid!

Discerning Satan's Schemes

Try a little experiment with me. Ask the Holy Spirit to help you discern evil powers and to protect your mind. Then ask Him to help you think through a few strategies of the devil. After all, Paul warns us "that Satan might not outwit us. For we are not unaware of his schemes" (2 Cor. 2:11). Ask yourself: If I were Satan, with evil powers and forces of darkness under my direct command, where would I assign them? Stop and think.

If it were me, I would assign some to governments and their leaders. I would assign some to the economy. I would assign some to the courts, to the legislative bodies, to the military and to educational systems. I would assign some to criminal warlords, organized crime and all kinds of street gangs. I would assign some to the media. I would assign some to the entertainment and music industries. I would assign some to attack institutions such as marriage and family. But you better believe I would especially assign some to churches, missions and Christian organizations!

If I (trying to play Satan) could slow down, immobilize, distract or derail the churches of Jesus Christ, everything else would be a piece of cake. If people remain blind to the gospel, they remain in the kingdom of darkness. The only human institutions that pray for God's light to dispel the darkness and then proclaim the gospel are churches and Christian organizations. I would therefore assign at least one fallen angel to every church. My point is this:

Probably Satan is much more intelligent and a better strategist than anyone who ever walked on earth, other than Jesus Christ. If we mortals can figure out that it would help the cause of evil to harass and hinder churches and their leaders, Satan must think it is too obvious even to mention.

Vulnerable Churches

Is it believable to you that the evil one snatches away some of the good seed of the gospel that is preached in your church (see Matt. 13:19)? Does it make sense that the devil sows weeds among the wheat in your fellowship (see Matt. 13:27,28,38,39)? Do you believe that someone in your church as close to Jesus as Peter can sometimes speak Satan's words (see Matt. 16:23)? Is it possible that the "rulers of this age" who caused Jesus to be crucified might attack His followers as well (see 1 Cor. 2:6-8)? Do you think the Bible means what it says when it talks about the dangers of Christians participating with demons (see 1 Cor. 10:20,21)? Do you ever consider it possible that deceitful workmen in your church are masquerading as Christ's representatives, just as Satan masquerades as an angel of light (see 2 Cor. 11:13,14)?

Do you see the point? Whether or not we believe that Satan assigns an evil angel to each local church, we have ample scriptural evidence to show that churches are in some ways vulnerable to Satan's deception and attacks. As New Testament scholar Clinton E. Arnold writes, "The powerful supernatural work of the devil and his powers sets itself against individual Christians and the church as a whole" (italics added).[1]

Seeing with Jesus' Eyes

Having this vulnerability in mind, let's look at our key passages in Revelation 2,3 once more. Please keep in mind that what people see in perplexing problems and what Jesus sees are quite different. People see other people who cause trouble; Jesus sees Satan and his henchmen who cause trouble.

To Smyrna: "I know the slander of those who say they are Jews and are not, but are a *synagogue of Satan.* Do not be afraid of what you are about to suffer. I tell you, *the devil* will put some of you in prison to test you, and you will suffer persecution for ten days" (Rev. 2:9,10, italics added).

What people saw were Jews who slandered the Christians in the Smyrna church. What Jesus saw was a "synagogue of Satan." What people saw were Roman rulers who threw Christians in jail. What Jesus saw was the devil who put some of them in prison. Not all synagogues were demonized, but this one was. Not all authorities believed lies about Christians, but in Smyrna the Roman overlords did. These enemies of the gospel were doing the devil's work, attacking the church in Smyrna.

To Pergamum: "I know where you live—*where Satan has his throne.* Yet you remain true to my name. You did not renounce your faith in me, even in the days of Antipas, my faithful witness, who was put to death in your city—*where Satan lives"* (Rev. 2:13, italics added).

What people saw was a city on a hill with major temples in it. What Jesus saw was Satan's throne. What people saw was the center of emperor worship in Asia. What Jesus saw was the city where Satan lived. This place was oppressive to Christians. It killed some of them and threatened the others. This was a dangerous place for a church. The "roaring lion" actually devoured people in this city (see 1 Pet. 5:8). Of course, that was only in Bible times, right? Satan does not actually headquarter in certain cities today, does he? Or could it be that his strategies have not changed that much?

To Thyatira: "Now I say to the rest of you in Thyatira, to you who do not hold to her teaching and have not learned *Satan's so-called deep secrets* (I will not impose any other burden on you): Only hold on to what you have until I come" (Rev. 2:24,25, italics added).

What people saw was a prophetess who taught that, since grace covered every sin, it was okay to indulge in the pagan temple feasts. What Thyatira church attenders might have heard was, "'Once saved, always saved,' and so what consenting adults do in a company party or in the privacy of their own bedrooms is not anyone's business." What Thyatira believers might have heard was, "Experimenting with New Age rituals and rites helps you understand non-Christians better so you can witness to them intelligently." What Jesus saw was that Satan's secrets were a deception for indulging in sexual sin and satanic rituals. What Jesus said was that church members were about to be struck dead for their sins (see Rev. 2:21-23).[2]

> **To Philadelphia:** "I will make those who are of *the synagogue of Satan,* who claim to be Jews though they are not, but are liars—I will make them come and fall down at your feet and acknowledge that I have loved you" (Rev. 3:9, italics added).

What people saw were two religious groups who had different interpretations about their beliefs. What Jesus saw was a demonized synagogue. What people saw was deep animosity that had religious roots. What Jesus saw was a pack of liars who were about to be proved wrong. What people saw were allegations of the dangerous practices and beliefs of Christians. What Jesus saw was a church wrongly accused. What Jesus saw was a faithful people to whom He was about to prove His love, even to their deceived enemies.

What people often see today are circumstances, group dynamics and various points of view. What Jesus sees is that the Church is under attack by Satan and his henchmen. What people see are groups who act in a way that can be explained by the culture, religion, politics, economy or one of the behavioral disciplines. What Jesus shows us is a Christian, supernatural world-view of the Church and its enemies. Dr. Timothy Warner, former missions professor at Trinity Seminary and currently vice president for International Ministries with Freedom in Christ, makes a telling comment in his lectures to missionaries around the world: "If our worldview does not allow for spirit activity in daily life, we will be easy targets for the enemy's deception and we will not reach out by faith to receive the resources available to us as God's children."

Corporate sins in a church are not the same as Satan's attacks but they do give the deceiver an advantage over us. Corporate sins give him a place to attack. He may deceive us into tolerating false teaching, and then use its lies to weaken our faith and lead us into heresy. He may dull our senses into tolerating some of our unmarried members living together and then use that "ground" to cause our youth to rationalize all kinds of sex sins. He may bombard us with noise and voices and demands and busyness until we spend little time in prayer and contemplation of the Word. Then he uses our neglect to make us apathetic and lukewarm toward Christ. He seizes on our wrongdoing for his own benefit.

Unfinished Story

From the beginning of this chapter, do you recall Main Street Church and its repeated pattern of church fights? There is more to the story. Several people retired and moved out of the community. The attendance continued to decline. As a last-ditch effort toward renewal, our denomination found an experienced interim pastor for one year whom we will call Pastor Joe. He was followed by a new pastor whom we will call Pastor Ed.

After arriving on the scene, Pastor Ed launched some research into the church's past, including its painful memories. The official minutes recorded some stormy sessions in detail. Forty years earlier the people were deeply divided about changing locations to the present site. Infighting and a gradual decline in attendance had been going on ever since. But that was not all. One of the former pastors reportedly died of syphilis. Another had to leave the church because of an adulterous affair. Although the church had many faithful pastors and good people, it appeared that the enemy had an advantage.

In more recent years, a newly started church rented Main Street Church's facilities in off-hours. Some of the members of Main Street Church did not like the new church's brand of theology nor their growth problems, constantly needing more and more space. Some of the members became fed up and began an effort to oust them from the facility. In time they succeeded.

Needing to replace the income, however, they quickly rented to a non-English speaking church that had ethnic roots in another country. Tragedy of tragedies, it turned out to be a cult that denied the deity of Christ and fouled up the Christian understanding of the Trinity. Pastor Joe, the one-year interim, objected strongly to heresy being taught in their own church building, but he found heavy resistance to canceling their lease. He did not give up, however. The local leaders of the cult group were interviewed about their false beliefs. After a stormy meeting or two among the church leaders, the renters were asked to vacate. Later, as Pastor Ed did his research, he wondered if the cult group left any lingering openings for the evil one.

Although the church had good memories, as well as the painful ones reported here, several of the recent pastors sensed a spiritual darkness and a gloom in the facility. Pastor Joe sensed it and led several people to pray from the four corners of the property. A series of special meetings with a guest speaker soon followed, and it bore fruit. The pastors of the first church that rented the facility had also sensed the same oppressive darkness. They had, in fact, confirmed it to their own satisfaction through one of their trusted visiting evangelists. Pastor Ed felt the same spirit of darkness, too, a sense of depression and despair. He began to read and study on the subject of spiritual warfare, and became convinced that the place needed a more thorough spiritual cleansing. He and a few others prayed through every room of the place, but did not yet sense any full release.

Pastor Ed called for a "Setting Your Church Free" conference. The process seemed to go well. The participants were honest in their evaluations and sincere in their prayers. But a most fascinating story emerged the next morning. Pastor Joe, a godly man of prayer, phoned from 1,500 miles away to say that he had been praying the day before. The Lord whispered to his heart, "Something powerful is happening today at Main Street Church." He phoned to confirm his sense of discernment from the Lord. When he learned that the "Setting Your Church Free" event was underway during the same time he was praying, he praised the Lord.

Pastor Ed soon sensed that the spiritual cleansing was effective. A freedom was felt in the facility. The old oppressiveness was gone. Gone, too, were the former patterns of conflict. Decisions, even tough decisions that did not please everyone, were made and implemented. Pastor Ed also began to make restitution on the church's behalf. He contacted the leadership of the church that had been ousted, seeking forgiveness. The sense of Christian fellowship was graciously restored. After this meeting, he felt a tremendous sense of release. He sensed that the old debts were canceled; the church was free and clear.

By this time, however, the church had no one to take action officially. The denominational leaders sensed that the best strategy was to close the church and plant a new, completely different congregation in the same facility after a reasonable period of time. Pastor Ed did not believe his calling was church planting.

At the time of this writing, the church has officially closed down, but the small group left has a sense of joy, cooperation and a desire to start over. They may start a Bible study during the interim time period. The cleansing of the facility, the restoration of ruptured relationships and the physical upgrades in the facility itself have prepared the way for a fresh start. From a denominational perspective, we expect a thriving church to emerge. This story is not yet finished.

What's Going On?

Having a case history before us, we can analyze the situation. Different people may reach various conclusions, but Neil and I discern a demonic presence at work in Main Street Church. We see a fallen angel or evil spirit targeting this church. The principle of Exodus 20:4-6 may apply here:

> You shall not make for yourself an idol in the form of anything in heaven above or on the earth beneath or in the waters below. You shall not bow down to them or worship them; for I, the Lord your God, am a jealous God, punishing the children for the sin of the fathers to the third and fourth generation of those who hate me, but showing love to a thousand generations of those who love me and keep my commandments.

The personal "Steps to Freedom" give this brief explanation:

> Familiar spirits can be passed on from one generation to the next if not renounced and your new spiritual heritage in Christ is not proclaimed. You are not guilty for the sin of any ancestor, but because of the sin, Satan has gained access to your family. This is not to deny that many problems are transmitted genetically or acquired from an immoral atmosphere. All three conditions can predispose an individual to a particular sin.

Because familiar spirits can follow generational lines within a single family, so they can within generations of church families. Just as physical or moral factors can play a role in a family, so social and psychological factors can enter into a church's repeated pattern of behavior. Main Street Church opened doors to the evil one through the scandal of sexual sin on the part of some former pastors. The church people repeatedly engaged in the corporate sin of divisiveness, disrupting unity within the fellowship. The refusal to forgive was evident to any objective observer. The evil powers did not lack opportunity to undermine this fellowship in corporate terms. Other than the sins of the pastors, no attempt was made to investigate the possible sinful practices of some of the members. Who knows whether familiar spirits also gained access through the sins of generations of families?

The practice of praying from the four corners of the property, and again through each room in the building, appeared to be of some help. However, it did not give full or lasting relief. Resisting the devil loosens his grip, but if the resistance does not include repentance of the personal and corporate sins as well as a commitment to obey Christ, it is unlikely that freedom will last (see Luke 11:24,25). It is fine for pastors to pray for the church, but it is much more powerful when all the responsible leaders renounce their sins, announce their resources in Christ, claim God's promises and commit themselves to replace the sin with positive action. When they follow through on their commitment, the shield of faith is held firmly in place. It extinguishes the flaming arrows of the evil one (see Eph. 6:16).

Christ's Judgments

What needs to be added here is that Christ's judgments also fall upon Christians *in this life* who fall into obvious sin and refuse to do anything about it. What is more, God's judgments come upon churches who indulge in corporate sins, or even tolerate them. Look again at Revelation 2,3:

To Ephesus: "If you do not repent, I will come to you and remove your lampstand from its place" (Rev. 2:5).

To Pergamum: "Repent therefore! Otherwise, I will soon come to you and will fight against them with the sword of my mouth" (Rev. 2:16).

To Thyatira: "I have given her time to repent of her immorality, but she is unwilling. So I will cast her on a bed of suffering, and I will make those who commit adultery with her suffer intensely, unless they repent of her ways. I will strike her children dead. Then all the churches will know that I am he who searches hearts and minds, and I will repay each of you according to your deeds" (Rev. 2:21-23).

To Sardis: "But if you do not wake up, I will come like a thief, and you will not know at what time I will come to you" (Rev. 3:3).

To Laodicea: "So, because you are lukewarm—neither hot nor cold—I am about to spit you out of my mouth" (Rev. 3:16).

Those whom I love I rebuke and discipline. So be earnest, and repent (Rev. 3:19).

The good news is that warnings of judgment are not the end of the story. Every church can turn around and follow Jesus. Every Christian can overcome and become a winner. The Spirit is speaking to the churches, and the risen Jesus walks among His people and knows what they do and what they teach. He is the living, powerful Christ revealed in the vision of Revelation 1. He has authority, power, splendor and strength to lift His people from personal and corporate sins into the joy of holy living and effective witnessing. What is more, He promises great rewards to every church that obeys Him.

Christ's Rewards

It is not the purpose of this book to become a commentary and try to explain all the symbolism of the rewards promised in Revelation 2,3. The lesson here is that Jesus does reward each Christian and every church who "overcomes." Every letter to the seven churches has a reference to overcoming, and a promise for those who share the victory of Christ's death, resurrection and powerful reign. In the New Testament, "overcomes" *(nikaó)* is a spiritual warfare word. *The New International Dictionary of New Testament Theology* tells us that *nikaó* always assumes the conflict between God or Christ and the opposing demonic powers.[3] Like Jesus, believers sometimes win by losing. They overcome by becoming martyrs, prisoners or the targets of slander and lies. They overcome by following Jesus' instructions to repent, remember, hold fast and obey.

CHURCH	PROMISED REWARD
Ephesus	"To him who overcomes, I will give the right to eat from the tree of life, which is in the paradise of God" (Rev. 2:7).
Smyrna	"Be faithful, even to the point of death, and I will give you the crown of life" (Rev. 2:10). "He who overcomes will not be hurt at all by the second death" (Rev. 2:11).
Pergamum	"To him who overcomes, I will give some of the hidden manna. I will also give him a white stone with a new name written on it, known only to him who receives it" (Rev. 2:17).
Thyatira	"To him who overcomes and does my will to the end, I will give him authority over the nations....I will also give him the morning star" (Rev. 2:26,28).
Sardis	"He who overcomes will, like them, be dressed in white. I will never blot out his

	name from the book of life, but will acknowledge his name before my father and his angels" (Rev. 3:5).
Philadelphia	"Him who overcomes I will make a pillar in the temple of my God. Never again will he leave it. I will write on him the name of my God and the name of the city of my God, the new Jerusalem, which is coming down out of heaven from my God; and I will also write on him my new name" (Rev. 3:12).
Laodicea	"To him who overcomes, I will give the right to sit with me on my throne, just as I overcame and sat down with my Father on his throne" (Rev. 3:21).

From the beginning of this chapter, do you recall Small Town Church and its pattern of rebellion against denominational authority? It hosted a "Setting Your Church Free" event. It was one of the early ones when the process was still in quite a primitive form. Nevertheless, the people identified several problem areas and dealt with them by prayer and action. Within a year, things began to happen. The church sold their present facility. Demonstrating their loyalty to God and to the denomination, they tithed their income from the sale. Most of the funds went to denominational missions, church planting and ministry projects designated by the church.

Their pastor from another church background did a fine job, but sensed the Lord's leading back to his home denomination. After a careful search, Small Town Church called a new pastor who had experience in relocating a congregation. They changed the church name and moved to a nearby community to start over. The new start was treated like a church planting project. The people worked and prayed hard, and today the church is twice its former size. The good news is that it is growing, healthy and loyal. The church found freedom from bondage and indeed is living free in Christ.

Not every "Setting Your Church Free" event produces measurable results in the life of the congregation. It is not a quick fix or a cure-all. It simply opens the way spiritually for godly, hardworking leaders to do their tasks. As Neil pointed out in the earlier chapters, leadership ability and practices hold a remarkable influence upon the ongoing life of the church. But even the best of leaders will still find themselves the bull's-eye of Satan's targeted attacks. The Christian life was never designed for luxury and ease. Christ built His Body to overcome, and to win in spiritual war!

Satan's Attacks

Let's make an important distinction before we go further. We will use the word "attacks" in a specialized way in the "Setting Your Church Free" process. Attacks from the evil one, in our terminology, are distinct from corporate sins. It is true that corporate sins give the devil an advantage. The judgments and missed rewards come upon us because of what we did wrong. But Satan's attacks, as we use the term, come because of what we do right. When churches or individual Christians love their neighbors, do good works, witness of Christ and glorify God, they can expect their adversary to oppose them. When God's people proclaim the truth, turn on the light and dispel the darkness, and see Christ set many free from bondage, Satan does not sit idly by.

How does the enemy attack churches and their people today? What kind of opposition comes from the evil one? Consider something that happens to almost every Christian family that has children. Why is it that more family hassles occur when getting ready for church than at any other time? Church usually starts later, goes for a shorter time period and expects less effort than work or school. So why the bickering and arguments on the way to church? Why is it so much harder than going to Little League or McDonald's or a school program? Have you ever noticed that when you get back into the car after church the tension is gone? No more abnormal hassles. No big arguments. Just normal family talk. Maybe, just maybe, the before-church tension is an attack from the enemy to disrupt worship and distract from the study of God's Word.

How do you know? How can you tell if such an attack is from the devil's forces? Try an experiment. For 30 days ask everyone in your family to pray for Christ's protection from the evil one on Sunday mornings (and any other regular service times). Out loud (or at least let your lips move), say something like this:

> In the name of the Lord Jesus Christ, and claiming my authority as a child of God seated in the heavenlies with Christ, I order you, Satan, to get out of here. Take all of your evil forces with you. By the authority of Jesus' shed blood and resurrected life, I command you not to harass us or even come close to us in any way except by the heavenly Father's perfect will. Go, and don't come back.

At the end of 30 days, evaluate your Sunday mornings. Our guess is that you will see a marked improvement.

A couple of other attacks are also common but seldom attributed to the enemy. Consider the problem of falling asleep during a church service, for example. Some people, of course, are so exhausted that they will sleep any time they become quiet and relaxed. But others sleep only in church, not in other settings. In those cases, it is not exhaustion at all, nor is it a boring sermon, but rather a deceitful ploy of the devil. (Of course, if too many people are consistently sleeping during sermons, the pastor may need to take a look at his delivery and content!)

What about people who never sing in church—not even a joyful noise? Some, of course, have perfectly normal reasons. They may not know the words or music. They may be embarrassed because they are tone deaf. But *others cannot sing hymns and choruses of praise to God.* They may not realize it but one of the symptoms of their bondage is that their spiritual enemy prevents them from singing. Neil reported to me that a particular elder who had made life miserable for him never sang in church. Most often these same people have fine-sounding excuses for why they do not sing. It is a good idea to test the spirits, however, and see if you are able to sing in church for at least one full service.

Leadership Attacks

One of the most common attacks identified in the "Setting Your Church Free" seminars is the harassment of Christian leaders. We believe in the priesthood of all believers and that every Christian has access to God through Christ. However, not everyone in the church is a leader. Not everyone has the same influence. Not everyone has the same gift-mix or personality or ability. Satan seems to know that Christian leaders hold strategic value to the progress of the church, and so he focuses his attacks on them.

To many people in the pew this seems strange. They seem to believe that pastors and Christian leaders live so close to God that they are immune from attack, that they live isolated from the world and protected by the ivory tower of the church's four walls. Pastors and leaders themselves know that they are under enemy fire. As I said earlier, they feel like the bull's-eye of the target for the evil one's flaming arrows. Some of the devil's attacks on Christian leaders are so common that they come up again and again.

Pastors battle to keep their priorities in balance. Priority pressures are normal, but satanic harassment is abnormal. Depression seems to strike for no apparent reason, and counseling professionals can find no cure. Slippage toward sexual immorality seems to happen to the very people who preach and teach against it. Marriage conflicts hit hard for no apparent reason and seemingly have no recourse. Unexplained hassles, far more than ordinary, sometimes come against the children of Christian leaders. Crazy thoughts of suicide or murder or running away come to kids in homes that are stable, secure and nonabusive.

Although the enemy is relentless in his attacks on Christian living and teaching within the church, he becomes even more aggressive and dangerous when we invade his territory. When a church actively engages in evangelism, backed by intercessory prayer, expect the enemy to stir up trouble. Frequent attacks and irritating harassments often occur just before activities or events that produce much for the kingdom of God. A church-planting executive complained that before every new church's opening his family would face major car trouble. It is not just that his cars broke down; after all, they were fairly old. What was amazing was the incredible timing. Attacks, harassments and irritations often hit in the week or two prior to the grand opening of a new church.

What the Devil Hates

Evangelistic events, church planting and pioneer missions can expect to meet with spiritual resistance from evil powers. Missionary experts sometimes warn against careless invasion of Satan's territory. Some of the most effective strategists are sending skilled intercessory prayer teams into the area first. After the spiritual battle is won in prayer, then the evangelists and church planters follow (see Eph. 6:18-20; Rom. 15:30).

Even then, however, expect the evil enemy to hit back to disrupt the ministry, discourage the workers, cause resistance from government officials and sometimes stir up violent persecution. What some Christians forget is that persecution is one of the promises of God. When is the last time you asked Sunday School students to memorize this Scripture: "In fact, *everyone* who wants to live a godly life in Christ Jesus will be persecuted" (2 Tim. 3:12, italics added)?

Next to non-Christians being rescued from the dominion of darkness and transferred to the Kingdom of light, what would you guess Satan hates most? Our guess is that he hates it when Christians become free in Christ. He strongly resists giving up his lies in our minds. He trembles when Christians know who they are in Christ and put on the whole armor of God. He despises their progress in holiness. He is repulsed when they honestly forgive and genuinely show love to everyone around them. He is genuinely threatened when they take sanctification seriously. He turns tail and runs when they submit to God, take their authority in Christ and then resist him by their verbal declarations.

Neil and I routinely experience the adversary's opposition before our conferences and seminars on spiritual conflicts. Some of these attacks are mere harassments of increased temptations or accusations; others are interpersonal in our marriages or families. A few are physical. If the Lord lays it on your heart to do so, our appeal is for all of our readers to pray for us and our families according to Ephesians 6:18-20:

> And pray in the Spirit on all occasions with all kinds of prayers and request. With this in mind, be alert and always keep on praying for all the saints. Pray also for me, that whenever I open my mouth, words may be given me so that I will fearlessly make known the mystery of the gospel, for which I am an ambassador in chains. Pray that I may declare it fearlessly, as I should.

Attacks on Ministry

Attacks come in direct relationship to local church ministry, too. Misunderstandings and miscommunication are normal, but deep conflicts that try to split a church from the top down are abnormal. What causes leaders to get at each other's throats, and then people start choosing up sides? Sometimes it is poor leadership, of course, but we are talking about something more malevolent that happens to good leaders. Consider another example. Discouragement seems normal enough, but how do you explain abnormal burnout or irrational desires to leave the ministry entirely?

Some attacks are subtle but do great damage to a church. It is normal, for example, to have a certain amount of turnover among lay leaders in the church because of people moving away. It is abnormal when the most promising people, often on the growing edge of ministry, move out of the community in unusual numbers and frequency. It is normal to have some periods of refreshing and some of dryness in our relationship with God. It is abnormal for Satan to lead our minds astray so that we seldom pray effectively. It is normal to be tempted; it is abnormal to feel compulsive about sinful behavior.[4] It is normal to get sick sometimes, but it is abnormal for leaders to have repeated and unexplainable recurrences of illness that devastate ministry progress.

The Bible makes it abundantly evident that Satan can hinder the direction and progress of Christian leaders. Paul wrote, "For we wanted to come to you—certainly I, Paul, did, again and again—but Satan stopped us" (1 Thess. 2:18). (For a few other biblical examples of Satan's activity, see Matt. 4:1; Acts 10:37,38; 2 Cor. 11:3.)

Protection or Perseverance?

How should we as God's people pray about Satan's attacks? Do we pray for protection? Do we pray that we will avoid pain and be exempt from hardship? Do we pray for a trouble-free church? Do we pray that we will avoid pressure and persecution at all costs? Is protection our ultimate goal?

Are we not to share the sufferings of Christ? Did not Jesus predict that we will face persecution? Should we then simply pray for perseverance; for strength to endure suffering and pain? Should we take up our cross, rejoice in the midst of evil, and put up with the attacks of the enemy? The quick answer is that we should pray for *both* protection and perseverance—but this answer is worth a little explanation.

Certainly Christians pray for protection from Satan and his evil forces. The Old Testament descriptions of God as our Rock, Refuge, Sword, Shield, Strong Tower and Fortress all suggest protection. In the New Testament, the full armor of God is protective gear and its description ends with an appeal for prayer (see Eph. 6:10-20; 1 Thess. 5:8,9). Jesus Himself prayed to the Father for our protection: "My prayer is not that you take them out of the world but that you protect them from the evil one" (John 17:15). He taught us to pray, "Deliver us from the evil one" (Matt. 6:13). Paul asked others to pray for him, and promised God's protection upon them: "And pray that we may be delivered from wicked and evil men, for not everyone has faith. But the Lord is faithful, and he will strengthen and protect you from the evil one" (2 Thess. 3:2,3).

At the same time, the Bible is clear that Christians will suffer for their faith and undergo trials of many kinds. "For it has been granted to you on behalf of Christ not only to believe on him, but also to suffer for him" (Phil. 1:29). Peter writes that Christians are not to be surprised when they suffer: "But rejoice that you participate in the sufferings of Christ, so that you may be overjoyed when his glory is revealed" (1 Pet. 4:13; also see 4:12-19). Christians overcome Satan, the accuser and deceiver, through Jesus' blood, their testimony and, if necessary, through their martyrdom. "They overcame him by the blood of the Lamb and by the word of their testimony; *they did not love their lives so much as to shrink from death*" (Rev. 12:11, italics added).

Two Exemptions
Obedient Christians, however, do not need to endure two kinds of sufferings. They do not endure the wrath of God (see 1 Thess. 1:10; 5:9; Rom. 5:9), nor do they need to suffer from the accusations, temptations and harassments of Satan, except by the perfect will of God.

When is an attack from Satan in the perfect will of God? We do not always know, but we are told that sometimes God disciplines His children for their own good (see Heb. 12:5-11). Even the apostle Paul was given a "messenger [literally angel] of Satan, to torment me" for a disciplinary purpose—"to keep me from becoming conceited" (2 Cor. 12:7). When sufferings come to faithful Christians, they need to persevere (see Heb. 10:32-36).

Praying for Protection

After the "Setting Your Church Free" sessions and after the church's leaders have worked hard to implement their findings, some pastors report intensified spiritual battles. They are making progress but not without each step being contested by the evil one. Our answer is: "Expect resistance. This is war! Spiritual warfare is not over when we start setting our churches free nor when we finish setting them free. Struggles with the world, the flesh and the devil are a normal part of the Christian's battle and the church's life. Get your church out of the hospital and onto the battlefield!"

How do you go about this? Based on Romans 12:1,2; Ephesians 6:10-18 and James 4:7, Neil strives for personal balance with the following prayer and declaration.

Prayer

Lord, I submit myself to You and yield my body as a living sacrifice. I ask You to fill me with your Holy Spirit. If what I'm experiencing is in accordance with Your will, than I gladly submit to this time of testing in order that my faith may be strengthened and my character may be made more like Yours. I believe that Your will is good, acceptable and perfect. I pray for Your protection. In Jesus' name. Amen.

Declaration

In the name and authority of the Lord Jesus Christ, I refuse and renounce any assignments by Satan that are directed at me, my family or my ministry that are not according to God's will. I command Satan to leave my presence. Since I bear the responsibility of being the head of my home, I lift the shield of faith over my family.

Church Protection Prayer

Although it is not part of the "Setting Your Church Free" process, here is a prayer and declaration of mine (Chuck) for your church's protection and perseverance. It claims Christ's resources and stands fast against the adversary:

252 DEFEATING SATAN'S ATTACKS

Prayer

Heavenly Father,

Thank You that our Lord Jesus disarmed the evil powers and authorities at the cross and in the resurrection and glorification. You made a public spectacle of them (Col. 2:15). Guide us in enforcing Your victory.

Lead us to remove the "high places" that the enemy gains in our lives through our personal and corporate disobedience, deception and disillusionment. Reveal to us our corporate sins that we may renounce, repent and reject them. Flood us with biblical truths that replace them. Forgive our lack of faith and trust in You. Forgive our lack of time in prayer. Forgive our disbelief in Your present, active power in response to prayer. Cleanse us of complacency and lukewarmness.

Cleanse us of our unwillingness to forgive one another. Forgive our withholding sacrificial love and giving only what costs us nothing. We now forgive one another from our hearts for the times we have neglected, betrayed, retreated, hurt, damaged, misunderstood, deceived or lied to one another.

Heal the pain left by attacks of Satan—and the damage caused—on our churches and leaders. Open our eyes to see any of the adversary's strongholds, and cause us to use the sword of the Spirit to stand against them in His power. Weaken whatever positions the enemy may have left.

Release Your angels to accomplish for us and for our church everything You send them to do. Remove the enemy's interference so that Your angels can minister to our church and our people unhindered.

Fill us afresh and anew with the fullness of the Holy Spirit. Lead us to live in Him, walk in Him, keep in step with Him. As Head of our church, Lord Jesus Christ, direct us, guide us, protect us. As bridegroom of Your bride, purify us, nourish us and satisfy us. As architect and builder, design us, build us, develop us. As author and finisher of the faith, teach us, instruct us and disciple us. Make us the beautiful church in Your sight that You intend us to be.

Stimulate us to respond to You with genuine faith, hope, love, obedience and holy living.

In the precious and powerful name of our Lord Jesus Christ. Amen.

Declaration

As shepherds of God's flock that is under our care, we stand our ground as overseers and examples (1 Pet. 5:1-4). We offer ourselves and our bodies to God as living sacrifices, holy and pleasing to Him, which is our spiritual worship (Rom. 12:1,2). As servants of Christ and as those entrusted with the secret things of God, we fulfill the requirement that is entrusted to us so that we may prove faithful (1 Cor. 4:1,2). We submit our ministries, our programs, our classes and groups, our activities, our facilities and all our members and attenders to God. In full union with our Lord Jesus Christ, including His protection and power, we now command Satan and all evil powers targeting our church to leave us and everything under our care. In the name and authority of Christ, we remove any advantage the adversary has gained. We forbid the evil one or his henchmen from attacking us. We accept only what is within our heavenly Father's will to accomplish His sovereign purposes. We declare that Satan and his forces are defeated through the death, resurrection and present reign of Christ at the right hand of the Father. We claim the promise of Jesus when He said, "I will build my church, and the gates of Hades will not overcome it" (Matt. 16:18).

Step Five: Identifying and Resisting Attacks

We turn now to the procedure used in the "Setting Your Church Free" day to identify and resist the attacks of the enemy. The facilitator will want to remind the group that this step has a different focus from the one on corporate sins. The last step dealt with the advantage gained by Satan because of what your church or its people have done wrong. The attacks you are going to identify in this step come because of the things that your church, your pastors and your leaders *are doing right.*

Satan will harass the pastors, leaders and people in your church at their points of greatest vulnerability. Not only are Christ's faithful followers being individually harassed, but deceived people are skillfully used by the adversary to cause disunity within the churches.

During the "Setting Your Church Free" retreat, the group prays a written prayer together, followed by silent prayer, asking the Lord to help discern accurately the nature of Satan's attacks upon the church. Group discernment is necessary once again. The facilitator may say something like, "Do we agree that this is a spiritual attack? Does anyone see it differently?" Most Western Christians have been taught that every effect has a natural explanation. Others want to see a demon as the cause of everything. It requires spiritual maturity to discern the difference. "But solid food is for the mature, who by constant use have trained themselves to distinguish good from evil" (Heb. 5:14). It takes a little longer to reach group consensus, but it is far better than listing only the ideas of one person.

Sample Attacks

Here are some examples of attacks discerned as coming from Satan and his forces of evil. The list results from conferences in several churches, but their own actual wording is used.

- On leadership—stress, division, burnout, marriage problems, anger against people;
- On families—divorce, problems with children, financial difficulties, unemployment, abuse, death, broken relationships;
- Deception that we're doing good enough;
- Attacks on pastor (and former pastors);
- Stimulate anger over false perceptions and assumptions;
- Creating apathy toward good things so they die;
- Distraction from spiritual disciplines;
- The spirit of deception;
- Things look right but are not;
- Believing rumors;
- Situations exaggerated;
- Christians have no problems, not like me.

Similar themes will come up in the various steps of the seminar, such as weaknesses, painful memories, corporate sins and attacks. This will happen naturally and will prove helpful in the next step, the Prayer Action Plan. We will discuss this repetition more in the next chapter. At this point it is enough to say that duplication is okay; in fact, it is good.

What are Christians to do about Satan's attacks? The Bible urges us to take action rather than passively withdraw. In the passage about testing the spirits (see 1 John 4:1-6), God gave us assurance of power to overcome every spirit that fails to acknowledge Jesus "because the one who is in you is greater than the one who is in the world" (1 John 4:4). When attacks from Satan or his demons strike, we are to hit back. Think of the famous passage in Ephesians 6:10-20:

- Be strong (v. 10);
- Put on the full armor (vv. 11,13);
- Stand your ground (v. 13);
- Stand firm (v. 14);
- Take up the shield of faith (v. 16);
- Take the helmet of salvation (v. 17);
- [Take] the sword of the Spirit (v. 17);
- Pray in the Spirit (v. 18).

In John's writings the key word is "overcome" (see 1 John 2:13,14; Rev. 2:7,11,17, etc.). In James and Peter, it is "submit to God" and "resist the devil" (see Jas. 4:8; 1 Pet. 5:8,9). In our terminology, we "renounce" Satan's attacks and "come against them in Jesus' powerful name." What is clear throughout the New Testament is that Christians have greater firepower than their adversary when they resist him in Christ. They are never told to fear the devil, only to fear God. One of the most devious lies from the pit is that ordinary Christians should not mess with Satan or they will really get hit. Christians are always told in Scripture to stand firm and resist. So in our procedure that is exactly what we do with the evil attacks that the group discerns.

When the list is complete, renounce, one by one, each attack as follows:

In the name and authority of our Lord Jesus Christ, we renounce Satan's attacks of (by, on, with, through [each one of the identified attacks listed]). We resist them and stand firm against them in Jesus' powerful name. Together we declare, "The Lord rebuke you, the Lord bind you" from any present or any future influence upon us.

Points of Caution

Testimonies of some former satanists and cult members would indicate that certain deceived or wicked people are deliberately out to destroy effective Christian ministries. Sometimes blood sacrifices are made to claim false ownership of Christian leaders or ministries. At other times, curses or satanic assignments are placed upon God's people or their leaders. In the past, this type of activity was more open in animistic cultures where belief in evil spirits is accepted by everyone. Western Christians have tended to dismiss the activity of witch doctors or shamans as mere superstition. As it begins to emerge in our country, however, more thinking Christians are taking a second look.

Satanists are becoming more bold. We know of one church (which can't be named because the court wisely ordered a media lid) where people from a satanic cult took children out of the nursery during worship, abused them and brought the little kids back before worship was over. Some of the accused were church members, considered to be infiltrators from the cult. In this court case, two people were convicted of child abuse and are now serving time.

Please hear our points of caution. Sometimes false memories are induced, either by Satan himself or by the subjective leading of irresponsible or unwise counselors. The result is that good people find themselves falsely accused of being everything from satanists to sex offenders when nothing could be further from the truth. The accuser of the brethren strikes again! The small percentage of false accusations then in turn causes the less informed to conclude wrongly that all memories are false. The point of caution is to make a thorough investigation before bringing any allegations. However, such allegations should not be dismissed out of hand but checked out first by church officials and then, if necessary, by civil authorities.

Breaking the Influence of Attacks

During the "Setting Your Church Free" seminar, the group will use the following declaration to break the influence of any of these attacks against the church, its leaders or its people:

Declaration

As leaders of this church and members of the Body of Christ, we reject and disown all influence and authority of demonic powers and evil spirits that cause resistance to Christ's work. As children of God, we have been delivered from the power of darkness and brought into the kingdom of God's dear Son.

Because we are seated with Christ in the heavenly realms, we renounce all satanic assignments that are directed toward our church and our ministry. We cancel every curse that deceived or wicked people have put on us. We announce to Satan and all his evil forces that Christ became a curse for us when He died on the cross.

We renounce any and all sacrifices by satanists or anyone else who would claim false ownership of us, our ministry, our leaders or our people. We announce that we have been bought and purchased by the blood of the Lamb. We accept only the sacrifice of Jesus, whereby we belong to Him.

This step concludes with a prayer for protection and dedication to God of the leaders, people and church facilities. This is more than a mere formality. Something of genuine spiritual significance takes place when we dedicate every part of our facilities to God. My own pastor, C. W. Perry of Rose Drive Friends Church, used to unlock all the doors and turn on the lights on Sunday mornings. (This was before the church became too large for him to continue.) As he turned on the physical lights, he prayed that God would turn on the light of Christ. He prayed for God's Word to flow freely from the Sunday School leaders and children's church leaders. God answered his prayers and the church built an effective Christian education ministry to people of all ages.

At a later time, the retreat participants may want to walk through every room in their church facility, rededicating it and all who use it to Christ. In this process, however, there will simply not be time nor energy to take this important step. Instead, the following prayer is used for protection and dedication to God of the leaders, people and church facilities.

Dear heavenly Father,
We worship You and You alone. You are the Lord of our lives and the Lord of our church. We offer our bodies to You as living sacrifices, holy and pleasing to God. We also present our church body to You as a sacrifice of praise.

258 DEFEATING SATAN'S ATTACKS

We pray for Your protection of our pastors, leaders, members, families, attenders and all of our ministries. Grant us the wisdom and grace to deal with heretics and spiritual wolves. We pray for discernment in order to judge between good and evil.

We dedicate all of our facilities to You, and all the property that You have entrusted to us, including our sound system, audiovisual equipment, kitchen and transportation. We rededicate our sanctuary, classrooms, offices and every part of our facility and property.

Lord Jesus Christ, You are the Head of this church, and we exalt You. May all that we do bring honor and glory to You. In Jesus' holy name we pray. Amen.

The next step is the most challenging. It involves discerning God's will for synthesizing all the input from the first five steps into a short, manageable Prayer Action Plan. This is what we have been building up to. Read on!

Notes

1. Clinton E. Arnold, *Powers of Darkness, Principalities and Powers in Paul's Letters* (Downers Grove, IL: InterVarsity Press, 1992), p. 213.
2. See the major commentaries for the interpretations that lead to this modern-day application.
3. Walther Günther, *The New International Dictionary of New Testament Theology*, Vol. 1, p. 650.
4. For practical help, see Neil Anderson's, *The Bondage Breaker* (Eugene, OR: Harvest House Publishers, 1990) and *Released from Bondage* (Nashville, TN: Thomas Nelson Publishers, 1991) and Charles Mylander's, *Running the Red Lights* (Ventura, CA: Regal Books, 1986).

THE PRAYER ACTION PLAN

(Step Six in the "Setting Your Church Free" Event)

The focal point of the "Setting Your Church Free" event is the Prayer
Action Plan. It is a plan that calls for prayer plus action. In this plan, the
group summarizes the big issues that are sinful or hurtful, and renounces
them. It then announces their resources in Christ and affirms a promise
from God's Word to overcome the sin or the pain. Finally, the group makes
a commitment to take action on each issue in a way that will correct the
wrong and advance the right. If this sounds complicated, please relax. The
final plan is really quite simple. Better yet, its goal is to respond to our living Lord Jesus so that He can glorify God through you and through your
church.

I have been looking up references in the Old Testament about splendor.
The concordance shows groupings in 1 Chronicles, Psalms and Isaiah, with
many other entries throughout the Bible. In the Chronicles and Psalms, the
emphasis is upon God's splendor rather than the splendor of nations, royalty

or creation. The Lord is robed with splendor and majesty. He calls us to worship Him in the splendor of His holiness.

> *Splendor* and majesty are before him strength and glory are in his sanctuary. Ascribe to the Lord, O families of nations, ascribe to the Lord glory and strength. Ascribe to the Lord the glory due his name; bring an offering and come into his courts. Worship the Lord in the *splendor* of his holiness; tremble before him, all the earth (Ps. 96:6-9, italics added).

Through the psalmist, God includes the "family of nations" and "all the earth" in this call to ascribe to the Lord the glory due His name. This is not for the nation of Israel alone, but for God's people everywhere. God intended for Israel to serve as a magnet to draw others to Himself, and Christ commissioned the Church to take His message to all the nations. Certainly the good news must include Christ's royal splendor and majesty, clothed in the humility of human flesh (and a crucified "criminal" at that!) and yet exalted to the highest place, the place of honor, glory, praise, majesty and splendor (see Phil. 2:4-11).

Display of Splendor

What amazed me was how often in the references from Isaiah the Lord revealed His intent to display His splendor among His people. Perhaps this is why the seven churches of Revelation 2,3 are pictured as lampstands. They hold the true light that gives light to everyone (see John 1:4,9). They radiate the splendor of the glory of God. "For God, who said, 'Let light shine out of darkness,' made his light shine in our hearts to give us the light of the knowledge of the glory of God in the face of Christ" (2 Cor. 4:6). I believe that churches living free in Christ will fulfill God's eternal purposes of revealing His glory and displaying His splendor.

> Surely you will summon nations you know not, and nations that do not know you will hasten to you, because of the Lord your God, the Holy One of Israel, for *he has endowed you with splendor* (Isa. 55:5, italics added).

Then will all your people be righteous and they will possess the land forever. They are the shoot I have planted, the work of my hands, *for the display of my splendor* (Isa. 60:21, italics added).

And provide for those who grieve in Zion—to bestow on them a crown of beauty instead of ashes, the oil of gladness instead of mourning, and a garment of praise instead of a spirit of despair. They will be called oaks of righteousness, a planting of the Lord *for the display of his splendor* (Isa. 61:3, italics added).

It is inevitable that some of this prophecy will find fulfillment when Christ comes again and gathers His people to Himself, but I believe there is a present fulfillment as well. God intends to display His splendor, the splendor of the exalted Christ, among His people today, including your church. Ask the Lord, "Where is the church that you have endowed with splendor? Where are the people who display your splendor? Could it not be our church? Could it not be our people?" Why not ask the Lord to set your church free and fill it with the splendor of His holiness?

God begins with leaders who are willing to seek Christ to display His splendor. As we have seen in Revelation 2,3, displaying His splendor requires facing up to weaknesses, painful memories, corporate sins and satanic attacks. His splendor is displayed when leaders encourage freedom in Christ to flow to others in their fellowship. Corporate freedom results, we believe, when leaders create an environment where all can grasp their identity in Christ, win the battle for their minds and go through the personal "Steps to Freedom" or some other means of finding their freedom in Christ. Certainly it occurs when church leaders pray and act so that the splendor of God's glory in the church is not eclipsed by corporate and personal sins. Jesus said, "Let your light shine before men, that they may see your good deeds and praise your Father in heaven" (Matt. 5:16).

In some ways, the glorious idea of displaying God's splendor in your church and your community may seem too high and lofty, too far removed from the violent and adulterous generation in which we live. But then, if there is no vision of Jesus' risen grandeur, of His majesty, glory and splendor, who will want to change? If there is no vision of the splendor and majesty of God, the people will perish.

Listen to the Lord of Splendor

The Lord Jesus gave some sharp commands to His churches about their weaknesses, memories, corporate sins and evil attacks. Let's review them and then consider our response:

Ephesus	Remember, repent.
Smyrna	Be faithful.
Pergamum	Repent.
Thyatira	Hold on.
Sardis	Wake up, strengthen what remains, remember, obey, repent.
Philadelphia	Hold on.
Laodicea	Be earnest, repent.

Our response to these commands is built into the Prayer Action Plan. It makes four declarations: "We renounce..." "We announce..." "We affirm..." and "We will..." Each one of these declarations captures our response to the marching orders from Jesus. Here are the connections:

- *We renounce* is our response to Christ's command, "Repent."
- *We announce* is our response to Christ's command, "Remember."
- *We affirm* is our response to Christ"s command, "Hold on."
- *We will* is our response to Christ's command, "Obey."

It is important that all the church leaders know what they are doing in the Prayer Action Plan. Let's carefully examine these four commands and our responses.

Repent and Renounce

Again and again Jesus commands His churches to repent. No messing around. No delays. No excuses. It is time to change and it is time to change now. Jesus wants quick, decisive action. He shouts, "Stop! Don't do that anymore!

Change your attitude! Change your lifestyle!" He wants His churches to make a clean break with their personal and corporate sins, once and for all.

Jesus is ordering His churches, including yours, to repent. This cold-water-in-the-face treatment is meant to shock you into a quick turnaround. These matters do not require six committees to study them for a year and a two-inch-thick document of environmental impact on your church. Jesus is talking about sin, offensive to Him and damaging to His people. He wants His church to abandon their sinful ways right now.

We respond by *renouncing* what so displeases Christ. We plead guilty and openly admit that we are in the wrong—but we do more. We repudiate the sin. We reject it, disown it, disavow it. We forsake it once and for all. We abandon it forever. We give up any right that we might claim to hang on to it. We reject the devil's lies about it that excuse our continued indulgence. We are through with it forever. We change our thinking and change our ways.

"We Renounce..."

One of the oldest declarations of the church is this: "I renounce you, Satan, and all your works and all your ways." It is in the *Book of Common Prayer* as part of the baptismal ritual, and many liturgical churches still use it. Why have other churches dropped it? When done from the heart and with the direction of the Holy Spirit, it holds decisive power. What kinds of things do churches renounce in the "Setting Your Church Free" process? Here is a representative list taken from various actual churches, again using their own wording:

- We renounce complacency and contentment.
- We renounce a critical and judgmental spirit.
- We renounce our passivity in spiritual disciplines.
- We renounce gossip and pettiness.
- We renounce moral failure.
- We renounce factions in the church that separate us from the love and unity of Christ.
- We renounce lukewarmness and weariness in doing the Lord's work.
- We renounce our distrust of God's chosen and faithful leaders.
- We renounce our sinful pride that keeps us from confessing our

sins and receiving salvation and healing.

- We renounce our poor stewardship of time, talent and treasures.
- We renounce our selfish pride that says, "We're good enough."
- We renounce our self-focus that produces apathy to the lost.

Although church leaders most often renounce corporate sins, they do not stop there. Some will renounce Satan's attacks or painful memories or simply weaknesses. Here are more examples:

- We renounce attacks of the devil in stimulating doubts and disagreements.
- We renounce ungodly values that the world imposes on our families.
- We renounce the spirit of darkness and heaviness that seeks to destroy our church.
- We renounce the spirit of fear that paralyzes open sharing, involvement, service and evangelism.
- We renounce attacks on leadership.
- We renounce any footholds gained by the evil one through past hurts and traumas.
- We renounce the spirit of criticism that divides rather than unites.
- We renounce Satan's use of discouragement as a tool against us.
- We renounce a spirit of division and defeat.
- We renounce the "destroyer" spirit and all his attacks on our church and community.

Having the "repent and renounce" declaration in mind, let's turn to the second response to Christ's commands. He commands us to remember, and we respond by announcing the riches we have in Christ.

Remember and Announce

It is so easy to forget. It is so easy to become absorbed in our problems instead of being intensely conscious of Christ's power. It is so easy to let His presence and riches slip out of memory and live as if we had seldom heard the truth. One of the challenges of the Christian life is to keep in mind who we are in

Christ, what He has done on our behalf and how rich we are in connection with Him. It is not that we do not know these things intellectually. We know, and Jesus wants us to keep reminding ourselves. This kind of memory jogging is more than a mental exercise; it is a spiritual discipline. It is a matter of calling on our God-given riches and claiming them in Christ.

We respond to Christ's call to remember by *announcing* our resources in Christ. We not only remember, we declare together that we remember. In so doing, we focus on our riches in Christ, rather than on our poverty without Him. We recall our position in Christ rather than the pain from our past. We feature Christ's helpfulness, rather than our helplessness. We fix in our minds the positive biblical opposite of what we renounced. The best way to make this clear is by example. As illustrations, let's look at part of our former list, along with the positive biblical opposites. Again these are actual declarations from real churches.

- We *renounce complacency and contentment.*
- We announce that in Christ we have vision, boldness, freedom and confidence.
- We *renounce a critical and judgmental spirit.*
- We announce that in Christ we have love and acceptance for one another.
- We *renounce our passivity in spiritual disciplines.*
- We announce that in Christ we have spiritual hunger for intimacy with God.
- We *renounce gossip and pettiness.*
- We announce that in Christ we have the Holy Spirit who brings unity.
- We *renounce moral failure.*
- We announce that in Christ we have moral fidelity.
- We *renounce factions in the church that separate us from the love and unity of Christ.*
- We announce that we are one in Christ Jesus.

If the renounce and announce pattern makes sense to you, then we are ready to consider the third declaration. Jesus commands us to hold on, and we respond by saying, "We affirm." Although what we announce focuses on our resources in Christ, what we affirm focuses on God's promises. In the affirmations, we look for motivational truths that encourage us to use the riches we have announced as ours in Christ.

Hold On and Affirm

The living truth of the gospel is worth holding on to. It helps us to get a grip on the great and precious promises of God and never let go. We hold on so we can hold up. When life is tough, we hold on to what Christ has given us so that we can hold up under the crushing burden of hard times. When life is easy, we must resist the deception of turning loose of our riches for the glitter of a cheap substitute. Whatever happens, hold on!

A closely related command comes from Christ: "Be earnest" (Rev. 3:19, *NIV*), or "Be zealous" *(NASB)*. The motivated Christian has passion as well as discipline. Fervent in faith, enthusiastic about Jesus, intense about obedience, glowing with the Holy Spirit and ardent in worship describe this kind of motivation. Hold on to what you know to be true and affirm what motivates you to use your God-given resources for Christ.

Let's consider some of our declarations again with the affirmation statement added:

- We *renounce complacency and contentment.*
- We announce that in Christ we have vision, boldness, freedom and confidence.
- We *affirm that we are children of God and have all His resources.*
- We *renounce a critical and judgmental spirit.*
- We announce that in Christ we have love and acceptance for one another.
- We *affirm that Christ brings unity and peace among us.*
- We *renounce our passivity in spiritual disciplines.*
- We announce that in Christ we have spiritual hunger for intimacy with God.
- We *affirm that we were created for fellowship with God.*
- We *renounce gossip and pettiness.*
- We announce that in Christ we have the Holy Spirit who brings unity.

- We *affirm that Christ can bridle our tongues and show us how to resolve problems.*

Sometimes the participants mix up the announce and the affirm declarations. In the most recent seminars we have found it helpful to keep the "We affirm" statements centered on the promises of Scripture. Here are a couple of examples:

- We *renounce acting independently of God.*
- We announce that in Christ we have God and all His resources.
- We *affirm that we can do all things through Christ who strengthens us* (see Phil. 4:13).
- We *renounce our lack of commitment to and practice of spiritual disciplines.*
- We announce that in Christ we have continual opportunity to commune with God.
- We *affirm that Christ is knocking at our heart's door, longing for intimacy with us* (see Rev. 3:20).

Will to Obey

Having the first three declarations in mind—renounce, announce, affirm—we are ready for the fourth. Jesus does not give us orders and commands without expecting us to obey them.

A young pastor told me of talking with his junior and senior high school youth. He asked them to be aware of his vocabulary while he was preaching. He did not want to use words that were out of date or that did not communicate. After listening for some time, the youths made a strange comment—at least, it seemed strange to my ears. They said "obey" was not a word in their regular vocabulary. It is a word they neither heard nor used. What does that say about the breakdown of authority in this country? In any case, Jesus has all authority and He does not hesitate to tell (not ask) us to obey.

The Prayer Action Plan calls for prayer plus action. The final declaration is the action step. In response to Christ's call to obey, we respond that *we will* do what He desires. It should be noted that each of the declarations are connected. It often helps in the "We will" stage to look back at what the group renounced in the first declaration. In light of that renunciation, what does Jesus want us to do to obey Him? How can we best comply with His orders? What action can we take to counter the corporate sin or attack that we renounced?

Consider our examples once more, this time the action step is added.

- We *renounce complacency and contentment.*
- We announce that in Christ we have vision, boldness, freedom and confidence.
- We *affirm that we are children of God and have all His resources.*
- We will step out in faith from our comfort zone.
- We *renounce a critical and judgmental spirit.*
- We announce that in Christ we have love and acceptance for one another.
- We *affirm that Christ brings unity and peace among us.*
- We will accept our differences as strengths.
- We *renounce our passivity in spiritual disciplines.*
- We announce that in Christ we have spiritual hunger for intimacy with God.
- We *affirm that we were created for fellowship with God.*
- We will teach, preach and regularly practice the spiritual disciplines.
- We *renounce gossip and pettiness.*
- We announce that in Christ we have the Holy Spirit who brings unity.
- We *affirm that Christ can bridle our tongues and show us how to resolve problems.*
- We will speak the truth in love.

Step Six of the "Setting Your Church Free" Procedure

The Prayer Action Plan (Step Six) synthesizes the information gathered in the earlier steps. It puts them into a one-page format that can be prayed individually and corporately. The facilitator or any of the group members will want to place four large sheets of paper side by side on the wall. All of the previous sheets should also be visible. On the first sheet write, "We renounce..." On the next three sheets jot down in order, "We announce..." "We affirm..." and "We will...." The group is now ready to combine everything discerned so far into the short, summary declarations.

The facilitator will briefly review what the group is summarizing.

1. We will want to *renounce the evil* (attacks, corporate sins, conflicts, weaknesses). For example, "We renounce division among us."
2. Next we will *announce the positive biblical opposite of what we renounced* worded in terms of our resources in Christ. ("We announce that in Christ we have the unity of the Spirit.")
3. Then we will *affirm in emotional language a scriptural promise or truth that encourages and motivates us* in regard to the same item. ("We affirm that in the depths of our hearts we are all one in Christ Jesus" [see Gal. 3:26-28].)
4. Finally, we will *commit to an action step that we will take.* ("We will talk to the right person in the right spirit when conflicts arise.")

Work out the first item on the list following the order of "We renounce," "We announce," "We affirm" and "We will." Then go on to the next item, and so on.

The goal in this crucial statement is to make the shortest list possible without leaving out any major pattern of bondage within the church. This list, along with the greatest strengths of the church, becomes the Prayer Action Plan, and so it holds special importance. (See the end of appendix B for an example.) Proceed with a group prayer, followed by silently listening to the Holy Spirit. It is important to ask for the Holy Spirit's discernment, unity, as well as the right words and order of items listed. Fatigue is a factor by now, so call upon God for divine energy and wisdom to make sense out of all the lists on the sheets (see Col. 1:29).

also see . 30
II Cor. 11 :23

Making Sense of It

By this time in the "Setting Your Church Free" day (or evening by now), the task of making a clear summary feels next to impossible. Some of the participants may find it hard to think, just when they need the mental energy the most. If it is any encouragement, every group can and does come up with an intelligible Prayer Action Plan. The facilitator, along with the more verbal people in the group, may lead the way in suggesting wording, but soon almost everyone will enter into the discussion. It is important to seek mutual agreement for how to word the items.

This part of the process is extremely valuable to the participants. It seems impossible to capture on paper the sense of discovery as the group interacts with one another. In some churches this environment for honest communication is just what is needed. What is so helpful is that the group is neither arguing nor problem solving, but simply coming to consensus. One person wrote that this feature of the seminar was the most helpful.

> My best memory from the hours the elders and pastors spent together was all the communication that finally took place. The people need an opportunity to communicate instead of gossiping to share their feelings. It was difficult to talk about some issues but they needed to be brought up! I believe a lot of people felt good about finally being able to share their feelings. I've always known how important communication is, but I really didn't realize how important it is to set an environment for people to be able to talk. It is important to help people feel free to open up. I will try to be aware of this now!

In the discussions, the typical group will discard some suggestions and modify many others. What they state will fit the theology, concerns and style of their own church because they, not the facilitator, are discerning the declarations. Each list is unique, stated in a way that only this church and this group of leaders can describe. Ownership grows because of this process of coming to unity.

When the process lags, the facilitator may use questions such as: "Is there any other major theme that we have not addressed?" or "What else do you see?" Then a "Do we have it; have we done it?" is a final check that this step is complete. Near the end of this step, the facilitator or someone in the group may sense that the Holy Spirit is giving a sense of completion. It is not necessary to cover every item on the sheet, but rather the major patterns. Five to eight items for each of the four declarations (on the four sheets) is the usual number to be completed.

Binding and Loosing

When the declarations are finished, all the group should stand and position themselves so they can read the four sheets. Then they hold hands and pray the Prayer Action Plan aloud. *This prayer is essential.* All the authority of heaven stands behind church leaders who fully agree and unite in prayer about a matter that they discern in the presence of Christ. When they declare it together, they are exercising the power of binding and loosing (see Matt. 16:19; 18:18-20). This is important enough to merit a good look at these two passages in the Bible.

> I [Jesus] will give you the keys of the kingdom of heaven; whatever you bind on earth will be bound in heaven, and whatever you loose on earth will be loosed in heaven (Matt. 16:19).

> I [Jesus] tell you the truth, whatever you bind on earth will be bound in heaven, and whatever you loose on earth will be loosed in heaven. Again, I tell you that if two of you on earth agree about anything you ask for, it will be done for you by my Father in heaven. For where two or three come together in my name, there am I with them (Matt. 18:18-20). *Thank you Jesus!*

Do we manipulate God like a puppet on a string? Do we make up our minds about something and then God must enforce it? Is this what Jesus teaches here? Hardly! An interesting footnote occurs in the *New International Version* and most other modern translations of the Bible. It indicates that the original Greek text reads, "Whatever you bind on earth will *have been* bound in heaven and whatever you loose on earth will *have been* loosed in heaven" (italics added). This strange grammatical construction suggests a vital truth. The task of church leaders is to discern what has already been bound or loosed in heaven; then they bind or loose it on earth. (In the Prayer Action Plan we bind by *renouncing* and loose by *announcing).* We never ask the Lord to capitulate to our will. In this process, we prayerfully seek to discern His will and then seek to carry it out.

The Gospel of Matthew repeats the same teaching in two different contexts. In chapter 16, the verse follows Peter's declaration that Jesus is the Christ, the Son of the living God (see Matt. 16:16). As part of His response Jesus promises, "I will build my church, and the gates of Hades will not overcome it" (Matt. 16:18).

R. E. Nixon writes, "The gates suggest the picture of a fortress or prison which lock in the dead and lock out their rescuers. This would imply that the church is on the offensive, and its Master will plunder the domain of Satan."[1] Please note the spiritual warfare reference in this passage and in Matthew 12:29. In the Prayer Action Plan, we renounce the efforts of the "gates of Hades" to hold people captive and hinder the building of Christ's Church. Then we announce our resources in Christ by which our Lord builds His Church.

Church Discipline

In Matthew 18, the context is church discipline and resolving conflicts between brothers in Christ. These are among the issues that the "Setting Your Church Free" process addresses. Again we are using the passage in context and for the purpose Jesus intended. The fact that this teaching is used in two different contexts in Matthew may indicate that the Church can use it wherever applicable. In any case, we are on safe biblical grounds in using our God-given authority to bind and loose, renounce and announce, what we agree upon as Christ's will for our local church.

Authorized by Christ
Let's be clear about what the Church is authorized by Christ to do.

The Church has prayer authority. When we agree in prayer about each issue in our Prayer Action Plan, we can claim the promise of two or more agreeing together (see Matt. 18:18-20). More than two of us agree as we ask God for the items mentioned and so He will honor our faith with His answer.

The Church has teaching authority. We have the God-given right to teach and preach what we scripturally discern as Christ's will for our church.

The Church has disciplinary authority. If we find that members, and especially leaders, of our church are living in defiance of clear scriptural teachings, and we agree about our discernment of Christ's direction for what we must do, He gives us the authority to take action within our church.

Church discipline is always a painful and touchy subject. Yet we dare not ignore what the Bible teaches. We are not to judge when the issue is a speck in our brother's eye (see Matt. 7:1-5). However, the church is committed to judge when the matter is an open disgrace (see 1 Cor. 6:1-6; 1 Tim. 5:19,20). Church discipline for certain public sins is a command of Jesus and the New Testament (see Matt. 18:15-17; 1 Cor. 5:3-13). Having a variety of actions to be taken, the Bible specifically names disorderly conduct, divisiveness, sexual immorality, false teaching, drunkenness, abusive speech, swindling and idolatry as issues requiring church discipline (see Rom. 16:17,18; 1 Cor. 6:9-11; 2 Thess. 3:6-15; 1 Tim. 1:20; 2 Tim. 2:17,18; Rev. 2:14-16).

Ignore church discipline, and you may suffer public scandal. Non-Christians use public church sins as an excuse for rejecting Christ. Weak Christians too often follow the example of a fallen leader in disobeying the Lord Jesus. The media love to exploit scandals of all kinds, including TV evangelists and high-profile pastors. Recent Christian leaders falling prey to sexual immorality or financial abuse fueled the media fire. Jim Jones and the mass suicide at Jonestown, or David Koresh and the fiery confrontation with authorities at Waco, also provide sober reminders of the danger when religious leaders become cultic. Wise church leaders must practice church discipline, but if they are smart they will do it as if they were handling a cobra—very carefully.

A Biblical View

For years, Neil taught biblical principles of church discipline in his seminary classes. As a denominational official, I have experienced my share of personal pain, not to mention witnessing the pain of others involved in disciplinary processes. When it comes to dealing with an unrepentant offender, there is no clean and easy way for it to be done. Open sin is scandalous and offensive. No simple way exists to fix it. The tension between the need to protect the church and the desire to restore the offenders will not go away. Often deceit and dishonesty on the part of the offenders complicate the issues even further. Church discipline is not to be done lightly or unadvisedly. Here are a few biblical principles and practical insights gleaned from what we have learned. Discipline is the proof of Christian love (see Heb. 12:5-11) and essential for the health of the church. To pray passively, asking God to do what He has already commanded church leadership and parents to do, is to fail in our responsibility as church leaders and as parents. The purpose for discipline is twofold. First, it is to carry out the ministry of reconciliation in restoring a Christian brother or sister caught in a sin (see Gal. 6:1). Always keep in mind, *the goal is not to expose the sin but to win back the offender.* The second goal of discipline is to maintain the purity of the church (see Acts 5:1-11; Heb. 12:10-12).

It is essential to base discipline upon prior instruction and observed behavior. If reputable witnesses observe behavior, if the evidence is beyond reasonable doubt or, most commonly, if the person confesses when confronted, there is no judgment in view at all. The person is "caught in a sin" (see Gal.6:1). When all attempts at reconciliation have failed, Scripture clearly teaches a breaking off of fellowship; in addition, the nature of the sin is to be told to the church (see Matt. 18:15-20; 1 Tim. 5:19,20).

Some major questions of interpretation must find their answers in church polity. Who decides when loss of fellowship or membership is required? Does knowledge on the part of the elders or church board constitute telling the church? *A word to the wise: Always honor the procedures of your church's polity in disciplinary matters. In a lawsuit-crazed society, following due process saves much grief.* However, no church polity or lack of it can nullify the commands given to church leaders in Scripture. (In addition to the passages already cited, please see 1 Thess. 5:14; 2 Thess. 3:14,15; Titus 3:9-11.)

Who Is Disciplined?

Most church discipline takes place in private, as it should. Pastors and church elders confront situations in their churches by using discretion and dignity. The offenders most often turn around in their lifestyle or quietly leave the church before any further action can be taken. When it comes to public church discipline, new Christians seldom if ever should receive it. They are growing in grace, trying to change their former way of life, and working themselves out of messes from their non-Christian days. The key issue to ask about a babe in Christ is, "Which way is this person going—toward Christ or away from Him?" If the answer is that the person is moving toward Christ, then public church discipline is most often inappropriate.

Entrenched church members of long standing are probably the most difficult to handle. These people have connections within the congregation, know the ropes politically and will appeal to people's sympathies. When it becomes known that they are living a double life and a refusal to change is evident, the church leaders need all the wisdom they can find, both from God and His people. This is the time to pray hard, stick close to Scripture, listen to the Holy Spirit, make personal appeals, take action discreetly but as boldly as necessary and consult legal counsel. Either hasty action or cowardly refusal to act can damage the church for years to come.

Most church discipline finds its focus on paid pastors and staff members or other full-time Christian workers. Most often they are asked to resign or are simply fired. The debates rage around how public to make their sins in order to obey Scripture, and whether or not they should be restored to full-time Christian ministry. The issues become complicated because almost all Christian professionals profess repentance, whether their lifestyle changes or not. Their own guilt stimulates them to do what is right, but their shame often drives them to do what is wrong. In most cases, the Spirit and the flesh have been battling for a long time, and secret sins have gone unchecked. It takes time and much accountability for genuine restoration to succeed.

Risking Lawsuits

What raises the stakes for many of us are the increasing number of cases in which offenders take the church to court. Although traditionally civil courts refuse to hear cases involving internal church disputes, a few recent suits indicate the courts may interfere if slander, libel, invasion of privacy or economic disaster are involved.

The specter of a church being taken to court because of church discipline toward members living in defiance of Scripture raises some important questions. What is the basis of a lawsuit against a church in a discipline case? How can a church protect itself and still obey the commands of Jesus? What

276 THE PRAYER ACTION PLAN

precautions can a church take to stay out of legal trouble? What are the limits of the law that everyone, including church leaders, must abide by? The Bible tells us, "Be wise in the way you act toward outsiders" (Col. 4:5; also see 1 Thess. 4:12; 1 Tim. 3:7; 1 Peter 3:16,17).

Legal Pitfalls

People who win lawsuits against churches usually base their case on violation of one or more sensitive legal issues; we strongly recommend that you confer with a Christian attorney for legal counsel. Every church leader, however, should know in advance about three common pitfalls.

1. Slander, libel or defamation of character is illegal. Slanderous statements are untrue, or they may be true but intended to damage a person's reputation. The legal key to this tricky lock is that it must be published to a third party before the matter is considered slander. It is not slander or libel for the pastor, elders or the official board to confront a church member about sexual immorality or a scandalous sin. It is slander if they publish it to others in a way that damages the person's reputation.

2. Invasion of privacy is illegal. This provision is difficult for churches because legitimate privacy rights are sometimes used as a cover for private sin. However, churches cannot legally take a private relationship and make it public in a harmful way. Church discipline by the pastor, elders or church board is not invasion of privacy if these standards are previously published and known by the offender. Even so, caution is needed. Any public censure or excommunication proceedings must use fairly general terms. All statements, written and oral, need to be prepared carefully and fall in line with Scripture and official church polity.

3. Inflicting a detrimental effect on a person's economic status is illegal. One church took disciplinary action against a member who worked as an insurance salesman. Most of his customers were also members of the same church. The church leaders advised the people not to aid him in any way. Many of the church members dropped their insurance policies purchased from him, and his business declined dramatically. He sued. The caution here is for churches not to go beyond their biblical limits of discipline. Dropping a person from membership and fellowship is legal; inflicting economic harm is not.

Wise Precautions

A church can do a few things to protect itself from losing a lawsuit.

1. A church can publish its standards of conduct and church discipline and communicate them to all members. The membership class may be the ideal place to explain Scripture relating to church discipline. In a positive way, the leaders can explain why we care so much about each other that we resolve conflict early and in private. Public discipline is a last resort that will be imposed only under the conditions stated in the church's standards of conduct and church discipline. Disciplinary matters in the church are never to be settled in public courts (see 1 Cor. 6:1-11). Independent Christian mediation organizations are often helpful in resolving disputes between church members.

2. A church can communicate what steps of disciplinary action it may take and in what kinds of cases (see 1 Cor. 5:1-5; 6:9-11; 2 Thess. 3:14,15; 1 Tim. 1:20; 2 Tim. 2:17,18; Rev. 2:14-16. Also see my chapter, "When the Church Must Get Tough" in *Running the Red Lights* for a more extensive treatment[2]). All church staff members should be notified in writing in advance of their hiring that immediate dismissal is the consequence of sexual immorality, financial fraud or any scandalous sin. After making the basic knowledge known, it is better to act than to talk. In other words, no threats allowed. The church must follow its stated polity and procedures explicitly and use due diligence. Counseling and restoration procedures must be part of the process so that the offender does not repeat the same sins in the next church.

3. A church needs to limit the number of people who are part of the process and give only general information to others. This is both gentle and wise (see Gal. 6:1; Eph. 5:15,16). Any written letters to the offenders need to show the biblical basis for the actions, review the steps taken and avoid anything that might be construed as slander. In most cases, it is wise to keep everything, including church minutes, out of print or in general terms. Written documents provide the kind of evidence attorneys love to use in court.

We purposely took a bird walk away from the procedure of Step Six. The subject of church discipline is simply too explosive today to ignore. Let's return now to the Prayer Action Plan that the participants have just prayed through. In prayer, they bind what has been bound in heaven and loose what has been loosed in heaven. They have discerned Christ's will for their church and have finished praying it together.

Praying in Unity

A sense of accomplishment sweeps across the group as they join together in declaring their Prayer Action Plan to God. The feeling of joy is almost tangible. But what participants remember most is the incredible unity. One pastor wrote, "My best memory from the 'Setting Your Church Free' seminar was the sense of unity with which everyone responded. Although each person had unique insights and comments, when it came to the *big* issues, there was unity and agreement and a sense of working together." His comments are typical and not the rare exception.

The Prayer Action Plan becomes a tangible way to submit to God and resist the devil on behalf of the whole church. "Submit yourselves, then, to God. Resist the devil, and he will flee from you" (Jas. 4:7). One church went through the "Setting Your Church Free" event and gained much helpful insight. Later, however, the pastor commented, "I didn't realize this was like a letter from Jesus. That would have added a lot of power to it!" Think of your Prayer Action Plan as a letter from Jesus. At the very least, think of it as your discernment of what Jesus would write in a letter to your church.

What has happened so far in the process is eye-opening. Most of the church's leaders arrive for this event, having only hazy ideas about their own corporate sins and attacks from the evil one. Now they are in unity about the actual spiritual health of their church, and have a plan that calls for prayer plus action. One person wrote, "Since completing the 'Setting Your Church Free' seminar, we have a concrete understanding of our strengths and weaknesses, areas where God is blessing and areas where the enemy has strongholds. We now have the ability to pray and work specifically to be completely free."

Act in obedience to the Holy Spirit and make the necessary changes in your lives and in your church. It is not by accident that each of the seven letters of Revelation contains the exhortation, "He who has an ear, let him hear what the Spirit says to the churches" (Rev. 2:7; also see Rev. 2:11,17,29; 3:6,13,22). Please recall: hearing in the Hebrew way of understanding meant hearing and obeying.

When our children, Kirk and Lisa, were small, they would sometimes procrastinate or stall when my wife, Nancy, and I had asked them to do something. We would then ask them, "Did you hear me?" We knew they heard us with their physical ears; that was not the question. The real question, which we knew they understood perfectly well, was, "Are you going to obey me now?" Let no hindrance keep you from hearing what the Holy Spirit says to your church. Let nothing stop you from applying Christ's message to your church and obeying Him now. Your church's angel is waiting with rewards or judgments to see how you respond to the living Lord Jesus!

A strategy for putting the message of this book into action is the subject of our last chapter.

Notes

1. R. E. Nixon, "Matthew," *The New Bible Commentary: Revised* (Grand Rapids, MI: Wm. B. Eerdmans Publishing Co., 1970), p. 837.
2. Charles Mylander, *Running the Red Lights* (Ventura, CA: Regal Books, 1986).

A LEADERSHIP STRATEGY

(Step Seven in the "Setting Your Church Free" Event)

What is the best strategy to defeat Satan's schemes against your church? What should you do to ensure that the people of your church become free in Christ? How can you encourage all of God's people to live fruitful, bondage-free lives of holiness?

Any church will be free only to the extent that its people are free in Christ. No corporate freedom can ever replace personal freedom. The two go hand in hand. All Christians need to know their true identity as children of God and the basics of living free in Christ. All church leaders need to understand servant leadership principles such as those found in Part One of this book. Some churches are communicating the message of freedom in Christ to the frontiers of their fellowship. This calls for a sustained motivation from Christ Himself, but the results are joyous.

A new church in Canada began by establishing their people free in Christ. They made a policy that all new members go through the personal "Steps to

Freedom." They wanted new members to come into their church having a fresh start and not bringing all their unresolved baggage from the past with them. People were taught how to release their past through forgiveness. They applied Christ's truth to win the battle for their minds. They faced up to their own personal sins and family bondages. Not only did the truth set people free, but it also led to remarkable growth in their new church. In just more than six months, their fellowship grew to 250 in attendance, and is still growing. Your church, too, can find rewarding benefits by communicating personal freedom in Christ to all of your people.

Freedom to the Frontiers

Crystal Evangelical Free Church in New Hope, Minnesota, spawned "Freedom Ministries" to mobilize their church, as well as others, to apply the message of "Freedom in Christ." Their ministry has three segments.

First, the church encourages everyone possible within their sphere of influence to make an *encourager appointment*. This is the opportunity to go through the "Steps to Freedom" with a trained encourager and a prayer partner. After explaining the steps and the purpose of helping people find the freedom that rightfully belongs to all who know Jesus Christ, their attractive brochure gives the following helpful description:

> Thousands of individuals have discovered the freedom of knowing who they are "in Christ" following a *Steps to Freedom* experience. The process is a one-time session, lasting anywhere from 2-5 hours during which an individual strategically works through the various areas in life that hinder the ability to enjoy God's abundant life. Each individual meets with a trained Encourager and a Prayer Partner, who gently guide the person through the process.
>
> If you are experiencing personal and/or spiritual oppression, or are having difficulty gaining control over chronic, destructive sins or habits, you may want to consider walking through the *Steps to Freedom*. You will learn who you really are as a child of God, and the truth regarding your new life in Christ.[1]

Second, the church organizes *encouragement groups.* The purpose of these groups is twofold—ongoing spiritual growth and personal development. In short, its goals are encouragement and edification. As their brochure states, "Encouragement groups provide the support and fellowship that prove so beneficial as one learns to walk in freedom." The group's interaction, discussion and prayer help those who may be fragile in their new freedom find reinforcement and spiritual strength. Each encouragement group consists of 7-12 people, permitting a high level of interaction. They continue weekly for 13-24 weeks. Participants are then invited to join an ongoing discipleship group sponsored by their home church or the host church.

Third, they provide *encourager training.* This is the training session required for those who will take others who have been referred from their church through the "Steps to Freedom." The session is also open to people from surrounding churches if they have a letter of recommendation from their pastor. The participants have attended Neil Anderson's "Resolving Personal and Spiritual Conflicts" seminar and the "Spiritual Conflicts and Counseling" advanced seminar in person or by video. The church gives further training, including more reading and a monthly Encouragers meeting for accountability. The supervision includes participating as a prayer partner for at least two appointments before helping someone who requested an appointment to go through the steps.

Every Member Free

At First Baptist Church in Modesto, California, the "Steps to Freedom" procedure is made available to every one of its members. The pastors and leaders at First Baptist believe it is beneficial for every Christian to go through the steps. For those in spiritual bondage, it leads to freedom. For those who are walking free in Christ already, it provides a daily tool in their lives to maintain their joy.

In a unique feature, they discovered that some people feel afraid of the unknown and hesitate to undergo the process. Often these people are in reconciliation or support ministries because of serious abuse or trauma in their lives. To familiarize them with the process, the pastors and lay leaders may use just one part of the steps as a teaching tool. They may, for example, ask the person to consider what pride looks like and talk about that one step. The goal is not to see an immediate transformation but rather to let the person see that the process is sane and sensible. Most often a decision to go through all the steps soon follows.

The pastors at Modesto First Baptist have helped some people in recovery ministries to see their identity in Christ in His light. For example, the typical Alcoholics Anonymous attender learns to say, "My name is John Jones and I am an alcoholic." After understanding their new identity in Christ, the introduction changes in a significant way. The person now says, "My name is John Jones, a child of God who struggles with alcohol." The shift in perception prepares the way for learning more about freedom in Christ and experiencing the steps.

Corporate Freedom

Personal freedom is the starting point but not the end of the battle. How can you stay alert to devious attempts to lure a church back into old patterns of corporate sin? How can you continue to stand against the evil one's attempt to undermine your church and your ministries? How does the Lord want you to implement the Prayer Action Plan? By going through the "Setting Your Church Free" process you take a giant step forward. Stop for a moment and think about what happens.

The Lord Jesus answers your prayers as you respond to Him. He heals painful memories, forgives corporate sins and thwarts Satan's attacks. He opens your eyes to your church's greatest strengths and weaknesses. He gives you a prayer plan with commitment to action. All this He accomplishes in one exhausting and rewarding day. But it is not finished. Just as people who find freedom in Christ still must deal with deeply ingrained behavioral patterns of the flesh, so churches must form new habits.

Corporate sins tend to surface again and again in a church's life. Discerning the major strongholds of the evil one is similar to good intelligence in a war. Repenting of those sins is similar to air strikes on enemy military targets; even then the ground troops must occupy the territory or it remains in the hands of our foes. So churches must follow their Lord beyond their present comfort zones to possess the land taken from the enemy. It is time to reject the old excuses and rationalizations. Jesus is calling His Church to obey Him, and He gives His resurrection power and personal presence to make it possible. This is the Lamb's war and the crucial battle is already won!

Common Strategies

At least seven strategies for implementing the Prayer Action Plan deserve careful consideration. Let's consider them one at a time.

The first and foremost strategy is personal prayer. Encourage all the participants to pray through the Prayer Action Plan on a daily basis. Wonderful benefits result. The pastors and leaders sensitize themselves to the corporate sins and common attacks from the enemy. These same patterns tend to reemerge weeks or months later, but the leaders spot them at once. It is not uncommon to hear comments such as, "We are about to repeat one of our old corporate sins" or "We just did one of the things we renounced." This kind of alertness to old bondage is essential in bringing about lasting change.

Our experience shows that most groups will not follow through on this daily prayer commitment without accountability. It is helpful to name one person besides the pastor or a paid staff member who has the assignment of reminding the group about this prayer commitment. This person may also take responsibility for leading the group regarding the other strategies. Pastors and staff members may, of course, do their part in implementing the Leadership Strategy (Step Seven).

The second strategy is similar: Pray through the Prayer Action Plan together at each of your regular meetings. These few moments reinforce the commitment to lead the church in obedience to Jesus. These are binding and loosing prayers all over again. Some groups ask, "How long should we pray through the Prayer Action Plan?" The best answer seems to be, until all of the action points are fulfilled and the items renounced no longer reappear. For many groups, this takes between 6 and 18 months. However, the "Setting Your Church Free" concept is new enough that further use by many more churches will help to verify or invalidate these findings.

Sermon Series

The third strategy is for the pastor to preach through the Prayer Action Plan in a sermon series. The pastor can present the leaders' findings with great sensitivity and care so that the congregation does not feel judged and condemned. Most of the people did not go through the seven-hour church freedom process and so they have no ownership and little knowledge of these truths. Some churches discovered that people who have not yet experienced the personal "Steps to Freedom" may feel the most offended. It makes sense that those who have no basis for understanding spiritual conflicts would struggle with the new terms and ideas. What is more, bondage in some lives may cause enough deception to reject the light that dispels the enemy's darkness.

Pastors who have the most success in the sermon series tackle one item each week that was renounced, announced, affirmed and willed. The "sandwich method" works well. In other words, place a positive biblical truth such as a "We announce" and "We affirm" truth on the top and bottom and have the meat, the "We renounce" item in the middle. Praising the church for their greatest strengths prepares the way for facing up to weaknesses. Some pastors will omit a few of the items if they apply only to the leaders of the church and not to the congregation as a whole.

At the close of the first sermon, lead the congregation in declaring together the four statements that relate to the subject. At the end of the second week, have them declare both the first week's statements and the second week's as well. By the end of the series, they are declaring most if not all of the Prayer Action Plan. The biblical background, practical explanations and personal style of the pastor helps this approach to prepare the congregation so that they respond well. It does not work to subtly slip parts into other messages (too weak) or preaching one sermon as an overview of the whole Prayer Action Plan (too strong).

Involving Leaders

Churches have various levels of leadership. Many people who were not a member of the group that participated in the "Setting Your Church Free" session serve capably and well in leadership capacities.

A fourth strategy is taking other groups of leaders in your church through the "Setting Your Church Free" process. This works best when it is applied, not to the church as a whole, but to members in their unique area of responsibility. In other words, the pastor or designated facilitator might lead a "Setting Our Sunday School Free" or "Setting Our Youth Ministry

Free" event. Each group needs to process the personal "Steps to Freedom" first, and insist on full attendance at the "Setting Our Group Free" event. The renounced and announced items, of course, will differ from the session by the church board and pastoral staff, but they will fit each unique ministry or organization.

Two Buckets

Those who experience the "Setting Your Church Free" process will have the greatest appreciation for it. Hopefully, all the leaders in your church have experienced personal freedom and heard the sermon series on the Prayer Action Plan. The timing is excellent for the pastor to teach the "two-bucket" principle. Every church leader carries two buckets—one full of water and the other full of gasoline. It makes all the difference in the world which one is used.

A little, church problem flares up like a fire. If life follows its usual course, a church leader hears about it before the pastor does. What happens next is crucial. If the leader pours gasoline on the problem, it will explode into a raging fire. If the leader douses it with water, it will die down or go out. The fire may flame from misunderstanding or gossip or jealousy or a critical spirit or some corporate sin. All the problem producer needs is an elder, deacon, committee chairperson or longtime member to dump gasoline on the problem and he or she has a fire going that will attract lots of misguided attention. Just the right amount of water, however, puts out the fire and sometimes extinguishes the problem.

A big fire needs attention at once. Instead of one bucket of water, it needs the fire department. Call for help! Phone the pastor or elders. Do not ignore it. No one in authority can deal with a problem that they do not know about. On the other hand, use some discernment. No one likes the stigma of the person who is always turning in false alarms.

I am grateful to my friend, John Maxwell, pastor of Skyline Wesleyan Church in San Diego, California, for this analogy. It occurred to me that the same comparison might apply in the opposite way to the fire of the Holy Spirit. The Bible says, "Do not put out the Spirit's fire" (1 Thess. 5:19). The fire of the Holy Spirit may come when a young believer experiences a dramatic answer to prayer, new freedom in Christ, or a special, personal surprise from God's sovereign hand. The church leader hears, yawns and changes the subject—and water drenches the Holy Spirit's fire. On the other hand, if the leader's eyes sparkle, the voice sounds enthusiastic and a big grin crosses the face, gasoline is poured on the Holy Spirit's fire.

The fire of the Holy Spirit may come when a new Christian discovers a familiar verse of Scripture for the first time. If the leader says, "I've known that one for years," having a tone of voice that implies, "Didn't you know that?", then the water bucket dumps on the Holy Spirit's fire. If, quite to the contrary, the leader gets excited, listens to why it is so meaningful, and shares a personal story of how God used the same verse in the leader's life, gasoline fuels the Spirit's fire. The fire of the Holy Spirit may be a desire to start a new ministry to the disadvantaged, abused children, cocaine users or any new group. It might be something this church has never done before. The leader can douse the idea or feed the flames.

The applications of how we might use the two buckets are many, but do not forget the basic rules. Use the water bucket to extinguish church problems; never use it to quench the Holy Spirit. Use the gasoline bucket to feed the fires that come from God; never use it to feed the egos of problem-producing personalities. Every church leader carries two buckets. Use each one wisely!

Prayerful Discussion

A fifth strategy is for the participants to discuss specific ways to obey each action point. This may happen in a series of regular meetings of the elders or the church board. Another option is to call a special session to prayerfully think through the church's purpose, strategies, goals, ministries and specific actions. The greatest danger is to consider the "Setting Your Church Free" event simply one more seminar, file the notes and go back to doing church as usual. It is so much better to let the Prayer Action Plan become a letter from Jesus that you must obey.

You might want to use the following questionnaire as a starting point for these discussions. We suggest that you customize it to fit your Prayer Action Plan. No magic exists in these particular questions. You may want to add specific questions that fit your church as well as retain some of the general questions that apply to all churches and all leaders. Pastors and staff members may be especially adept at writing questions that will stimulate good thinking about follow-through. Ask the participants to fill out the questionnaire before the meeting. The advance thinking and praying will help your discussion.

The greatest danger!

Jill Cundy —
Need a Projector
for Feb 19
20 people

th gift discernment
thing — seeking the gifts +
not th fruit

The fruit of th Spirit is love

If that same Spirit that
raised Christ from th dead
dwelling in —

Strategy Questionnaire
Prayer Action Plan

Please remember to pray through the Prayer Action Plan daily. Before our next meeting please fill out this questionnaire. It will serve as our basis for discussion. Thank you for taking time to prepare in advance.

1. What must we do to become the leaders God has called us to be?

2. How can we keep Christ as the center of all we are and do as a church?

3. What must we do to ensure that our people are living free and productive lives in Christ?

4. Including prayer, what steps can we take to ensure that our people are spiritually protected?

5. As a letter from Jesus, what parts of His prayer action plan must we act on at once?

6. Which parts of the plan require only alertness and prayer?

7. Who should we designate as leaders to implement various parts of the plan?

A sixth strategy is a summary report to the congregation. Rather than projecting the items renounced onto the congregation as "their problem," it is far wiser to begin with the responsibilities of the leaders. Nothing sets the example of genuine repentance quite like the board or other key decision makers humbling themselves before the congregation. Wise church leaders who were participants in the event will take responsibility for what they learned. They will share what the Lord revealed to them, how they discovered their painful memories and corporate sins, and how they confessed and forgave. The one doing the reporting might say, "We haven't been the leaders that we should be, but we are committing ourselves to pray and take action." When leaders model repentance it is far easier for the congregation to follow their example, as the Scriptures so clearly illustrate:

> All of you, clothe yourselves with humility toward one another, because, "God opposes the proud but gives grace to the humble." Humble yourselves, therefore, under God's mighty hand, that he may lift you up in due time. Cast all your anxiety on him because he cares for you. Be self-controlled and alert. Your enemy the devil prowls around like a roaring lion looking for someone to devour. Resist him, standing firm in the faith, because you know that your brothers throughout the world are undergoing the same kind of sufferings (1 Pet. 5:5-9).

Then the leaders may want to present the Prayer Action Plan or a summary of it to the congregation. Some churches adopt it as part of their official church minutes. Be careful to observe one major "no-no." Caution: Please avoid this mistake. Other churches have learned the hard way—*it does not work well to try to involve the whole congregation directly in the Prayer Action Plan.* People feel unfairly judged and condemned if they have not gone through the "Setting Your Church Free" process themselves. Although the sermon series mentioned earlier does work well, trying to impose the findings directly on others is often offensive. The better approach is to let the leaders lead.

Letting Leaders Lead

Some people have inborn leadership; they are strong natural leaders. Wherever they go, whatever they do, they end up leading the pack. It often shows up as children. Certain girls and boys set the pace. Others look to them, take their cue from them, imitate them—in short, they follow them. Let's pursue this subject of letting leaders lead in a little more detail.

The Holy Spirit gives the spiritual gift of leadership to some but not to all. "If it [the spiritual gift] is leadership, let him govern diligently" (Rom. 12:8; also see 1 Cor. 12:28 for the related gift of administration). Just as all do not have gifts of teaching, mercy or healing, so all do not have the gift of leadership. But some do have this gift, and those in the church recognize it and follow them. Often (but not always) they are the same people who have the natural talent of leadership that was evident in them even as children.

Others learn the art of leadership. They work so diligently at developing their skills that they earn a following. When leaders have enough years of experience you can hardly tell the gifted leaders from those who learned the role the hard way. Good leaders show us what to do next and why it is necessary. Good leaders love and serve. Good leaders influence, motivate, inspire or organize to get the job done; the best leaders find the resources to finish the task.

One of the dangers we face is that something foul within us resists letting leaders lead. We acknowledge with our lips that God called and gifted leaders in our congregation, but we rebel in our hearts. We make excuses. We think that in a democracy everyone should have an equal voice. This is true enough, but not all voices have the same wisdom, discernment or influence.

Followers' Responsibilities

Sometimes we followers foul up our leaders. We give responsibility without authority. We ask our pastors, staff members and other leaders to produce; then we question their every move and block their initiatives. We want leadership but no change. Impossible! We often reject authority from any source that displeases us, and especially our own chosen leaders. In a culture that specializes in giving each person many choices in everything, we find it hard to settle for the leader's one choice.

How much better to seek excellence through biblical submission. Recently Brent Bailey, a friend of mine, asked a member of a superb choir why they were so good. What was their secret of excellence? Having some pain in her voice, the choir member replied that the director insisted on absolute submission of everyone in the choir to his musical authority. He in turn gave them love, respect and enthusiasm. As the talented voices submitted totally to their gifted director, the music that resulted was phenomenal. Brent then made his point that submission to a gifted leader is a way of achieving the excellence that most of us have forgotten today.

Leaders' Responsibilities

The best leaders listen to wise and godly counsel. They especially respect those who have spiritual discernment. The two roles are not the same. Discerners have an essential role that is different from leaders. They support their leaders with love, but sometimes point out a flaw or spot a wrong direction. They almost always know the difference between the authentic and the phony. Elders and overseers in particular are charged with the task of spiritual discernment. They are to counsel, support and sometimes correct pastors and staff members. A group of godly elders or deacons who honestly seek God's will and come to genuine unity always deserve a careful hearing. Most often their counsel is from the Lord and is invaluable. Wise is the pastor or leader who will listen and heed. A fine resource is Neil Anderson's *Walking in the Light.*[2] The chapter on "Spiritual Discernment" is excellent, and the book is filled with solid counsel on divine guidance and detecting spiritual counterfeits.

We must always balance leadership and discernment. A common shortcoming, however, lies in criticizing our leaders when we are not in a position to know the facts and discern what is best. The Bible gives a crisp command: "Obey your leaders and submit to their authority. They keep watch over you as men who must give an account. Obey them so that their work will be a joy, not a burden, for that would be of no advantage to you" (Heb. 13:17).

High Tuesdays

A seventh strategy is to recruit committed intercessors to pray for the pastor and paid staff members. Pastors and staff will more likely lead the church in making the changes and fulfilling the challenges of the Prayer Action Plan if they feel the prayer support of intercessory partners. What is more, Christ's own power will enable them to do it in a way that will build up the church rather than damage it. C. Peter Wagner, in his excellent book *Prayer Shield,* makes this bold statement: "The most underutilized source of spiritual power in our churches today is intercession for Christian leaders."[3] Frankly, he is right.

Every pastor wishes for more of God's power. This is not selfish; it is a healthy desire for God's best in the ministry. And it is available. Some pastors and Christian leaders are tapping into a known but often unused resource—receiving intercession. In contrast to the pastor praying for church members, receiving intercession means a few people praying intensely for their pastor and for the church's ministry.

One of my pastor friends was unusually candid with me. He is a young man and remembers well his days before engaging in full-time ministry.

"It's harder to be in the ministry and still live the Christian life than it was before. It's harder to pray, and I have more trouble with my thought life—except on Tuesdays."

"What happens on Tuesdays?" I asked.

"I have a group of men in my church who take turns praying for me each day of the week. The man who prays on Tuesdays really takes it seriously. He feels it's a call from God. On Tuesdays I can pray easily and I seldom struggle with my thought life."

"Maybe you should schedule your most important things to do on Tuesday," I suggested.

"I've already started doing that," he replied. "It works, too." Frankly, he enjoyed high Tuesdays. They were the most effective day of his week.

Another friend of mine, Jerry Johnson, currently serves as the executive pastor of Lake Avenue Congregational Church in Pasadena, California. During one time period, between the church's senior pastors, he carried the major responsibility for leadership in the church. As if the load were not heavy enough already, the church was struggling with overwhelming debt from a major building program. He called for prayer partners—many of them. He asked them to sign up for different days of the week. Every day a group of people were praying for him. They were all to pray on Sunday.

Not only did Jerry lead the church with distinction during the interim period, but the finances actually improved; they ended the year having a surplus. He is quick to credit his prayer partners and to give God the glory. "I have learned to tap into the power of intercession," Johnson says.

Why don't more pastors and Christian leaders call for prayer partners?

Some may not recognize the potential blessing available. Some may feel as though it is a selfish request. Some may not want to be vulnerable. But all pastors need to take this bold step.

The more powerful the intercessor, the greater the blessing that comes. Some time ago I prayed for a couple of strong intercessors as prayer partners. God answered, and two prayer warriors lifted me before the throne of grace. Since then I have appealed, on a somewhat lower commitment basis, for a prayer team. Today, 25 or 30 people regularly hold me and my ministry before the Lord in intercessory prayer. My own ministry took a turn for the better once this started. Before seminars, speaking engagements, important meetings (and writing my part of this book) I write or phone my intercessors and request special prayer. The result is that the events almost always have a greater sense of God's blessing and power than before.

Why don't you begin praying daily for your pastor? Or why not join with some others so that several of you are praying fervently every day of the week? Only heaven will reveal the results. The one you pray for could have a high Tuesday every day.

Procedure for Step Seven

Keeping these strategies in mind, let's turn to the procedure for the final step. The task before your group is to discern what Jesus wants you to do to carry out your Prayer Action Plan. The participants will pray together the prepared prayer, asking the Lord if anything was missed. If so, the facilitator should add the item into the Prayer Action Plan. The primary purpose of this group prayer, however, is to ask the Lord Jesus what steps the church leaders should take next.

As in the other steps, the participants spend a few moments in silent prayer asking for the Holy Spirit's direction. The facilitator, or two of the members, will close this time in spoken prayers. Because of fatigue from the process, it is essential that each person in the group ask the Lord to impress strongly His strategy upon everyone's minds and hearts. The facilitator will again write the suggestions on the large sheets of paper up front. In this step, as in the last three, it is vital to seek group unity. This last step, important as it is, often moves more quickly than the others. Some groups enjoy a fellowship meal together at the close of their "Setting Your Church Free" event. Plan in advance what you will do to celebrate.

It Works

Recently I received an encouraging letter from a pastor whose church went through the "Setting Your Church Free" process about nine months ago. Here is part of what he wrote:

> Since the "Setting Your Church Free" mini-retreat, I have noticed significant healing and growth in the church as an organization and as an instrument. I know that I may be a bit naive being so young, but I am constantly amazed to find skeleton after skeleton in this church's closet.
>
> The good news is we are bringing old issues and deep hurts out into the open. People say our church is laid back, friendly and very relational. This assessment seems fair on the surface of things. I am learning, however, that if you dig beneath the surface, you begin to see incredible pains that have not been resolved.
>
> Having an outside person who is qualified to deal with spiritual issues do what you did in that retreat has offered us hope. Our corporate sins are enough to close this place down. They have already severely stunted our growth and effectiveness to do God's work.
>
> You have helped us to start a tremendous and often very painful healing process. We have been faithful in following through with the six steps listed in our Prayer Action Plan. I am guessing that before this retreat we wouldn't have finished any of them. God has used you to bless us. We are truly thankful.

A "Setting Your Church Free" conference takes one day in the life of your church. Skeletons may continue to emerge from carefully concealed closets. We hope you now know how to deal with them when they do emerge. Neil and I suspect that some churches have such a long history of bondage, the Lord may peel off one layer at a time similar to peeling an onion. This has certainly been the case in personal counseling.

Becoming free and staying free are two different issues. The moment we take our freedom for granted, we will lose it. Remember what Jesus taught: "If you hold to my teaching, you are really my disciples. Then you will know the truth, and the truth will set you free" (John 8:31,32). What is more, "It is for freedom that Christ has set us free" (Gal. 5:1). May the Lord enable you to be free in Christ. May He equip you to become the spiritual leader who can lead the way in setting your church free. May He build you up in Christ until you are the leader He called you to be!

Notes

1. For a copy of this attractive brochure entitled "Freedom Ministries," send a self-addressed, stamped envelope to: Crystal Evangelical Free Church, 4225 Gettysburg Ave. North, New Hope, MN 55428, Attn: Freedom Ministries.
2. Neil T. Anderson, *Walking in the Light* (Nashville, TN: Thomas Nelson Publishers, 1991).
3. C. Peter Wagner, *Prayer Shield* (Ventura, CA: Regal Books, 1992), p. 19.

APPENDICES

LEVELS OF CONFLICT AND GROWTH IN CHRIST

LEVELS OF CONFLICT

Level I	Level II	Level III
(Col. 2:10, NKJV) "You are complete IN Him."	(Col. 2:7, NASB) "Having been firmly rooted and now being built up IN Him."	(Col. 2:6, NASB) "You...have received Christ Jesus the Lord, so walk IN Him."

	Level I	Level II	Level III
SPIRITUAL	Lack of salvation or assurance (Eph. 2:1-3)	Walking according to the flesh (Gal. 5:19-21)	Insensitive to the Holy Spirit's leading (Heb. 5:11-14)
RATIONAL	Darkened in their understanding (Eph. 4:18)	Wrong belief or philosophy of life (Col. 2:8)	Pride (1 Cor. 8:1)
EMOTIONAL	Fear (Matt. 10:26-33)	Anger (Eph. 4:31) Anxiety (1 Pet. 5:7) Depression (2 Cor. 4:1-18)	Discouragement and sorrow (Gal. 6:9)
VOLITIONAL	Rebellion (1 Tim. 1:9)	Lack of self-control, compulsive (1 Cor. 3:1-3)	Undisciplined (2 Thess. 3:7,11)
RELATIONAL	Rejection (Eph. 2:1-3)	Unforgiveness (Col. 3:13)	Selfishness (Phil. 2:1-5) (1 Cor. 10:24)

LEVELS OF GROWTH

	Level I	Level II	Level III
	(Col. 2:10, *NKJV*) "You are complete IN Him."	(Col. 2:7, *NASB*) "Having been firmly rooted and now being built up IN Him."	(Col. 2:6, *NASB*) "You...have received Christ Jesus the Lord, so walk IN Him."
SPIRITUAL	Child of God (1 John 3:1-3) (1 John 5:11-13)	Walking according to the Spirit (Gal. 5:22,23)	Led by the Holy Spirit (Rom. 8:14)
RATIONAL	Renewed mind (Rom. 12:2) (Eph. 4:23)	Handling accurately the word of truth (2 Tim. 2:15)	Adequate, equipped for every good work (2 Tim. 3:16,17)
EMOTIONAL	Free (Gal. 5:1)	Joy Peace Patience (Gal. 5:22)	Contentment (Phil. 4:11)
VOLITIONAL	Submissive (Rom. 13:1,2)	Self-control (Gal. 5:23)	Disciplined (1 Tim. 4:7,8)
RELATIONAL	Acceptance (Rom. 5:8) (Rom 15:7)	Forgiveness (Eph. 4:32)	Devoted to one another in brotherly love (Rom. 12:10) (Phil. 2:1-5)

APPENDIX

SEVEN STEPS TOWARD SETTING YOUR CHURCH FREE

Prior to the retreat, please read this book before attempting the "Setting Your Church Free" process. Explanations, biblical background and directions for the facilitator and the recorder are in the book. This outline gives the bare-bones process, having few of the whys and hows. As you read the book, you will discover the biblical background and a working understanding of what the event intends to accomplish. It also explains practical questions such as when to schedule the event, how to set up the room, how the facilitator conducts the process and what the participants actually do. Studying the process is essential advance preparation for the event.

It is vital for the participants to experience personal freedom in Christ prior to engaging in the "Setting Your Church Free" event. All of the participants must have gone through the personal "Seven Steps to Freedom" recently (see appendix C). (You may order these materials from Freedom in Christ, 491 East Lambert Road, La Habra, CA 90631. Each participant should have a copy of these "Seven Steps Toward Setting Your Church Free" as well. This appendix can be used or copies can be ordered from Freedom in Christ, which will have the latest revision.) We recommend a day of fasting and prayer by the participants and their prayer partners prior to the event. Ask for prayer partners to intercede in prayer before and during this time together.

It is essential that 100 percent of the elders or board members and all full-time pastoral staff be present for the first time a church goes through the process. Please postpone if even one member cannot attend. The process works best when every member is present and is greatly weakened if even one is missing. We also recommend that an unbiased outside facilitator lead your church leadership through these steps. The pastor and staff members need to be a part of the process. Although the time may vary with different groups, the "Setting Your Church Free" event normally takes about seven hours.

Day of Retreat

At the beginning of the day of the event, pray the follow personal renewal prayer—once silently and then out loud together:

Dear heavenly Father,

Open my eyes to see Your truth. Give me ears to hear and a compelling desire to respond in faith to what the Lord Jesus Christ has already done for me.

I confess Jesus Christ—crucified, risen and reigning—as my one and only Lord and Savior. I renounce any past involvement with non-Christian religions or experiences. I announce that Christ died on the cross for me and for my sins and rose again bodily from the dead for my justification.

I confess that the Lord Jesus Christ rescued me from the dominion of darkness and transferred me into His kingdom of light. I renounce Satan in all his works and all his ways. I announce that Jesus Christ is my Lord, Savior, Teacher and Friend. I give myself to obey everything that He commanded. I yield myself fully to Christ to do whatever He wants me to do, to be whatever He wants me to be, to give up whatever He wants me to give up, to give away whatever He wants me to give away, to become whatever He wants me to become.

I confess, reject, renounce and utterly disown every sin in which I have ever been involved. I announce that in Christ I have received redemption, the forgiveness of sins. I accept His reconciliation to the heavenly Father and welcome peace with God.

As an expression of my faith of Christ's forgiveness of me, I forgive every person who has ever hurt, abused or taken advantage of me. I let them off my hook and let God settle the score as the final Judge who metes out perfect justice.

I open all the doors of my life to the Lord Jesus Christ and ask Him to take control of every part of my being. I gladly accept the filling of the Holy Spirit into every part of my life. I surrender myself to live in union with the Lord Jesus Christ from this moment until I stand before the Judgment Seat of Christ and hear my name read from the Lamb's Book of Life.

Thank You, heavenly Father, for uniting me with the Lord Jesus Christ and with all those who truly belong to You and live under Your gracious reign.

In Jesus' powerful name.
Amen.

Processing these steps is not business as usual. To move out of your comfort zone in a meaningful way, engage in a form of prayer that is not your church's usual custom. For instance, in many countries Christians pray out loud, all together at the same time. If you have not done this before, stand in a circle holding hands, praying aloud at the same time. Ask the Lord to fill you with His Holy Spirit, guide you and your church and protect you from the evil one. Claim Christ's resources against Satan and his evil forces. Conclude this time with the Lord's Prayer. (If this is customary for your group, find a way to pray that is not your usual practice.)

Bible Study

First, discuss the power of binding and loosing (see Matt. 16:19; 18:18-20). The fact that this teaching is used in two different contexts in Matthew may indicate that it may have more than one application in the Church. We bind what we renounce and loose what we announce as the Holy Spirit leads us to discern what has already been bound or loosed in heaven.

Second, read the letters to the seven churches in Revelation 2,3. It is helpful to take turns, reading one letter apiece. Then all the participants look for the following items, one or two at a time.

- Note the love of the risen Lord Jesus for His churches and His encouragement to them. Christ wants all of His churches to become free. Count how many times Jesus uses "I" in each letter. The major emphasis in these seven letters is on the near presence of the living Christ among the churches.
- Note that each church has an angel (see Rev. 1:9-20). Two common functions of angels in the book of Revelation are (1) to praise and worship God and (2) to carry out the promises and judgments of Christ. The angel assigned by Christ to your church may do these very things.
- Note the corporate sins of the churches in Revelation 2,3. Many Christians are not used to thinking about corporate sins, although the concept is taught in Nehemiah 9, Daniel 9 and Revelation 2,3.
- Note the phrases that indicate Satan's attacks or opposition to the churches (Rev. 2:9,10,13,24; 3:9).
- Note the Lord's judgments for disobedience and promises for obedience.
- Note the repeated phrase, "To him who overcomes." In the New Testament, "overcomes" is a word most often used for the Christian's battle against the world, the flesh and the devil.

During this "Setting Your Church Free" event, each person needs to be sensitive to God's leading. To each of the churches in Revelation 2,3, John writes, "He who has an ear, let him hear what the Spirit says to the churches." If the Lord Jesus wrote a letter to your church, would you obey Him? Or would some hindrance keep you from really applying His message and making the necessary changes?

Pray together the following prayer, and then read aloud the Church Renunciations that follow:

Dear heavenly Father,

Open our eyes to see Your truth and our ears to hear what Your Holy Spirit is saying to our church. We acknowledge that the Lord Jesus Christ is the Head of our church, and we renounce any claim of ownership on our part. This is Your church, not ours, and You are the Head. We renounce any independent spirit and declare our full dependence upon You.

We come together to discern Your will for our church. We renounce any and all desires or attempts to exert our own wills through arguing, manipulating or intimidating. You are light and in You there is no darkness at all. We choose to walk in the light in order to have fellowship with You and with one another. We ask You to fill us with Your Holy Spirit and guide us through these steps to our church's freedom. Set us free to fulfill Your purpose for our being here.

Lead us not into temptation but deliver us from the evil one. Because we are seated with Christ in the heavenlies and because the Church is commissioned to go into all the world and make disciples of all nations, we take our stand against the evil one and all his forces. We gladly submit to You, heavenly Father, and obey Your command to resist the devil. We ask You to ban the adversary from our presence so that we will be free to know Your will and to choose to obey it.

In Jesus' precious name.

Amen.

Read aloud the following church renunciations. The first one is an ancient declaration of the early church. The others are based on Revelation 2,3. Although they may not precisely fit your church, they are a biblical example of corporate sins all churches should avoid. Make the following declaration together.

Church Renunciations

We renounce...	We announce....
We renounce you, Satan, in all your works and in all your ways.	We announce that Christ is Lord of our lives and choose to follow only His ways.

We renounce forsaking
our first love.

We renounce tolerating
false teaching.

We renounce overlooking
non-Christian beliefs
and practices among our
members.

We renounce tolerating
sexual immorality among
some of our members.

We renounce our
reputation of being
alive when we are dead.

We renounce our
incomplete deeds,
starting to do God's
will and then not
following through.

We renounce disobe-
dience to God's Word,
including the Great
Commandment and the
Great Commission.

We renounce our luke-
warmness, being neither
hot nor cold for Christ.

We announce that Christ is
our first love because He first loved
us and gave Himself an atoning
sacrifice for our sins.

We announce that God's truth
is revealed to us through the
living and written Word of God.

We announce that Christ is our
true identity and the only way
to salvation and fellowship
with God.

We announce that our sexuality
is God's gift, and that sexual
intercourse is to be enjoyed
only within the marriage of
one man and one woman.

We announce that Christ alone
is our Resurrection and
our Life.

We announce that Christ is
the Head of His Body, the
Church, and that as His
members we find freedom and
strength to finish the work
He has given us to do.

We announce that God energizes
us to desire and to do His
will so that we can obey
Christ.

We announce that Christ
is our refining fire Who
disciplines us for our own
good so that our faith may
prove genuine.

| We renounce our false pride in financial "security" that blinds us to our actual spiritual needs. | We announce that Christ is our true wealth, security and insight—and outside of Him we are wretched, pitiful, poor, blind and naked. |

What if the Lord Jesus were to write a letter to your church? What would He commend? What would He rebuke? Although you cannot have a letter with the authority of Scripture, you can ask the Holy Spirit to help you discern how the Head of the Church views this local congregation. He can help you apply scriptural truths to your lives and to your church.

Discerning the Lord's View of Our Church

If you have not already done so, appoint a recorder to write down all the lists that are compiled by the group.

Step One: Our Church's Strengths

In this first step, you are seeking to discern the strengths of your church. Pray together the following prayer, then follow with a few moments of silent prayer. Allow the Lord to impress upon your hearts what you are doing right. The facilitator, or those appointed, will close the time in prayer.

Dear heavenly Father,
Thank You for calling and choosing us as shepherds of the flock and servant leaders in Your Church. Thank You for this church and what You have done through it. Thank You for the people who worship and serve You here.
Show us what the living Lord Jesus commends in our church. Remind us of what we are doing right, and the strengths You have given to our church. As we wait silently before You, show us our good works that glorify our Father in heaven (Matt. 5:16).

This step has two parts. In the first part, the facilitator asks the group to list the church's strengths as the Holy Spirit brings them to mind. Encourage all the participants to identify as many strengths of the church as possible.

The second part takes place after all of the strengths are listed. The facilitator asks the group to summarize the greatest strengths God has given to your church. Good questions to ask here are: "What are the things we always do best?" "What works for us every time?" "How has God uniquely gifted us as a church body?" Keep this list short, having only the greatest strengths identified, normally five to seven items.

The facilitator writes on the poster or butcher paper the greatest strengths, beginning each one with "We thank God for...." State them in complete sentences and save the statements for the final summary in the Prayer Action Plan (Step Six).

Conclude this step by praying in unison the following prayer:

Dear heavenly Father,

Thank You for the strengths You have given to us and to our church. Thank You for gracing us with Your presence and for working through the gifts, talents and service of Your people. We bow in gratitude for the ways that You have ministered through our church. We know that apart from Christ we can do nothing. So we gladly acknowledge that every good and perfect gift is from above.

Continue to equip us to be good stewards of these strengths as well as responsible managers of all the relationships and all of the resources You have given us. In Jesus Christ our Lord we pray. Amen.

Step Two: Our Weaknesses

In Step Two, the group will ask the Holy Spirit to help discern the weaknesses of the church. What are your shortcomings, faults, failures? What are you not doing well? What should your church be doing that is not being done?

Pray together the following prayer. Then spend a couple of minutes in silent prayer, allowing the Lord to impress upon your hearts the weaknesses of your church.

Dear heavenly Father,
    We have not fully utilized the gifts, talents and strengths that You
have made available to us. We slip into patterns of thinking and acting
that displease You. We fall short of Your best and of all that You intend for
us. We ask You to open our eyes so that we may see our weaknesses as You
do. We wait silently before You in the powerful name of Jesus. Amen.

    The facilitator will ask the group to list the weaknesses that the Holy
Spirit brings to their minds. Encourage the participants to express their own
opinions. This is not a time for any objection or defensiveness from others.
Absolute accuracy is not essential this early in the process. You are not trying
to identify your greatest weaknesses (as with strengths in Step One), but simply listing them for future reference.
    When you have finished listing your church's weaknesses, pray the fol-
lowing prayer together.

Heavenly Father,
    You know our weaknesses as well as our strengths, and You love us
just the same. Forgive us for the times we have placed our confidence in
ourselves instead of in Christ. We put no confidence in our flesh but
instead we declare our dependence upon You. We are confident that the
good work You have begun in us will be completed.
    Show us how we can strengthen our weaknesses and live with our
limitations. May Your power be made perfect in our weakness. In Jesus'
strong name we pray. Amen.

Step Three: Memories

In this step, you are asking the Lord to remind you of both the best memories,
and the traumatic events in your church's past. If yours is an older church,
consider it decade by decade, beginning in the earliest recalled or researched
past. What happened in the 1930s, '40s, '50s, '60s, '70s, '80s, '90s? If yours is a
younger church, you may want to divide its history into halves or thirds.
What happened in the first five years, the last five years?

Make two lists for this step, one titled "Good Memories" and the other titled "Painful Memories." List all of the good memories first. The good memories are fun to recall, and are an occasion for thanksgiving to God for His blessings upon His people.

Begin with the following prayer:

Dear heavenly Father,

Thank You for the wonderful experiences we have shared together that have built such special memories. We thank You for Your blessings upon us and for all the good times You have given us. With joy and thanksgiving we ask You to bring the good memories of our church into our minds. With grateful hearts, we pray in the name of Jesus. Amen.

When the list of good memories is complete, the facilitator will ask the participants to lift them before the Lord in thanksgiving and praise. Encourage everyone to pray aloud, beginning with the following words:

Lord, I thank you for (name the good memory)...

After thanking the Lord for the good memories throughout the church's past, pray together the following prayer. Then follow with a few moments of silent prayer, allowing the Lord to bring to your memories the painful experiences of your church's past.

Dear heavenly Father,

We thank You for the riches of Your kindness, forbearance and patience, knowing that Your kindness has led us to repentance. We acknowledge that we have not extended that same patience and kindness toward those who have offended us. We have not acted gracefully and wisely in all our past dealings.

Sometimes pain has come to others even when we were using our best judgment in following You. Sometimes the actions and attitudes of others have deeply wounded us. Show us where we have allowed a root of bitterness to spring up, causing trouble and defiling many. As we wait silently before You, bring to our minds all the painful memories of our church's past. In Jesus' compassionate name we pray. Amen.

Make another list of painful memories. Use real names. It is nearly impossible to get in touch with the emotional core of pain without using people's names.
Everything said here is to be spoken with respect. Carefully avoid placing blame
or making disparaging remarks. Absolute confidentiality must be assured. No
person will be permitted to share this confidential information outside the group.
Ask the recorder *not* to write down the painful memories section. After the
process is finished, you will want to destroy this large sheet up front.

You can't fix the past, but you can free yourselves from it by facing it,
forgiving and seeking forgiveness. Once again the group interacts and the
facilitator writes the painful memories on the sheets up front. Then each person is to lift the painful memories before the Lord, asking for courage to face
the pain honestly, and grace to forgive fully. Releasing the offenses results in
relieving the pain. Item by item, individually and silently, forgive each person
you recall and release the offenses as follows:

Lord, I forgive (name the person) for (specifically name every painful
memory).

Prayerfully focus on each person you know until every remembered pain
has surfaced. Each person should also forgive themselves as needed. Forgiveness softens the heart. When every head is lifted from this time of silent
prayer, then proceed.

In unison, release these painful memories to the Lord in the following
declaration and prayer. Before you say "Amen," all the participants are encouraged to pray individually and audibly. One at a time, lift spontaneous prayers
before the Lord, beginning with, "We forgive..." "We release..." "We bless..."
Then proceed with the following declaration and prayer:

Declaration

By the authority of the Lord Jesus Christ Who is seated at Your
right hand, we assume our responsibility to resist the devil. In Jesus' all-
powerful name we retake any ground that Satan may have gained in
our lives and in our church through these painful memories. Because

we are seated with Christ in the heavenly realms we command Satan to leave our presence, our ministries and our church.

Prayer

Dear heavenly Father,

We forgive each and every person who has hurt us or our church. We forgive as the Lord forgave us.

We release our resentments and regrets into Your hands. You alone can heal our broken hearts and bind up our wounds. We ask You to heal the pain in our hearts and in the corporate memory of our church. We ask for Your forgiveness for allowing a root of bitterness to spring up and defile many. We also ask You to forgive us for the times we did not seek to resolve these painful memories according to Your Word.

We commit ourselves to think of these memories, whenever we may happen to recall them, from the vantage point of our union with Christ. We will recall our forgiveness and Your healing.

May Your grace and mercy guide us as we seek to live out our calling as spiritual leaders. We ask You, heavenly Father, to fill us with Your Holy Spirit. We surrender full control of our church body to our crucified, risen and reigning Head.

We ask You to bring healing to those who have hurt us. Also bring healing to those who may have been hurt by us. Bless those who curse us and give rich and satisfying ministries to all who belong to You but have gone away from us. We bless them all in the name of our Lord Jesus Christ Who taught us, "Love your enemies, do good to those who hate you, bless those who curse you, pray for those who mistreat you" (Luke 6:27,28). According to Your Word, we pray for those who have hurt us:

We forgive...	(Individually, as the Lord leads,
We release...	pray for people and situations
We bless...	beginning with these phrases.)

In Jesus' name we pray. Amen.

This is a good time to take a break—and to ask yourself, "Is there someone I need to talk with right now?"

Step Four: Corporate Sins

In this fourth step, you are going to identify corporate sins. Individual sins that do not corporately affect the body will not be a part of this process; they must be dealt with individually. Corporate sins need not involve the whole church, but they must involve a significant group within the church.

Pray together the following prayer. Then follow with a few moments of silent prayer. Ask the Lord to impress upon your minds the past and present corporate sins of your church or of any significant group within it:

Dear heavenly Father,
As we seek Your face, bring to our minds all the corporate sins that we, or any significant group within our church, have committed. Like Ezra and Daniel we stand before You, ready to repent of the sins of our spiritual ancestors in this church. We also ask for your discernment to identify and renounce our own sins. As we wait silently before You, bring to our minds all the corporate sins that we, and the spiritual leaders before us, have tolerated or not adequately dealt with. Then grant us the grace that we may confess, renounce and forsake them. In Jesus' forgiving name we pray. Amen.

The facilitator will now ask you to share your church's corporate sins. Usually this step starts slowly but gradually gains momentum. Unlike the first steps, the facilitator will seek discernment from the group. Write on the sheets up front only those corporate sins that have group consensus. From this step onward group discernment is vital, rather than only listing each person's ideas. Be patient and wait for general agreement.

Pray the following prayer aloud together for each corporate sin you have listed on the large sheet on the wall:

Heavenly Father,
We confess (name one sin each time) as sinful and displeasing to our Lord Jesus Christ. We ask Your forgiveness for it, turn from it, forsake it and renounce it.
In Jesus' name. Amen.

When every corporate sin has been confessed and renounced, pray the following prayer together:

Heavenly Father,
As spiritual leaders in our church, we acknowledge that these corporate sins are unacceptable to You. We renounce every use of our corporate body as an instrument of unrighteousness by ourselves and by those who have gone before us. We reject and disown all the sins of our ancestors. We cancel out all advantages, schemes and other works of the devil that have been passed on to our church from them.

By the authority of Christ, the Head of His Body, the Church, we demolish every satanic foothold and stronghold in our church gained because of our own corporate sins. We retake all ground given to the adversary in our church, in our related organizations and in our life together as a congregation. We release control of that territory to the Holy Spirit.

We invite the Holy Spirit to cleanse us, renew us, fill us and lead us into all truth. Cause us to obey Your truth so that our church will be set free.

We submit ourselves and our church to the sovereignty and ownership of the heavenly Father, the Lordship and fullness of Christ and the presence and power of the Holy Spirit. By Your grace and according to Your Word, we acknowledge that we are fellow citizens with the saints, and we belong to God's household. We affirm that we have been built upon the foundation of the apostles and prophets, Christ Jesus Himself being the Chief Cornerstone. We praise our Lord Jesus Christ for His headship of our church and see ourselves as His Body, bride and building.

"Now to him who is able to do immeasurably more than all we ask or imagine, according to his power that is at work within us, to him be glory in the church and in Christ Jesus throughout all generations, for ever and ever! Amen" (Eph. 3:20,21).

At this point, the facilitator will invite everyone to search their own hearts. Ask for the Holy Spirit to reveal each one's participation in the church's corporate sins. Each person, as directed by the Holy Spirit, should then pray out loud, confessing personal involvement in these corporate sins. Alert everyone that it is off-limits to confess someone else's sins. After this prayer time, you may want to talk during the break with anyone in the room with whom you need to reconcile, make amends or ask forgiveness. These can be powerful moments of healing hurts and conflicts within the group.

Step Five: Attacks of Spiritual Enemies

The last step dealt with the ground given over to Satan because of what your church or its people have done wrong. This step has a different focus. The attacks you are going to identify in this step come because of the things that your church, your pastors and your leaders are *doing right.*

Pray together the following prayer; then engage in moments of silent prayer. Ask the Lord to help you discern accurately the nature of Satan's attacks upon your church, its leaders and its people because of what you are doing right.

Dear heavenly Father,
We thank You for our refuge in Christ. We choose to be strong in the Lord and in His mighty power. In Christ Jesus we put on the full armor of God. We choose to stand firm and be strong in our faith. We accept the truth that our struggle is not against flesh and blood, but against the spiritual forces of evil in the heavenly realms.

We desire to be aware of Satan's schemes, not ignorant of them. Open our eyes to the reality of the spiritual world that we live in. We ask You for the ability to discern spiritually so that we can rightly judge between good and evil.

As we wait silently before You, reveal to us the attacks of Satan against us, our pastors, our people and our ministries in order that we may stand against them and expose the father of lies. In Jesus' discerning name we pray. Amen.

Once again the group needs to discern the spiritual attacks, not just list people's ideas. It takes a little longer to reach group consensus, but it is far better than listing only the ideas of one person.

When the list is complete, renounce each attack one by one as follows:

In the name and authority of our Lord Jesus Christ, we renounce Satan's attacks of (or by, on, with, through [each of the identified attacks listed one at a time]). We resist them and come against them in Jesus' all-powerful name. Together we declare, "The Lord rebuke you, the Lord bind you" from any present or any future influence upon us.

Testimonies of some former satanists and cult members would indicate that certain deceived or wicked people are deliberately out to destroy effective Christian ministries. Sometimes blood sacrifices are made to claim false ownership of Christian leaders or ministries. At other times, curses or satanic assignments are placed upon God's people or their leaders. Use the following declaration to break the influence of any of these attacks against your church, its leaders or its people:

Declaration

As leaders of this church and members of the Body of Christ, we reject and disown all influence and authority of demonic powers and evil spirits that cause resistance to Christ's work. As children of God we have been delivered from the power of darkness and brought into the kingdom of God's dear Son.

Because we are seated with Christ in the heavenly realms, we renounce all satanic assignments that are directed toward our church and our ministry. We cancel every curse that deceived or wicked people have put on us. We announce to Satan and all his forces that Christ became a curse for us when He died on the cross.

We renounce any and all sacrifices by satanists or anyone else who would claim false ownership of us, our ministry, our leaders or our people. We announce that we have been bought and purchased by the blood of the Lamb. We accept only the sacrifice of Jesus whereby we belong to Him.

Conclude this step with the following prayer for protection and an act of dedication of yourselves and your facilities to God:

Dear heavenly Father,

We worship You and You alone. You are the Lord of our lives and the Lord of our church. We offer our bodies to You as living sacrifices, holy and pleasing to God. We also present our church body to You as a sacrifice of praise.

We pray for Your protection of our pastors, leaders, members, families, attenders and all of our ministries. Grant us the wisdom and grace to deal with heretics and spiritual wolves. We pray for discernment in order to judge between good and evil.

We dedicate all of our facilities to You, and all the property that You have entrusted to us, including our sound system, audiovisual equipment, kitchen and transportation. We rededicate our sanctuary, classrooms, offices and every part of our facility and property.

Lord Jesus Christ, You are the Head of this church, and we exalt You. May all that we do bring honor and glory to You. In Jesus' holy name we pray. Amen.

Step Six: Prayer Action Plan

Place four large sheets of paper side by side on the wall. All of the previous sheets should also be visible. On the first sheet write, "We renounce." On the next write, "We announce" and then "We affirm" and "We will" on the other sheets. Turn to the last page of this appendix for an example and how the wording begins for each item.

You are now ready to synthesize everything you have discerned in the last five steps. Especially look for recurring patterns that can be put together.

You will want to renounce the evil (attacks, corporate sins, conflicts, weaknesses). For example, "We renounce division among us."

Next, you will announce the positive biblical opposite of what you renounced, worded in terms of your resources in Christ. ("We announce that in Christ we have the unity of the Spirit.")

Then you will affirm in emotional language a scriptural promise or truth that encourages and motivates you in regard to the same item. ("We affirm that in the depths of our hearts we are all one in Christ Jesus" [see Gal. 3:26-28]).

Finally, you will commit to an action step you will take. ("We will talk to the right person in the right spirit when conflicts arise.")

Your goal in this crucial statement is to make the shortest list possible without leaving out any major pattern of bondage within your church. You will want to set your church free by using this list as a prayer and action guide in removing the advantages of the evil one. Therefore, it holds special importance. Pray the following prayer together, and spend a few moments silently seeking God's wisdom. Ask for the Holy Spirit's discernment, unity and the right words and order of items.

Dear heavenly Father,

We thank You for opening our eyes to see the strengths, weaknesses, good memories, painful memories, corporate sins and spiritual attacks of evil enemies. Thank You for helping us grasp our spiritual battle with the demonic powers.

Provide us with discernment into the true condition of our church. You know our church intimately. Give us Your plan of action. Teach us to pray it with Your power.

We ask for Your divine guidance in formulating this prayer action plan. We thank You that the Holy Spirit helps us in our weakness because we don't really know how or what to pray. Give us unity. Grant us wisdom. Supply us with the right words and Your order of subjects for us to list.

Open our eyes to the truth of Your Word. Convict us of the need to follow through with what You cause us to see. In Jesus' all-wise name we pray. Amen.

For each subject, work across the four sheets—We renounce, We announce, We affirm, We will—before going on to the next item. Fatigue is a factor now, so call upon the Holy Spirit for divine energy to make sense out of all the lists on the sheets (see Col. 1:29).

When you have finished the list, ask all the participants to stand, face the four sheets, hold hands and pray the Prayer Action Plan aloud. Explain that these are binding and loosing prayers, as discussed at the beginning. We are binding what we renounce and loosing what we announce, affirm and commit to do. This prayer is essential.

Step Seven: Leadership Strategy

Your Prayer Action Plan is similar to a letter from Jesus to your church. In it, He calls you to repent ("We renounce"), to remember ("We announce"), to hold on ("We affirm") and to obey ("We will"). With this view of your church, how does the Lord want you to implement the Prayer Action Plan? Pray together the following prayer, followed by moments of silent prayer. In spite of fatigue from this process, ask the Lord to impress upon your minds and hearts what you as leaders should do.

Dear heavenly Father,
We come before You in worship, adoration and thanksgiving. Thank You for revealing to us Your view of our church. Show us if there is anything else that is keeping our church in bondage. We commit ourselves to renounce it, stand against it in Christ, hold fast to Your promises and obey Your will.

We ask You to reveal what we should do with our Prayer Action Plan. Unveil to us the practical steps that You want us as leaders to take. Make Your will for us known in order that we may fully obey Your direction for our church. In Jesus' powerful name we pray. Amen.

Some strategies for implementing the Prayer Action Plan are as follows:

- Pray through it on a daily basis.
- Pray through it together in each of your regular meetings.
- Preach through it in a sermon series.
- Take other groups of leaders in your church through the "Setting Your Church Free" process.
- Discuss in future meetings specific ways to obey each action point (see the Strategy Questionnaire in chapter 13).
- Present a summary report to the congregation.
- Recruit committed intercessors to pray for the pastor and paid staff members in their leadership of the strategy.

Caution: Other churches have found that it does not work well to try to involve the whole congregation directly in the Prayer Action Plan. People feel judged and condemned if they have not been through the process themselves. We recommend a summary report to the congregation in which the leaders who went through the process take responsibility for what they learned. ("We haven't been the leaders we should be, but we are committing ourselves to pray and take action.") A sermon series also works well in most churches.

Implementation works best if the leaders and pastors pray the Prayer Action Plan until it becomes a part of their lives and their thinking. Think of it as a letter from Jesus—not new revelation but conviction and guidance from the Holy Spirit that your church must obey. Expect resistance, as this is a spiritual battle.

The facilitator will again list on the paper sheets up front the action points reached by group consensus. At this point, name one person besides the pastor or a paid staff member to hold the group accountable for following through on this Leadership Action Plan. (Pastors and staff may also take leadership in implementing it.)

Conclude the session by praying together the following prayer:

Heavenly Father,

Thank You, Lord, that we can call You our heavenly Father. Thank You for Your love and acceptance of us. Thank You for all You have done for us today. Thank You for hearing our prayers, forgiving our corporate sins and setting us free from the damaging influence of Satan's schemes against our church.

Thank You for opening our eyes to see and our ears to hear. Now give us a heart to obey. We commit ourselves to follow through on the Leadership Action Plan You have given us. Teach us to pray and apply this plan as You have directed.

We praise You for uniting us with the Lord Jesus Christ. We praise You that the Son of God came to destroy the works of the devil. We ask for Your protection for our marriages, our families, our ministries and our church. Keep us from scandal. We love You, and commit ourselves to become the people that You have called us to be. Empower us to walk in the light and to speak the truth in love.

"Now to the King eternal, immortal, invisible, the only God, be honor and glory for ever and ever. Amen" (1 Tim. 1:17).

After Completing the Seven Steps

Appoint someone to destroy the sheet for "Step Three—Painful Memories." Ask the recorder or a church secretary to compile all the other lists for the participants in this retreat. Compile the Prayer Action Plan on a single sheet for easy use by the participants. Place the strategy steps on the reverse side of the sheet. Follow the following format.

Our Greatest Strengths

1.

2.

3.

Our Prayer Action Plan

We renounce...	We announce...	We affirm...	We will...
1	1.	1.	1.
2.	2.	2.	2.
3.	3.	3.	3.

Some groups enjoy a fellowship meal together at the close of this time. Plan in advance what you will do to celebrate what Christ has done among you.

OUR GREATEST STRENGTHS

1. We have a strong unity in Christ that creates a close family feeling and loving relationships.
2. We preach the truth and desire to live it out in holiness and righteousness.
3. We pursue unity, humility and the Holy Spirit's direction.
4. We have leadership with a servant's heart.
5. We encourage personal participation in Christ.
6. We have a strong and active children's ministry.
7. We have a Christ-led vision for health, growth, reproduction and optimism.

OUR PRAYER ACTION PLAN

We Renounce

1. We renounce acting independently of God.
2. We renounce acting independently of one another.
3. We renounce our lack of commitment to and practice of spiritual disciplines.
4. We renounce our self-focus that produces apathy to the lost.
5. We renounce inappropriate dependence on the pastor that excuses us from our God-given ministries.
6. We renounce sexual immorality in all its forms.

We Announce

1. We announce that in Christ we have God and all His resources.
2. We announce that in Christ we have mutual dependence on and submission to one another.
3. We announce that in Christ we have continual opportunity to commune with God.
4. We announce that in Christ alone we have the freedom and power to love the unsaved as ourselves.
5. We announce that in Christ we are each equipped for the ministries to which He calls us.
6. We announce that in Christ we have freedom from the power of sin.

We Affirm

1. We affirm that we can do all things through Christ who strengthens us.

2. We affirm that we are united as one body in Christ.

3. We affirm that Christ is knocking at our heart's door, longing for spiritual intimacy with us.

4. We affirm that Christ so loved the lost that He died for their sins to bring them to God.

5. We affirm that it's a high privilege and honor to serve the living God.

6. We affirm that there is no sin that is worth breaking our communion with Christ.

We Will

1. We will be diligent in prayer, seeking to obey the will of God.

2. We will be sensitive to one another and yield our rights to one another, seeking the Lord's best for the body.

3. We will renew our commitment to the spiritual disciplines by cutting out or giving up less important things in order to practice them.

4. We will set aside our fear and inconvenience to prayerfully and actively share the love of Christ.

5. We will make ourselves available to exercise our gifts, strengths and abilities as the Holy Spirit leads us.

6. We will hold each other accountable and pray for one another's purity.

APPENDIX

STEPS TO FREEDOM IN CHRIST

It is my deep conviction that the finished work of Jesus Christ and the presence of God in our lives are the only means by which we can resolve our personal and spiritual conflicts. Christ in us is our only hope (see Col. 1:27), and He alone can meet our deepest needs of life, acceptance, identity, security and significance. The discipleship counseling process upon which these steps are based should not be understood as just another counseling technique we learn. It is an encounter with God. He is the Wonderful Counselor. He is the one who grants repentance that leads to a knowledge of the truth that sets us free (see 2 Tim. 2:24-26).

The Steps to Freedom in Christ do not set you free. *Who* sets you free is Christ, and *what* sets you free is your response to Him in repentance and faith. These steps are just a tool to help you submit to God and resist the devil (see Jas. 4:7). Then you can start living a fruitful life by abiding in Christ and becoming the person He created you to be. Many Christians will be able to work through these steps on their own and discover the wonderful freedom Christ purchased for them on the cross. Then they will experience the peace of God that surpasses all comprehension, and it shall guard their hearts and their minds (see Phil. 4:7).

Before You Begin

The chances of that happening and the possibility of maintaining that freedom will be greatly enhanced if you read *Victory over the Darkness* and *The Bondage Breaker* first. Many Christians in our Western world need to understand the reality of the spiritual world and our relationship to it. Some can't read these books or even the Bible with comprehension because of the battle that is going on for their minds. They will need the assistance of others who have been trained. The theology and practical process of discipleship counseling is presented in my book *Helping Others Find Freedom in Christ,* and the study guide that accompanies it. The book attempts to biblically integrate the reality of the spiritual and the natural world so we can have a whole answer for a whole person. In doing so, we cannot polarize into psychotherapeutic ministries that ignore the reality of the spiritual world or attempt some kind of deliverance ministry that ignores developmental issues and human responsibility.

You May Need Help

Ideally, it would be best if everyone had a trusted friend, pastor or counselor who would help them go through this process because it is just applying the wisdom of James 5:16: "Therefore, confess your sins to one another, and pray for one another, so that you may be healed. The effective prayer of a righteous man can accomplish much." Another person can prayerfully support you by providing objective counsel. I have had the privilege to help many Christian leaders who could not process this on their own. Many Christian groups throughout the world are using this approach in many languages with incredible results because the Lord desires for all to come to repentance (see 2 Pet. 3:9), and to know the truth that sets us free in Christ (see John 8:32).

Appropriating and Maintaining Freedom

Christ has set us free through His victory over sin and death on the cross. Appropriating our freedom in Christ through repentance and faith and maintaining our life of freedom in Christ, however, are two different issues. It was for freedom that Christ set us free, but we have been warned not to return to a yoke of slavery that is legalism in this context (see Gal. 5:1) or to turn our freedom into an opportunity for the flesh (see Gal. 5:13). Establishing people as free in Christ makes it possible for them to walk by faith according to what God says is true, and to live by the power of the Holy Spirit and not carry out the desires of the flesh (see Gal. 5:16). The true Christian life avoids both legalism and license.

If you are not experiencing freedom, it may be because you have not stood firm in the faith or actively taken your place in Christ. It is every Christian's responsibility to do whatever is necessary to maintain a right relationship with God and humankind. Your eternal destiny is not at stake. God will never leave you nor forsake you (see Heb. 13:5), but your daily victory is at stake if you fail to claim and maintain your position in Christ.

Your Position in Christ

You are not a helpless victim caught between two nearly equal but opposite heavenly superpowers. Satan is a deceiver. Only God is omnipotent, omnipresent and omniscient. Sometimes the reality of sin and the presence of evil may seem more real than the presence of God, but that's part of Satan's deception. Satan is a defeated foe and we are **in Christ**. A true knowledge of God and knowing our identity and position in Christ are the greatest determinants of our "mental health." A false concept of God, a distorted understanding of who we are as children of God and the misplaced deification of Satan are the greatest contributors to "mental illness."

Many of our illnesses are psychosomatic. When these issues are resolved in Christ, our physical bodies will function better and we will experience greater health. Other problems are clearly physical, and we need the services of the medical profession. Please consult your physician for medical advice and prescriptions. We are both spiritual and physical beings who need the services of both the church and the hospital.

Winning the Battle for Your Mind

The battle is for the mind, which is the control center of all that we think and do. The opposing thoughts you may experience as you go through these steps can control you only if you believe them. If you are working through these steps alone, don't be deceived by any lying, intimidating thoughts in your mind. If a trusted pastor or counselor is helping you find your freedom in Christ, he or she must have your cooperation. You must share any thoughts you are having in opposition to what you are attempting to do. As soon as you expose the lie, the power of Satan is broken. The only way you can lose control in this process is if you pay attention to a deceiving spirit and believe a lie.

You Must Choose

The following procedure is a means of resolving personal and spiritual conflicts that have kept you from experiencing the freedom and victory Christ purchased for you on the cross. Your freedom will be the result of what *you* choose to believe, confess, forgive, renounce and forsake. No one can do that for you. The battle for your mind can only be won as you personally choose truth. As you go through this process, understand that Satan is under no obligation to obey your thoughts. Only God has complete knowledge of your mind because He is omniscient (all-knowing). So we can submit to God inwardly, but we need to resist the devil by reading aloud each prayer and by verbally renouncing, forgiving, confessing, etc.

This process of reestablishing our freedom in Christ is nothing more than a fierce moral inventory and a rock-solid commitment to truth. It is the first step in the continuing process of discipleship. There is no such thing as instant maturity. It will take you the rest of your life to renew your mind and conform to the image of God. If your problems stem from a source other than those covered in these steps, you may need to seek professional help.

May the Lord grace you with His presence as you seek His face and help others experience the joy of their salvation.

Neil T. Anderson

Prayer

Dear heavenly Father,

We acknowledge Your presence in this room and in our lives. You are the only omniscient (all knowing), omnipotent (all powerful) and omnipresent (always present) God. We are dependent upon You, for apart from You we can do nothing. We stand in the truth that all authority in heaven and on earth has been given to the resurrected Christ, and because we are in Christ, we share that authority in order to make disciples and set captives free. We ask You to fill us with Your Holy Spirit and lead us into all truth. We pray for Your complete protection and ask for Your guidance. In Jesus' name, Amen.

Declaration

In the name and authority of the Lord Jesus Christ, we command Satan and all evil spirits to release (name) in order that (name) can be free to know and choose to do the will of God. As children of God seated with Christ in the heavenlies, we agree that every enemy of the Lord Jesus Christ be bound to silence. We say to Satan and all your evil workers that you cannot inflict any pain or in any way prevent God's will from being accomplished in (name's) life.

Preparation

Before going through the Steps to Freedom, review the events of your life to discern specific areas that might need to be addressed.

Family History
_____ Religious history of parents and grandparents
_____ Home life from childhood through high school
_____ History of physical or emotional illness in the family
_____ Adoption, foster care, guardians

Personal History

_____ Eating habits (bulimia, bingeing and purging, anorexia, compulsive eating)

_____ Addictions (drugs, alcohol)

_____ Prescription medications (what for?)

_____ Sleeping patterns and nightmares

_____ Rape or any sexual, physical, emotional abuse

_____ Thought life (obsessive, blasphemous, condemning, distracting thoughts, poor concentration, fantasy)

_____ Mental interference in church, prayer or Bible study

_____ Emotional life (anger, anxiety, depression, bitterness, fears)

_____ Spiritual journey (salvation: when, how and assurance)

Now you are ready to begin. The following are seven specific steps to process in order to experience freedom from your past. You will address the areas where Satan most commonly takes advantage of us and where strongholds have been built. Christ purchased your victory when He shed His blood for you on the cross. Realizing your freedom will be the result of what you choose to believe, confess, forgive, renounce and forsake. No one can do that for you. The battle for your mind can only be won as you personally choose truth.

As you go through these Steps to Freedom, remember that Satan will only be defeated if you confront him verbally. He cannot read your mind and is under no obligation to obey your thoughts. Only God has complete knowledge of your mind. As you process each step, it is important that you submit to God inwardly and resist the devil by reading aloud each prayer—verbally renouncing, forgiving, confessing, etc.

You are taking a fierce moral inventory and making a rock-solid commitment to truth. If your problems stem from a source other than those covered in these steps, you have nothing to lose by going through them. If you are sincere, the only thing that can happen is that you will get very right with God!

Step 1: Counterfeit Versus Real

The first Step to Freedom in Christ is to renounce your previous or current involvement with satanically inspired occult practices and false religions. You need to renounce any activity and group that denies Jesus Christ, offers guidance through any source other than the absolute authority of the written Word of God or requires secret initiations, ceremonies or covenants.

In order to help you assess your spiritual experiences, begin this Step by asking God to reveal false guidance and counterfeit religious experiences.

Dear heavenly Father,
I ask You to guard my heart and my mind and reveal to me any and all involvement I have had either knowingly or unknowingly with cultic or occult practices, false religions or false teachers. In Jesus' name, I pray. Amen.

Using the "Non-Christian Spiritual Experience Inventory" on the following page, carefully check anything in which you were involved. This list is not exhaustive, but it will guide you in identifying non-Christian experiences. Add any additional involvement you have had. Even if you "innocently" participated in something or observed it, you should write it on your list to renounce, just in case you unknowingly gave Satan a foothold.

Non-Christian Spiritual Experience Inventory
(Please check those that apply.)

Occult

Astral-projection
Ouija board
Table or body lifting
Dungeons and Dragons
Speaking in trance
Automatic writing
Magic eight ball
Telepathy
Using spells or curses
Seance
Materialization
Clairvoyance
Spirit guides
Fortune-telling
Tarot cards
Palm reading
Astrology/horoscopes
Rod and pendulum
    (dowsing)
Self-hypnosis
Mental manipulations or
    attempts to swap
    minds
Black and white magic
New Age medicine
Blood pacts (or cutting
    yourself in a destruc-
    tive way)

Cult

Christian Science
Unity
The Way International
Unification Church
Mormonism
Church of the Living
    Word
Jehovah's Witnesses
Children of God (Love)
Swedenborgianism
Unitarianism
Masons
New Age
The Forum (EST)
Spirit worship
Other _____

Other Religions

Buddhism
Hare Krishna
Bahaism
Rosicrucian
Science of the Mind
Science of Creative
    Intelligence
Transcendental Medita-
    tion
Hinduism
Yoga
Eckankar
Roy Masters
Silva Mind Control
Father Divine
Theosophical Society
Islam
Black Muslim
Religion of Martial Arts
Other _____

Fetishism (objects of
    worship, crystals,
    good-luck charms)
Incubi and succubi (sex-
    ual spirits)
Other _____

1. Have you ever been hypnotized, attended a New Age or parapsychology seminar, consulted a medium, Spiritist or channeler? Explain.

2. Do you or have you ever had an imaginary friend or spirit guide offering you guidance or companionship? Explain.

3. Have you ever heard voices in your mind or had repeating and nagging thoughts condemning you or that were foreign to what you believe or feel, as though a dialog was going on in your head? Explain.

4. What other spiritual experiences have you had that would be considered out of the ordinary?

5. Have you ever made a vow, covenant or pact with any individual or group other than God?

6. Have you been involved in satanic ritual or satanic worship of any form? Explain.

When you are confident that your list is complete, confess and renounce each involvement, whether active or passive, by praying aloud the following prayer, repeating it separately for each item on your list:

> Lord,
> I confess that I have participated in _____,and
> I renounce_____. Thank You that in Christ I am forgiven.

If you have had any involvement in satanic ritual or heavy occult activity, you need to state aloud the following special renunciations that apply. Read across the page, renouncing the first item in the column of the Kingdom of Darkness and then affirming the first truth in the column of the Kingdom of Light. Continue down the page in this manner.

All satanic rituals, covenants and assignments must be specifically renounced as the Lord allows you to recall them. Some who have been subjected to satanic ritual abuse may have developed multiple personalities to survive. Nevertheless, continue through the Steps to Freedom in order to resolve all you consciously can. It is important that you resolve the demonic strongholds first. Every personality must resolve his/her issues and agree to come together in Christ. You may need someone who understands spiritual conflict to help you maintain control and not be deceived into false memories. Only Jesus can bind up the broken-hearted, set captives free and make us whole.

KINGDOM OF DARKNESS	KINGDOM OF LIGHT
I renounce ever signing my name over to Satan or having had my name signed over to Satan.	*I announce that my name is now written in the Lamb's Book of Life.*
I renounce any ceremony where I may have been wed to Satan.	*I announce that I am the Bride of Christ.*
I renounce any and all covenants that I made with Satan.	*I announce that I am a partaker of the New Covenant with Christ.*
I renounce all satanic assignments for my life, including duties, marriage and children.	*I announce and commit myself to know and to do only the will of God and accept only His guidance.*
I renounce all spirit guides assigned to me.	*I announce and accept only the leading of the Holy Spirit.*
I renounce ever giving of my blood in the service of Satan.	*I trust only in the shed blood of my Lord Jesus Christ.*
I renounce ever eating of flesh or drinking of blood for satanic worship.	*By faith I eat only the flesh and drink only the blood of Jesus in Holy Communion.*
I renounce any and all guardians and satanist parents that were assigned to me.	*I announce that God is my Father and the Holy Spirit is my Guardian by which I am sealed.*
I renounce any baptism in blood or urine whereby I am identified with Satan.	*I announce that I have been baptized into Christ Jesus and my identity is now in Christ.*
I renounce any and all sacrifices that were made on my behalf by which Satan may claim ownership of me.	*I announce that only the sacrifice of Christ has any hold on me. I belong to Him. I have been purchased by the blood of the Lamb.*

Step 2: Deception Versus Truth

Truth is the revelation of God's Word, but we need to acknowledge the truth in the inner self (see Ps. 51:6). When David lived a lie, he suffered greatly. When he finally found freedom by acknowledging the truth, he wrote: "How blessed is the man...in whose spirit there is no deceit" (Ps. 32:2). We are to lay aside falsehood and speak the truth in love (see Eph. 4:15,25). A mentally healthy person is one who is in touch with reality and relatively free of anxiety. Both qualities should characterize the Christian who renounces deception and embraces the truth.

Begin this critical step by expressing aloud the following prayer. Don't let the enemy accuse you with thoughts such as: "This isn't going to work" or "I wish I could believe this but I can't" or any other lies in opposition to what you are proclaiming. Even if you have difficulty doing so, you need to pray the prayer and read the Doctrinal Affirmation.

Dear heavenly Father,

I know that You desire truth in the inner self and that facing this truth is the way of liberation (John 8:32). I acknowledge that I have been deceived by the father of lies (John 8:44) and that I have deceived myself (1 John 1:8). I pray in the name of the Lord Jesus Christ that You, heavenly Father, will rebuke all deceiving spirits by virtue of the shed blood and resurrection of the Lord Jesus Christ. By faith I have received You into my life and I am now seated with Christ in the heavenlies (Eph. 2:6). I acknowledge that I have the responsibility and authority to resist the devil, and when I do, he will flee from me. I now ask the Holy Spirit to guide me into all truth (John 16:13). I ask You to "Search me, O God, and know my heart; try me and know my anxious thoughts; and see if there be any hurtful way in me, and lead me in the everlasting way" (Ps. 139:23,24). In Jesus' name, I pray. Amen.

You may want to pause at this point to consider some of Satan's deceptive schemes. In addition to false teachers, false prophets and deceiving spirits, you can deceive yourself. Now that you are alive in Christ and forgiven, you never have to live a lie or defend yourself. Christ is your defense. How have you deceived or attempted to defend yourself according to the following?

Self-deception
_____ Hearing God's Word but not doing it (see Jas. 1:22; 4:17)
_____ Saying we have no sin (see 1 John 1:8)
_____ Thinking we are something when we aren't (see Gal. 6:3)
_____ Thinking we are wise in our own eyes (see 1 Cor. 3:18,19)
_____ Thinking we will not reap what we sow (see Gal. 6:7)
_____ Thinking the unrighteous will inherit the Kingdom (see 1 Cor. 6:9)
_____ Thinking we can associate with bad company and not be corrupted (see 1 Cor. 15:33)

Self-defense
(defending ourselves instead of trusting in Christ)
_____ Denial (conscious or subconscious refusal to face the truth)
_____ Fantasy (escaping from the real world)
_____ Emotional insulation (withdrawing to avoid rejection)
_____ Regression (reverting back to a less threatening time)
_____ Displacement (taking out frustrations on others)
_____ Projection (blaming others)
_____ Rationalization (making excuses for poor behavior)

For those things that have been true in your life, pray aloud:

Lord,
I agree that I have been deceived in the area of _____.
Thank You for forgiving me. I commit myself to know and follow Your truth. Amen.

Choosing the truth may be difficult if you have been living a lie (been deceived) for many years. You may need to seek professional help to weed out the defense mechanisms you have depended upon to survive. The Christian needs only one defense—Jesus. Knowing that you are forgiven and accepted as God's child is what sets you free to face reality and declare your dependence on Him.

Faith is the biblical response to the truth, and believing the truth is a choice. When someone says, "I want to believe God, but I just can't," he or she is being deceived. Of course you can believe God. Faith is something you decide to do, not something you feel like doing. Believing the truth doesn't make it true. It's true; therefore, we believe it. The New Age movement is distorting the truth by saying we create reality through what we believe. We can't create reality with our minds; we face reality. It is what or who you believe in that counts. Everybody believes in something, and everybody walks by faith according to what he or she believes. But if what you believe isn't true, then how you live (walk by faith) won't be right.

Historically, the Church has found great value in publicly declaring its beliefs. The Apostles' Creed and the Nicene Creed have been recited for centuries. Read aloud the following affirmation of faith, and do so again as often as necessary to renew your mind. Experiencing difficulty in reading this affirmation may indicate where you are being deceived and under attack. Boldly affirm your commitment to biblical truth.

Doctrinal Affirmation

I recognize that there is only one true and living God (Exod. 20:2,3) who exists as the Father, Son and Holy Spirit and that He is worthy of all honor, praise and glory as the Creator, Sustainer and Beginning and End of all things (Rev. 4:11; 5:9,10; Is. 43:1,7,21).

I recognize Jesus Christ as the Messiah, the Word who became flesh and dwelt among us (John 1:1,14). I believe that He came to destroy the works of Satan (1 John 3:8), that He disarmed the rulers and authorities and made a public display of them, having triumphed over them (Col. 2:15).

I believe that God has proven His love for me because when I was still a sinner, Christ died for me (Rom. 5:8). I believe that He delivered me from the domain of darkness and transferred me to His kingdom, and in Him I have redemption, the forgiveness of sins (Col. 1:13,14).

I believe that I am now a child of God (1 John 3:1-3) and that I am seated with Christ in the heavenlies (Eph. 2:6). I believe that I was saved by the grace of God through faith, that it was a gift, and not the result of any works on my part (Eph. 2:8,9).

I choose to be strong in the Lord and in the strength of His might (Eph. 6:10). I put no confidence in the flesh (Phil. 3:3) for the weapons of warfare are not of the flesh (2 Cor. 10:4). I put on the whole armor of God (Eph. 6:10-20), and I resolve to stand firm in my faith and resist the evil one.

I believe that apart from Christ I can do nothing (John 15:5), so I declare myself dependent on Him. I choose to abide in Christ in order to bear much fruit and glorify the Lord (John 15:8). I announce to Satan that Jesus is my Lord (1 Cor. 12:3), and I reject any counterfeit gifts or works of Satan in my life.

I believe that the truth will set me free (John 8:32) and that walking in the light is the only path of fellowship (1 John 1:7). Therefore, I stand against Satan's deception by taking every thought captive in obedience to Christ (2 Cor. 10:5). I declare that the Bible is the only authoritative standard (2 Tim. 3:15,16). I choose to speak the truth in love (Eph. 4:15).

I choose to present my body as an instrument of righteousness, a living and holy sacrifice, and I renew my mind by the living Word of God in order that I may prove that the will of God is good, acceptable and perfect (Rom. 6:13; 12:1,2). I put off the old self with its evil practices and put on the new self (Col. 3:9,10), and I declare myself to be a new creature in Christ (2 Cor. 5:17).

I trust my heavenly Father to fill me with His Holy Spirit (Eph. 5:18), to lead me into all truth (John 16:13) and to empower my life that I may live above sin and not carry out the desires of the flesh (Gal. 5:16). I crucify the flesh (Gal. 5:24) and choose to walk by the Spirit.

I renounce all selfish goals and choose the ultimate goal of love (1 Tim. 1:5). I choose to obey the two greatest commandments: to love the Lord my God with all my heart, soul and mind, and to love my neighbor as myself (Matt. 22:37-39).

I believe that Jesus has all authority in heaven and on earth (Matt. 28:18) and that He is the head over all rule and authority (Col. 2:10). I believe that Satan and his demons are subject to me in Christ since I am a member of Christ's Body (Eph. 1:19-23). Therefore, I obey the command to submit to God and to resist the devil (Jas. 4:7), and I command Satan in the name of Christ to leave my presence.

Step 3: Bitterness Versus Forgiveness

We need to forgive others in order to be free from our pasts and to prevent Satan from taking advantage of us (see 2 Cor. 2:10,11). We are to be merciful just as our heavenly Father is merciful (see Luke 6:36). We are to forgive as we have been forgiven (see Eph. 4:31,32). Ask God to bring to mind the names of those people you need to forgive by expressing the following prayer aloud:

Dear heavenly Father,
I thank You for the riches of Your kindness, forbearance and patience, knowing that Your kindness has led me to repentance (Rom. 2:4). I confess that I have not extended that same patience and kindness toward others who have offended me, but instead I have harbored bitterness and resentment. I pray that during this time of self-examination You would bring to my mind those people I need to forgive in order that I may do so (Matt. 18:35). I ask this in the precious name of Jesus. Amen.

As names come to mind, make a list of only the names. At the end of your list, write "myself." Forgiving yourself is accepting God's cleansing and forgiveness. Then write "thoughts against God." Thoughts raised up against the knowledge of God will usually result in angry feelings toward Him. Technically, we can't forgive God because He cannot commit any sin of commission or omission. But you need to specifically renounce false expectations and thoughts about God and agree to release any anger you have toward Him.

Before you pray to forgive these people, stop and consider what forgiveness is, what it is not, what decision you will be making and what the consequences will be.

In the following explanation, the main points are highlighted in bold print:
Forgiveness is not forgetting. People who try to forget find they cannot. God says He will remember our sins "no more" (see Heb. 10:17), but God, being omniscient, cannot forget. Remember our sins "no more" means that God will never use the past against us (see Ps. 103:12). Forgetting may be the result of forgiveness, but it is never the means of forgiveness. When we bring up the past against others, we are saying we haven't forgiven them.

Forgiveness is a choice, a crisis of the will. Since God requires us to forgive, it is something we can do. However, forgiveness is difficult for us because it pulls against our concept of justice. We want revenge for offenses suffered. We are told, however, never to take our own revenge (see Rom. 12:19). You say, "Why should I let them off the hook?" That is precisely the problem. You are still hooked to them, still bound by your past. You will let them off your hook, but they are never off God's. He will deal with them fairly, something we cannot do.

You say, "You don't understand how much this person hurt me!" But don't you see, they are still hurting you! How do you stop the pain? **You don't forgive someone for their sake; you do it for your own sake so that you can be free. Your need to forgive isn't an issue between you and the offender; it's between you and God.**

Forgiveness is agreeing to live with the consequences of another person's sin. Forgiveness is costly. You pay the price of the evil you forgive. You're going to live with those consequences whether you want to or not; your only choice is whether you will do so in the bitterness of unforgiveness or the freedom of forgiveness. Jesus took the consequences of your sin upon Himself. All true forgiveness is substitutionary because no one really forgives without bearing the consequences of the other person's sin. God the Father "made Him who knew no sin to be sin on our behalf, that we might become the righteousness of God in Him" (2 Cor. 5:21). Where is the justice? It is the Cross that makes forgiveness legally and morally right: "For the death that He died, He died to sin, once for all" (Rom. 6:10).

Decide that you will bear the burdens of their offenses by not using that information against them in the future. This doesn't mean that you tolerate sin. You must set up scriptural boundaries to prevent future abuse. Some may be required to testify for the sake of justice, but not for the purpose of seeking revenge from a bitter heart.

How do you forgive from your heart? You acknowledge the hurt and the hate. If your forgiveness doesn't visit the emotional core of your life, it will be incomplete. Many feel the pain of interpersonal offenses, but they won't or don't know how to acknowledge it. Let God bring the pain to the surface so He can deal with it. This is where the healing takes place.

Don't wait to forgive until you feel like forgiving; you will never get there. Feelings take time to heal after the choice to forgive is made and Satan has lost his place (see Eph. 4:26,27). Freedom is what will be gained, not a feeling.

As you pray, God may bring to mind offending people and experiences you have totally forgotten. Let Him do it even if it is painful. Remember, you are doing this for your sake. God wants you to be free. Don't rationalize or explain the offender's behavior. Forgiveness is dealing with your pain and leaving the other person to God. Positive feelings will follow in time; freeing yourself from the past is the critical issue right now.

Don't say, "Lord, please help me to forgive," because He is already helping you. Don't say, "Lord, I want to forgive," because you are bypassing the hard-core choice to forgive, which is your responsibility. Stay with each individual until you are sure you have dealt with all the remembered pain—what they did, how they hurt you, how they made you feel (rejected, unloved, unworthy, dirty).

You are now ready to forgive the people on your list so that you can be free in Christ; those people no longer having any control over you. For each person on your list, pray aloud:

Lord,
        I forgive (name the person) for (verbally share every hurt and pain the Lord brings to your mind and how it made you feel).

After you have forgiven every person for every painful memory, then finish this step by praying:

Lord,
        I release all these people to You, and my right to seek revenge. I choose not to hold on to my bitterness and anger, and I ask You to heal my damaged emotions. In Jesus' name, I pray. Amen.

Step 4: Rebellion Versus Submission

We live in rebellious times. Many believe it is their right to sit in judgment of those in authority over them. Rebelling against God and His authority gives Satan an opportunity to attack. As our commanding general, the Lord says, "Get into ranks and follow Me. I will not lead you into temptation, but I will deliver you from evil" (see Matt. 6:13).

We have two biblical responsibilities regarding authority figures: Pray for them and submit to them. The only time God permits us to disobey earthly leaders is when they require us to do something morally wrong before God or attempt to rule outside the realm of their authority. Pray the following prayer:

Dear heavenly Father,

You have said that rebellion is as the sin of witchcraft and insubordination is as iniquity and idolatry (1 Sam. 15:23). I know that in action and attitude I have sinned against You with a rebellious heart. I ask Your forgiveness for my rebellion and pray that by the shed blood of the Lord Jesus Christ all ground gained by evil spirits because of my rebelliousness will be canceled. I pray that You will shed light on all my ways that I may know the full extent of my rebelliousness. I now choose to adopt a submissive spirit and a servant's heart. In the name of Christ Jesus, my Lord. Amen.

Being under authority is an act of faith. You are trusting God to work through His established lines of authority. There are times when employers, parents and husbands are violating the laws of civil government that are ordained by God to protect innocent people against abuse. In these cases, you need to appeal to the state for your protection. In many states, the law requires such abuse to be reported.

In difficult cases, such as continuing abuse at home, further counseling help may be needed. And in some cases, when earthly authorities have abused their position and are requiring disobedience to God or a compromise in your commitment to Him, you need to obey God, not man.

We are all admonished to submit to one another as equals in Christ (see Eph. 5:21). Specific lines of authority in Scripture, however, are provided for the purpose of accomplishing common goals:

Civil Government (see Rom. 13:1-7; 1 Tim. 2:1-4; 1 Pet. 2:13-17)
Parents (see Eph. 6:1-3)
Husband (see 1 Pet. 3:1-4) or Wife (see Eph. 5:21; 1 Pet. 3:7)
Employer (see 1 Pet. 2:18-23)
Church Leaders (see Heb. 13:17)
God (see Dan. 9:5,9)

Examine each area and confess those times you have not been submissive by praying:

Lord,
I agree I have been rebellious toward _____. I choose
to be submissive and obedient to your Word. In Jesus' name. Amen.

Step 5: Pride Versus Humility

Pride is a killer. Pride says, "I can do it! I can get myself out of this mess without God or anyone else's help." Oh no, we can't! We absolutely need God, and
we desperately need each other. Paul wrote: "We worship in the Spirit of
God and glory in Christ Jesus and put no confidence in the flesh" (Phil. 3:3).
Humility is confidence properly placed. We are to be "strong in the Lord and
in the strength of His might" (Eph. 6:10). James 4:6-10 and 1 Peter 5:1-10
reveal that spiritual conflict follows pride. Use the following prayer to express
your commitment to live humbly before God:

Dear heavenly Father,
You have said that pride goes before destruction and an arrogant
spirit before stumbling (Prov. 16:18). I confess that I have lived independently and have not denied myself, picked up my cross daily and followed You (Matt. 16:24). In so doing, I have given ground to the enemy
in my life. I have believed that I could be successful and live victori-
ously by my own strength and resources. I now confess that I have
sinned against You by placing my will before Yours and by centering my
life around myself instead of You. I now renounce the self-life and by so
doing cancel all the ground that has been gained in my members by
the enemies of the Lord Jesus Christ. I pray that You will guide me so
that I will do nothing from selfishness or empty conceit, but with humility of mind I will regard others as more important than myself (Phil.
2:3). Enable me through love to serve others and in honor prefer others
(Rom. 12:10). I ask this in the name of Christ Jesus, my Lord. Amen.

Having made that commitment, now allow God to show you any specif-
ic areas of your life where you have been prideful, such as:
_____ Stronger desire to do my will than God's will
_____ More dependent upon my strengths and resources than God's

_____ Too often believe that my ideas and opinions are better than others'
_____ More concerned about controlling others than developing self-
control
_____ Sometimes consider myself more important than others
_____ Tendency to think I have no needs
_____ Find it difficult to admit that I was wrong
_____ Tendency to be more of a people-pleaser than a God-pleaser
_____ Overly concerned about getting the credit I deserve
_____ Driven to obtain the recognition that comes from degrees, titles and
positions
_____ Often think I am more humble than others
_____ Other ways _____

For each of these that has been true in your life, pray aloud:

Lord,
    I agree I have been prideful by _____. I
choose to humble myself and place all my confidence in You. Amen.

Step 6: Bondage Versus Freedom

The next Step to Freedom deals with habitual sin. People who have been
caught in the trap of sin-confess-sin-confess may need to follow the instructions of James 5:16, "Confess your sins to one another, and pray for one another, so that you may be healed. The effective prayer of a righteous man can
accomplish much." Seek out a righteous person who will hold you up in prayer
and to whom you can be accountable. Others may only need the assurance of
1 John 1:9: "If we confess our sins, He is faithful and righteous to forgive us our
sins and to cleanse us from all unrighteousness." Confession is not saying "I'm
sorry"; it is saying "I did it." Whether you need the help of others or just the
accountability to God, pray the following prayer:

Dear heavenly Father,
    You have told us to put on the Lord Jesus Christ and make no provi-

sion for the flesh in regard to its lust (Rom. 13:14). I acknowledge that I have given in to fleshly lusts that wage war against my soul (1 Pet. 2:11). I thank You that in Christ my sins are forgiven, but I have transgressed Your holy law and given the enemy an opportunity to wage war in my physical body (Rom. 6:12,13; Eph 4:27; Jas. 4:1; 1 Pet. 5:8). I come before Your presence to acknowledge these sins and to seek Your cleansing (1 John 1:9) that I may be freed from the bondage of sin. I now ask You to reveal to my mind the ways I have transgressed Your moral law and grieved the Holy Spirit. In Jesus' precious name, I pray. Amen.

The deeds of the flesh are numerous. Many of the following issues are taken from Galatians 5:19-21. Check those that apply to you and any others you have struggled with that the Lord has brought to your mind. Then confess each one with the concluding prayer. Note: sexual sins, eating disorders, substance abuse, abortion, suicidal tendencies and perfectionism will be dealt with later.

___ stealing	___ criticizing	___ greediness
___ lying	___ lusting	___ laziness
___ fighting	___ cheating	___ divisiveness
___ jealousy	___ gossiping	___ gambling
___ envying	___ controlling	other_____
___ outbursts of anger	___ procrastinating	_____
___ complaining	___ swearing	_____

Dear heavenly Father,
   I thank You that my sins are forgiven in Christ, but I have walked by the flesh and therefore sinned by _____.
Thank You for cleansing me of all unrighteousness. I ask that You would enable me to walk by the Spirit and not carry out the desires of the flesh. In Jesus' name, I pray. Amen.

It is our responsibility not to allow sin to reign in our mortal bodies by not using our bodies as instruments of unrighteousness (see Rom. 6:12,13). If you are or have struggled with sexual sins (pornography, masturbation, sexual promiscuity) or are experiencing sexual difficulty in your marriage, pray as follows:

Lord,

I ask You to reveal to my mind every sexual use of my body as an instrument of unrighteousness. In Jesus' precious name, I pray. Amen.

As the Lord brings to your mind every sexual misuse of your body, whether it was done to you (rape, incest or other sexual abuse) or willingly by you, renounce every occasion:

Lord,

I renounce (name the specific misuse of your body) with (name the person) and ask You to break that bond.

Now commit your body to the Lord by praying:

Lord,

I renounce all these uses of my body as an instrument of unrighteousness and by so doing ask You to break all bondages Satan has brought into my life through that involvement. I confess my participation. I now present my body to You as a living sacrifice, holy and acceptable unto You, and I reserve the sexual use of my body only for marriage. I renounce the lie of Satan that my body is not clean, that it is dirty or in any way unacceptable as a result of my past sexual experiences. Lord, I thank You that You have totally cleansed and forgiven me, that You love and accept me unconditionally. Therefore, I can accept myself. And I choose to do so, to accept myself and my body as cleansed. In Jesus' name. Amen.

Special Prayers for Specific Problems

Homosexuality

Lord,

I renounce the lie that You have created me or anyone else to be homosexual, and I affirm that You clearly forbid homosexual behavior. I accept myself as a child of God and declare that You created me a man (woman). I renounce any bondages of Satan that have perverted my relationships with others. I announce that I am free to relate to the opposite sex in the way that You intended. In Jesus' name. Amen.

Abortion

Lord,

I confess that I did not assume stewardship of the life You entrusted to me and I ask your forgiveness. I choose to accept your forgiveness, and I now commit that child to You for Your care in eternity. In Jesus' name. Amen.

Suicidal Tendencies

Lord,

I renounce suicidal thoughts and any attempts I have made to take my own life or in any way injure myself. I renounce the lie that life is hopeless and that I can find peace and freedom by taking my own life. Satan is a thief, and he comes to steal, kill and destroy. I choose to be a good steward of the physical life You have entrusted to me. In Jesus' name, I pray. Amen.

Eating Disorders or Self-Mutilation

Lord,

I renounce the lie that my value as a person is dependent upon my physical beauty, my weight or size. I renounce cutting myself, vomiting, using laxatives or starving myself as a means of cleansing myself of evil or altering my appearance. I announce that only the blood of the Lord Jesus Christ cleanses me from sin. I accept the reality that there may be sin present in me due to the lies I have believed and the wrongful use of my body, but I renounce the lie that I am evil or that any part of my body is evil. My body is the temple of the Holy Spirit and I belong to You, Lord. I receive Your love and acceptance of me. In Jesus' name. Amen.

Substance Abuse

Lord,

I confess that I have misused substances (alcohol, tobacco, food, prescription or street drugs) for the purpose of pleasure, to escape reality or to cope with difficult situations—resulting in the abuse of my body, the harmful programming of my mind and the quenching of the Holy Spirit. I ask Your forgiveness. I renounce any satanic connection or influence in my life through my misuse of chemicals or food. I cast my anxiety onto Christ Who loves me, and I commit myself to no longer yield to substance abuse, but to the Holy Spirit. I ask You, heavenly Father, to fill me with Your Holy Spirit. In Jesus' name. Amen.

Drivenness and Perfectionism

Lord,

I renounce the lie that my self-worth is dependent upon my ability to perform. I announce the truth that my identity and sense of worth are found in who I am as Your child. I renounce seeking the approval and acceptance of other people, and I choose to believe that I am already approved and accepted in Christ because of His death and resurrection for me. I choose to believe the truth that I have been saved, not by deeds done in righteousness, but according to Your mercy. I choose to believe that I am no longer under the curse of the law, because Christ became a curse for me. I receive the free gift of life in Christ and choose to abide in Him. I renounce striving for perfection by living under the law. By Your grace, heavenly Father, I choose from this day forward to walk by faith according to what You have said is true by the power of Your Holy Spirit. In Jesus name. Amen.

Plaguing Fears

Dear heavenly Father,

I acknowledge You as the only legitimate fear object in my life. You are the only omnipresent (always present) and omniscient (all knowing) God and the only means by which all other fears can be expelled. You are my sanctuary. You have not given me a spirit of timidity, but of power and love and discipline. I confess that I have allowed the fear of man and the fear of death to exercise control over my life, instead of trusting in You. I now renounce all other fear objects and worship You only. I pray that You would fill me with Your Holy Spirit that I may live my life and speak Your word with boldness. In Jesus' name, I pray. Amen.

Prejudice and Bigotry

Dear heavenly Father,

I know that You love everyone equally and that You do not show favoritism, but You accept people from every nation who fear You and do what is right (Acts 10:34). You do not judge people based on race, gender, culture, economic or social status (Gal. 3:28). I confess that I have too often prejudged others or regarded myself superior because of these things. I have not always been a minister of reconciliation, but have been a proud agent of division through my attitudes, words and deeds. I repent of all hateful bigotry and proud prejudice and I ask You, Lord, to reveal to my mind all the specific ways in which this form of pride has corrupted my heart and mind. I confess and renounce the prideful sin of prejudice against (name the group). I thank You for Your forgiveness, Lord, and ask You to change my heart and make me a loving agent of reconciliation with (name the group). In Jesus' name. Amen.

After you have confessed all known sin, pray:

I now confess these sins to You and claim my forgiveness and cleansing through the blood of the Lord Jesus Christ. I cancel all ground that evil spirits have gained through my willful involvement in sin. I ask this in the wonderful name of my Lord and Savior, Jesus Christ. Amen.

Step 7: Acquiescence Versus Renunciation

Acquiescence is passively giving in or agreeing without consent. The last Step to Freedom is to renounce the sins of your ancestors and any curses that may have been placed on you. In giving the Ten Commandments, God said: "You shall not make for yourself an idol, or any likeness of what is in heaven above or on the earth beneath or in the water under the earth. You shall not worship them or serve them; for I, the Lord your God, am a jealous God, visiting the iniquity of the fathers on the children, on the third and fourth generations of those who hate Me" (Exod. 20:4,5).

Familiar spirits can be passed on from one generation to the next if not renounced and if your new spiritual heritage in Christ is not proclaimed. You are not guilty for the sin of any ancestor, but because of their sin, Satan may have gained access to your family. This is not to deny that many problems are transmitted genetically or acquired from an immoral atmosphere. All three conditions can predispose an individual to a particular sin. In addition, deceived people may try to curse you, or satanic groups may try to target you. You have all the authority and protection you need in Christ to stand against such curses and assignments. Ask the Lord to reveal to your mind the sins and iniquities of your ancestors by praying the following prayer:

Dear heavenly Father,
I thank You that I am a new creation in Christ. I desire to obey Your command to honor my mother and my father, but I also acknowledge that my physical heritage has not been perfect. I ask you to reveal to my mind the sins and iniquities of my ancestors in order to confess, renounce and forsake them. In Jesus' name, I pray. Amen.

Now claim your position and protection in Christ by making the following declaration verbally, and then by humbling yourself before God in prayer.

Declaration

I here and now reject and disown all the sins and iniquities of my ancestors, including (name them). As one who has been delivered from the power of darkness and translated into the kingdom of God's dear Son, I cancel out all demonic working that has been passed on to me from my ancestors. As one who has been crucified and raised with Jesus Christ and who sits with Him in heavenly places, I renounce all satanic assignments that are directed toward me and my ministry, and I cancel every curse that Satan and his workers have put on me. I announce to Satan and all his forces that Christ became a curse for me (Gal. 3:13) when He died for my sins on the cross. I reject any and every way in which Satan may claim ownership of me. I belong to the Lord Jesus Christ who purchased me with His own blood. I reject all other blood sacrifices whereby Satan may claim ownership of me. I declare myself to be eternally and completely signed over and committed to the Lord Jesus Christ. By the authority I have in Jesus Christ, I now command every spiritual enemy of the Lord Jesus Christ to leave my presence. I commit myself to my heavenly Father to do His will from this day forward.

Prayer

Dear heavenly Father,
I come to You as Your child purchased by the blood of the Lord Jesus Christ. You are the Lord of the universe and the Lord of my life. I submit my body to You as an instrument of righteousness, a living sacrifice, that I may glorify You in my body. I now ask You to fill me with Your Holy Spirit. I commit myself to the renewing of my mind in order to prove that Your will is good, perfect and acceptable for me. All this I do in the name and authority of the Lord Jesus Christ. Amen.

Once you have secured your freedom by going through these seven Steps, you may find demonic influences attempting reentry, days or even months later. One person shared that she heard a spirit say to her mind, "I'm back" two days after she had been set free. "No, you're not!" she proclaimed aloud. The attack ceased immediately. One victory does not constitute winning the war. Freedom must be maintained. After completing these Steps, one jubilant lady asked, "Will I always be like this?" I told her that she would stay free as long as she remained in right relationship with God. "Even if you slip and fall," I encouraged, "you know how to get right with God again."

One victim of incredible atrocities shared this illustration: "It's like being forced to play a game with an ugly stranger in my own home. I kept losing and wanted to quit, but the ugly stranger wouldn't let me. Finally I called the police (a higher authority), and they came and escorted the stranger out. He knocked on the door trying to regain entry, but this time I recognized his voice and didn't let him in."

What a beautiful illustration of gaining freedom in Christ. We call upon Jesus, the ultimate authority, and He escorts the enemy out of our lives. Know the truth, stand firm and resist the evil one. Seek good Christian fellowship, and commit yourself to regular times of Bible study and prayer. God loves you and will never leave or forsake you.

Aftercare

Freedom must be maintained. You have won a very important battle in an ongoing war. Freedom is yours as long as you keep choosing truth and standing firm in the strength of the Lord. If new memories should surface or if you become aware of "lies" you have believed or other non-Christian experiences you have had, renounce them and choose the truth. Some have found it helpful to go through the Steps again. As you do, read the instructions carefully.

For your encouragement and further study, read *Victory over the Darkness* (adult or youth version), *The Bondage Breaker* (adult or youth version) and *Released from Bondage*. If you are a parent, read *Spiritual Protection for Your Children*. *Walking in the Light* was written to help people understand God's guidance and discern counterfeit guidance. To maintain your freedom, we also suggest the following:

1. Seek legitimate Christian fellowship where you can walk in the light and speak the truth in love.
2. Study your Bible daily. Memorize key verses.
3. Take every thought captive to the obedience of Christ. Assume responsibility for your thought life, reject the lie, choose the truth and stand firm in your position in Christ.
4. Don't drift away! It is very easy to get lazy in your thoughts and revert back to old habit patterns of thinking. Share your struggles openly with a trusted friend. You need at least one friend who will stand with you.
5. Don't expect another person to fight your battle for you. Others can help, but they can't think, pray, read the Bible or choose the truth for you.
6. Continue to seek your identity and sense of worth in Christ. Read *Living Free in Christ* and the devotional, *Daily in Christ*. Renew your mind with the truth that your acceptance, security and significance is in Christ by saturating your mind with the following truths. Read the entire list of who you are "in Christ" and the Doctrinal Affirmation (in Step 2) aloud morning and evening during the next several weeks (and look up the verses referenced).
7. Commit yourself to daily prayer. You can pray the following suggested prayers often and with confidence:

Daily Prayer

Dear heavenly Father,

I honor You as my sovereign Lord. I acknowledge that You are always present with me. You are the only all-powerful and wise God. You are kind and loving in all Your ways. I love You and thank You that I am united with Christ and spiritually alive in Him. I choose not to love the world, and I crucify the flesh and all its passions.

I thank You for the life that I now have in Christ, and I ask You to fill me with Your Holy Spirit that I may live my life free from sin. I declare my dependence upon You, and I take my stand against Satan and all his lying ways. I choose to believe the truth, and I refuse to be discouraged. You are the God of all hope, and I am confident that You will meet my needs as I seek to live according to Your Word. I express with confidence that I can live a responsible life through Christ who strengthens me.

I now take my stand against Satan and command him and all his evil spirits to depart from me. I put on the whole armor of God. I submit my body as a living sacrifice and renew my mind by the living Word of God in order that I may prove that the will of God is good, acceptable and perfect. I ask these things in the precious name of my Lord and Savior, Jesus Christ. Amen.

Bedtime Prayer

Thank You, Lord, that You have brought me into Your family and have blessed me with every spiritual blessing in the heavenly realms in Christ. Thank You for providing this time of renewal through sleep. I accept it as part of Your perfect plan for Your children, and I trust You to guard my mind and my body during my sleep. As I have meditated on You and Your truth during this day, I choose to let these thoughts continue in my mind while I am asleep. I commit myself to You for Your protection from every attempt of Satan or his emissaries to attack me during sleep. I commit myself to You as my rock, my fortress and my resting place. I pray in the strong name of the Lord Jesus Christ. Amen.

Cleansing Home/Apartment

After removing all articles of false worship from home/apartment, pray aloud in every room, if necessary:

Heavenly Father, we acknowledge that You are Lord of heaven and earth. In Your sovereign power and love, You have given us all things richly to enjoy. Thank You for this place to live. We claim this home for our family as a place of spiritual safety and protection from all the attacks of the enemy. As children of God seated with Christ in the heavenly realm, we command every evil spirit claiming ground in the structures and furnishings of this place, based on the activities of previous occupants, to leave and never return. We renounce all curses and spells utilized against this place. We ask You, heavenly Father, to post guardian angels around this home (apartment, condo, room, etc.) to guard it from attempts of the enemy to enter and disturb Your purposes for us. We thank You, Lord, for doing this, and pray in the name of the Lord Jesus Christ. Amen.

Living in a Non-Christian Environment

After removing all articles of false worship from your room, pray aloud in the space allotted to you:

Thank You, heavenly Father, for my place to live and to be renewed by sleep. I ask You to set aside my room (portion of my room) as a place of spiritual safety for me. I renounce any allegiance given to false gods or spirits by other occupants, and I renounce any claim to this room (space) by Satan based on activities of past occupants or me. On the basis of my position as a child of God and a joint-heir with Christ who has all authority in heaven and on earth, I command all evil spirits to leave this place and never to return. I ask You, heavenly Father, to appoint guardian angels to protect me while I live here. I pray this in the name of the Lord Jesus Christ. Amen.

Freedom in Christ Ministries

Purpose: Freedom in Christ Ministries is an interdenominational, international, Bible-teaching Church ministry which exists to glorify God by equipping churches and mission groups, enabling them to fulfill their mission of establishing people free in Christ.

Freedom in Christ Ministries offers a number of valuable video, audio, and print resources that will help both those in need and those who counsel. Among the topics covered are:

Resolving Personal Conflicts
Search for Identity ▪ Walking by Faith ▪ Faith Renewal
Renewing the Mind ▪ Battle for the Mind ▪ Emotions
▪ Relationships ▪ Forgiveness

Resolving Spiritual Conflicts
Position of Believer ▪ Authority ▪ Protection ▪ Vulnerability
▪ Temptation ▪ Accusation ▪ Deception & Discernment
Steps to Freedom

Spiritual Conflicts and Biblical Counseling
Biblical Integration ▪ Theological Basis ▪ Walking by the Spirit
Surviving the Crisis ▪ The Process of Growth ▪ Counseling and
Christ ▪ Counseling the Spiritually Afflicted ▪ Ritual Abuse

The Seduction of Our Children
God's Answer ▪ Identity and Self-Worth ▪ Styles of Communication
Discipline ▪ Spiritual Conflicts and Prayer ▪ Steps to Freedom

Resolving Spiritual Conflicts and Cross-Cultural Ministry
Dr. Timothy Warner
Worldview Problems ▪ Warfare Relationships ▪ Christians and
Demons ▪ The Missionary Under Attack ▪ Practical Application for
Missionaries ▪ Steps to Freedom in Christ

**For additional resources from Dr. Anderson's
ministry write or call us at:**

Freedom in Christ Ministries
*491 E. Lambert Road, La Habra, California 90631
Phone: (562) 691-9128 Fax: (562) 691-4035*

More books from Neil Anderson to help you and those you love find freedom in Christ.

Victory over the Darkness
Regal Books

Victory over the Darkness Study Guide
Regal Books

The Bondage Breaker
Harvest House Publishers

The Bondage Breaker Study Guide
Harvest House Publishers

Spiritual Warfare
(Timothy M. Warner)
Crossway Books

Winning Spiritual Warfare
Harvest House Publishers

Walking in the Light
Thomas Nelson Publishers

The Seduction of Our Children
Harvest House Publishers

Released from Bondage
Thomas Nelson Publishers

Breaking Through to Spiritual Maturity
Regal Books

Living Free in Christ
Regal Books

Daily in Christ
Harvest House Publishers

The Bondage Breaker Youth Edition
Harvest House Publishers

The Slimeball Memos
(Richard Miller)
Harvest House Publishers

Stomping Out the Darkness
Regal Books

Setting Your Church Free
Regal Books

These and many other helpful resources are available at your local Christian bookstore.